Deut - 33:27
Ps 26:3

COME BOLDLY

COME BOLDLY

Timeless Daily Encouragements on Prayer

NAVPRESS

Discipleship Inside Out®

NAVPRESS
Discipleship Inside Out®

NavPress is the publishing ministry of The Navigators, an international Christian organization and leader in personal spiritual development. NavPress is committed to helping people grow spiritually and enjoy lives of meaning and hope through personal and group resources that are biblically rooted, culturally relevant, and highly practical.

For a free catalog go to www.NavPress.com
or call 1.800.366.7788 in the United States or 1.800.839.4769 in Canada.

ISBN-13: 978-1-61747-901-4 (hardback)
ISBN-13: 978-1-61291-381-0 (paperback)

Cover design by Arvid Wallen
Cover image by Sundari/Shutterstock

Some of the anecdotal illustrations in this book are true to life and are included with the permission of the persons involved. All other illustrations are composites of real situations, and any resemblance to people living or dead is coincidental.

Unless otherwise identified, all Scripture quotations in this publication are taken from the Holy Bible, *English Standard Version*® (ESV®) Copyright © 2001 by Crossway, a publishing ministry of Good News Publishers. Used by permission. All rights reserved. Other versions used include: the *Holy Bible, New International Version*® (NIV®), Copyright © 1973, 1978, 1984, 2011 by Biblica, Inc.®, used by permission of Zondervan, all rights reserved worldwide. The "NIV" and "New International Version" are trademarks registered in the United States Patent and Trademark Office by Biblica, Inc.® ; *New American Standard Bible*® (NASB) ©1960, 1977, 1995 by the Lockman Foundation. Used by permission; the New King James Version® (NKJV). Copyright © 1982 by Thomas Nelson, Inc. Used by permission. All rights reserved; the King James Version (KJV); the *Amplified Bible* (AMP), © 1954, 1958, 1962, 1964, 1965, 1987 by The Lockman Foundation; and the Weymouth New Testament (WNT).

Excerpts from Dietrich Bonhoeffer, *The Cost of Discipleship*, © 1963, Collier Books, used by permission.
Excerpts from E. M. Bounds, *The Essentials of Prayer, The Necessity of Prayer, The Possibilities of Prayer, Prayer and Praying Men, Purpose in Prayer, The Reality of Prayer*, and *The Weapon of Prayer*, public domain.
Excerpts from Lee Brase with Henry Helsabek, *Praying from God's Heart*, © 1993, NavPress, used by permission.
Excerpts from John Bunyan, *Pilgrim's Prayer Book*, © 1986, Tyndale, used by permission.
Excerpts from Captain E. G. Carré, *A Present-Day Challenge to Prayer*, public domain.
Excerpts from D. A. Carson, *A Call to Spiritual Reformation*, © 1992, Baker Academic, used by permission.
Excerpts from Samuel Chadwick, *The Path of Prayer*, public domain.
Excerpts from Oswald Chambers, *If You Will Ask*, public domain.
Excerpts from Wesley L. Duewel, *Touch the World Through Prayer*, © 1986, Zondervan, used by permission.
Excerpts from Jonathan Edwards, *The Life and Diary of David Brainerd*, public domain.
Excerpts from Elisabeth Elliot, *God's Guidance*, © 1992, Revell, used by permission.
Excerpts from Charles Finney, *Power from on High*, public domain.
Excerpts from P. T. Forsyth, *The Soul of Prayer*, public domain.
Excerpts from Jeanne Guyon, *A Short and Easy Method of Prayer*, public domain.
Excerpts from Ole Hallesby, *Prayer*, © 1959, Augsburg, used by permission.
Excerpts from Brother Lawrence, *The Practice of the Presence of God*, public domain.
Excerpts from C. S. Lewis, *Letters to Malcolm: Chiefly on Prayer*, © 1964, Harcourt Brace & Company, used by permission.
Excerpts from David McIntyre, *The Hidden Life of Prayer*, public domain.
Excerpts from D. L. Moody, *Prevailing Prayer*, public domain.
Excerpts from George Müller, *Answers to Prayer* and *The Autobiography of George Müller*, public domain.
Excerpts from Andrew Murray, *With Christ in the School of Prayer*, public domain.
Excerpts from John Owen, *Of Communion with God the Father, Son and Holy Ghost*, public domain.
Excerpts from Marcus Rainsford, *Our Lord Prays for His Own*, public domain.
Excerpts from Rosalind Rinker, *Prayer: Conversing with God*, public domain.
Excerpts from R. C. Sproul, *The Prayer of the Lord*, © 2009, Reformation Trust Publishing, a division of Ligonier Ministries, used by permission.
Excerpts from Charles Spurgeon, *Morning by Morning*, public domain.
Excerpts from Dr. and Mrs. Howard Taylor, *Hudson Taylor's Spiritual Secret*, public domain.
Excerpts from R. A. Torrey, *How to Pray* and *The Power of Prayer*, public domain.
Excerpts from A. W. Tozer, *The Pursuit of God*, public domain.
Excerpts from An Unknown Christian, *The Kneeling Christian*, public domain.
Excerpts from Thomas R. Yeakley, *Praying Over God's Promises*, © 2007, NavPress, used by permission.

Printed in the United States of America

2 3 4 5 6 7 8 / 18 17 16 15 14 13

Contents

FOREWORD

The collection you hold in your hands is a gathering in one place of some of the best writing of our time — as well as of earlier days — on prayer. The entries have been carefully arranged to address the essential biblical elements of prayer each week: preparation, confession, examination, worship, and request. In addition, every weekend entry relates a true story of prayer in action to inspire your faith. These are stunning and memorable words that have deeply influenced generations in the movement of discipleship to Jesus. The best books are timeless, and most often they cross cultural barriers. Created by dozens of outstanding authors, the selections in this book have stood the test of time and shown the power to touch a new generation of disciples in many settings around the world.

Jesus said, "Every teacher of the law who has been instructed about the kingdom of heaven is like the owner of a house who brings out of his storeroom new treasures as well as old" (Matthew 13:52, NIV). At NavPress, we are conscious of both the old and the new, and we treasure both. We live in a world of profound change in publishing, and NavPress is at the forefront of keeping up with the new media. But we are also looking to our faith's heritage for classic writing that never lets us forget where we have come from and to pass along those timeless messages that have proven to change lives. That's the kind of writing you hold in your hands: some of the greatest selections on the nature of our God.

The ministry of The Navigators began in the 1930s through the call of God to Dawson Trotman. Trotman's vision was to teach others, one to one, the biblical principles of discipleship he found beneficial in his own life. He began to teach high school students and local Sunday school classes. In 1933, he and his friends extended their work to reach out to sailors in the U.S. Navy. From there, Trotman met and established a partnership with the then up-and-coming evangelist Billy Graham.

One of the men Trotman chose to lead the work with Billy Graham was Lorne Sanny. Sanny went on to become Trotman's successor and served The Navigators for thirty years as its president. This book contains writing that is what Lorne Sanny used to call "life-borne" messages. These are messages that grow out of a life steeped in the Scriptures and lived out in passionate love and obedience to God. They are tested in real life, and they have a practical authenticity that prompts genuine transformation.

Over the years, I personally have been touched by all the messages in this collection. These books on prayer reflect the incredibly vast thinking and counsel on prayer. Their counsel guides, models, and encourages us in our experiencing of prayer. Each one is part of the fabric of my own discipleship. Now I'm convinced that you, too, will find in them an abundance of godly stimulation and transformative guidance for your own walk with God.

Dr. Michael D. Miller
president, NavPress
chief business officer, The Navigators

INFINITE FULLNESS

He is also able to save to the uttermost
those who come to God through Him.
(HEBREWS 7:25, NKJV)

We are not of this world, though we are in it. We have been translated out of the kingdom of darkness, we have been introduced into the kingdom of God's dear Son; our title has not to be made out, it has been already secured to us. The precious blood is our title, and He who shed it has gone within the veil to present it, as our Representative. Our meetness and qualification for heaven and for glory has not to be bestowed, it has been already given. Our meetness is the Holy Ghost who dwelleth in us. The moment the Holy Ghost enters the soul of a believing sinner, that man is as "meet for glory" as if he lived in the school of grace for a thousand years.

Our inheritance is secure, and, "Our fellowship is with the Father, and with his Son Jesus Christ" (1 John 1:3, KJV).

And if we are left here it is because the Lord has need of our emptiness, our weakness, the variety of our temptations and temperaments, the peculiar character of our corruptions, the disappointments, the dangers and difficulties with which His poor people are possessed and surrounded, that it may be made manifest that there never was a case, or a circumstance, or a sorrow, or a sin, or a difficulty, for which there was not a remedy and a supply in His fullness and in His love. Our need suits His fullness, and His fullness corresponds to our need; there must needs be the infinite variety of cases, and of characters, of temptations, and necessities, which exist among the children of God, in order that there may be full scope, occasion and opportunity for displaying the infinite varieties of the fullness, the love, grace, mercy, and salvation, laid up in the Lord Jesus Christ for His dear people, and that in their relief and deliverance from all their troubles, He might win for Himself an everlasting name.

MARCUS RAINSFORD, IN *OUR LORD PRAYS FOR HIS OWN*

Resolved to Do His Will

I have come down from heaven,
not to do my own will but the will of him who sent me.
(John 6:38)

I fear it is common for professed Christians to overlook the state of mind in which God requires them to be as a condition of answering their prayers. For example, in offering the Lord's Prayer, "Thy kingdom come," it is plain that sincerity in offering this petition implies the whole heart and life devotion of the petitioner to the building up of this kingdom. It implies the sincere and thorough consecration of all that we have and all that we are to this end. To utter this petition in any other state of mind involves hypocrisy and is an abomination. So [it is] in the next petition, "Thy will be done on earth as it is in heaven." God has not promised to hear this petition unless it is sincerely offered. But *sincerity* implies a state of mind that accepts the whole revealed will of God, so far as we understand it, as they accept it in heaven. It implies a loving, confiding, universal obedience to the whole *known* will of God, whether that will is revealed in His Word, by His Spirit, or in His Providence. It implies that we hold ourselves and all that we have and are as absolutely and cordially at God's disposal as do the inhabitants of heaven. If we fall short of this and withhold anything whatever from God, we "regard iniquity in our hearts," and God will not hear us.

Sincerity in offering this petition implies a state of entire and universal consecration to God. Anything short of this is withholding from God that which is His due. It is "turning away our ear from hearing the law." But what saith the Scriptures? "He that turneth away his ear from hearing the law, even his prayer shall be an abomination." Do professed Christians understand this?

Charles Finney, in *Power from on High*

Self-Examination and the Love of God

*If we walk in the light, as he is in the light, we have fellowship with one
another, and the blood of Jesus his Son cleanses us from all sin.*

(1 John 1:7)

Self-examination should always precede Confession. The business of those
that are advanced to the degree of which we now treat, is to lay their whole
souls open before God, who will not fail to enlighten them, and enable
them to see the peculiar nature of their faults. This examination, however,
should be peaceful and tranquil, and we should depend on God for the
discovery and knowledge of our sins, rather than on the diligence of our
own scrutiny.

When we examine with constraint, and in the strength of our own
endeavours, we are easily deceived and betrayed by self-love into error; "we
believe the evil good, and the good evil" (Isaiah 5:20); but when we lie in
full exposure before the Sun of Righteousness, His Divine beams render
the smallest atoms visible.

When souls have attained to this, no fault escapes reprehension. Such
is the scrutiny of Him who suffers no evil to be concealed; and under His
purifying influence the one way is to turn affectionately to our Judge, and
bear with meekness the pain and correction He inflicts. Experience will
convince the soul that it is a thousand times more effectually examined by
His Divine Light than by the most active and vigorous self-inspection.

Those who tread these paths should be informed of a matter respecting their Confession in which they are apt to err. When they begin to give
an account of their sins, instead of the regret and contrition they had been
accustomed to feel, they find that love and tranquility sweetly pervade and
take possession of their souls: now those who are not properly instructed
are desirous of withdrawing from this sensation, to form an act of contrition, because they have heard, and with truth, that it is requisite: but they
are not aware that they lose thereby the genuine contrition, which is this
Intuitive Love, infinitely surpassing any effect produced by self-exertion.

Jeanne Guyon, in *A Short and Easy Method of Prayer*

HOPING IN GOD ALONE

Why are you cast down, O my soul, and why are you in turmoil within me? Hope in God; for I shall again praise him, my salvation and my God.

(PSALM 42:5-6)

There is in prayer an unbosoming of a person's self, an opening of the heart to God, a deeply felt pouring out of the soul in requests, sighs, and groans. "All my longings lie open before you, O Lord, my sighing is not hidden from you," says David (Psalm 38:9, NIV). This is the prayer to which the promise is made for the delivering of the poor creature out of captivity: "But if from there you seek the Lord your God, you will find him if you look for him with all your heart and with all your soul" (Deuteronomy 4:29, NIV).

Prayer must be a pouring out of the heart and soul *to God*. This shows the excellency of the spirit of prayer. It is the great God of the universe to whom prayer attends. When shall we come and appear before God? We pray when we see an emptiness in all things under heaven. We see that in God alone there is rest and satisfaction for the soul. "The widow who is really in need and left all alone puts her hope in God and continues night and day to pray and to ask God for help" (1 Timothy 5:5, NIV). So says David, "In you, O Lord, I have taken refuge; let me never be put to shame. Rescue me and deliver me in your righteousness; turn your ear to me and save me. Be my rock of refuge, to which I can always go; give the command to save me, for you are my rock and my fortress. Deliver me, O my God, from the hand of the wicked, from the grasp of evil and cruel men. For you have been my hope, O Sovereign Lord, my confidence since my youth" (Psalm 71:1-5, NIV). To pray rightly, you must make God your hope, stay, and all. Right prayer sees nothing substantial or worth being concerned about except God. And that, as I said before, it does in a sincere, sensible, and affectionate way.

JOHN BUNYAN, IN *PILGRIM'S PRAYER BOOK*

THE MOUNTAIN IS STILL OPEN

I will lift up my eyes to the hills — from whence comes my help? My help comes from the LORD, who made heaven and earth. He will not allow your foot to be moved; He who keeps you will not slumber.

(PSALM 121:1-3, NKJV)

After forty years of exile for his championship of God's people, the shepherd-prince found the God of Israel. He was not a stranger to Him in Egypt. He had renounced the privileges and pleasures of a royal palace and cast in his lot with the afflicted people of his race. He had given proof of his zeal for the Most High, but he had never had a personal revelation of Him till he found Him that day in the mount. It is there He reveals Himself as nowhere else. He manifests Himself to those who pray in secret as He cannot to those who have no inner sanctuary of the soul.

Moses found the will of God in the mount. It was there he received the law. After forty days alone with God he brought heaven's laws to earth on two tablets of stone. Those laws remain to this day the foundation of all righteous government among men. After centuries of progress they are still the basis of civilization.

He not only received the Commandments which were to be the corner-stones of good government for all time; he also received directions concerning local and personal details. The way to the mount is still open. The divine pattern of each life is still to be seen in the secret place of the Most High God. The humblest follower of Jesus may know the Divine Will at first hand. It is every man's privilege to be fully assured in the will of God. The Divine attention to detail is amazing. Nothing is too trivial for Omniscience. Come straight to God. Do not bother other people. Lay all questions naked before Him, and He will make it plain to you what is His will. When God speaks, His speech is easily understood. All questions of the plain should be settled in the mount, and where there is certainty in the mount there will be victory on the levels and in the valleys.

SAMUEL CHADWICK, IN *THE PATH OF PRAYER*

Faith to Grasp His Faithfulness

Seek first the kingdom of God and his righteousness,
and all these things will be added to you.

(Matthew 6:33)

Though his father and the Society which ultimately sent him to China both offered to help with his expenses, he felt he must not lose the opportunity of further testing the promises of God. There was nothing between him and want in [London] save the faithfulness of God. Before leaving he had written to his mother:

> I am indeed proving the truth of that word, "Thou wilt keep him in per-fect peace whose mind is stayed on thee, because he trusteth in thee." My mind is quite as much at rest as, nay more than, it would be if I had a hundred pounds in my pocket. May He keep me ever thus, simply depending on Him for every blessing, temporal as well as spiritual.

And to his sister Amelia:

> No situation has turned up in London that will suit me, but I am not con-cerned about it, as HE is "the same yesterday, and today, and forever." His love is unfailing, His Word unchangeable, His power ever the same; there-fore the heart that trusts Him is kept in "perfect peace." I know He tries me only to increase my faith, and that it is all in love. Well, if He is glori-fied, I am content.

For the future, near as well as distant, Hudson Taylor had one all-sufficient confidence. If that could fail, it were better to make the discovery in London than far away in China. Deliberately and of his own free will, he cut himself off from possible sources of supply. It was God, the living God he needed — a stronger faith to grasp His faithfulness, and more experi-ence of the practicability of dealing with Him about every situation. Comfort or discomfort in London, means or lack of means, seemed a small matter compared with deeper knowledge of the One on whom everything depends.

Dr. and Mrs. Howard Taylor, in *Hudson Taylor's Spiritual Secret*

COME HELPLESS

Whom have I in heaven but you? And there is nothing on earth
that I desire besides you.

(PSALM 73:25)

Prayer and helplessness are inseparable. Only he who is helpless can truly pray. Listen to this, you who are often so helpless that you do not know what to do. At times you do not even know how to pray. Your mind seems full of sin and impurity. Your mind is preoccupied with what the Bible calls the world. God and eternal and holy things seem so distant and foreign to you that you feel that you add sin to sin by desiring to approach God in such a state of mind. Now and then you must ask yourself the question, "Do I really desire to be set free from the lukewarmness of my heart and my worldly life? Is not my Christian life always lukewarm and half-hearted for the simple reason that deep down in my heart I desire it that way?" Thus an honest soul struggles against the dishonesty of his own being. He feels himself so helplessly lost that his prayers freeze on his very lips. Listen, my friend! Your helplessness is your best prayer. It calls from your heart to the heart of God with greater effect than all your uttered pleas. He hears it from that very moment that you are seized with helplessness, and He becomes actively engaged at once in hearing and answering the prayer of your helplessness. He hears today as He heard the helpless and wordless prayer of the man sick with the palsy.

If you are a mother, you will understand very readily this phase of prayer. Your infant child cannot formulate in words a single petition to you. Yet the little one prays the best way he knows how. All he can do is to cry, but you understand very well his pleading. Moreover, the little one need not even cry. All you need to do is to see him in all his helpless dependence upon you, and a prayer touches your mother-heart, a prayer which is stronger than the loudest cry.

OLE HALLESBY, IN *PRAYER*

Acknowledging Sin

In your light do we see light.
(Psalm 36:9)

When Job was confessing his sin, God turned his captivity and heard his prayer. God will hear our prayer and turn our captivity when we take our true place before Him and confess and forsake our transgressions. It was when Isaiah cried out before the Lord, "I am undone," that the blessing came; the live coal was taken from the altar and put upon his lips; and he went out to write one of the most wonderful books the world has ever seen. What a blessing it has been to the church! It was when David said, "I have sinned!" that God dealt in mercy with him. "I acknowledge my sin unto Thee, and mine iniquity have I not hid. I said, 'I will confess my transgressions unto the Lord; and Thou forgavest the iniquity of my sin.'" Notice how David made a very similar confession to that of the prodigal in the fifteenth of Luke: "I acknowledge my transgressions; and my sin is ever before me. Against Thee, Thee only, have I sinned, and done this evil in Thy sight!" There is no difference between the king and the beggar when the Spirit of God comes into the heart and convicts of sin.

Always in the Presence

In your presence there is fullness of joy;
at your right hand are pleasures forevermore.
(Psalm 16:11)

After having given myself wholly to God, that He might take away my sin, I renounced, for the love of Him, everything that was not He, and I began to live as if there was none but He and I in the world. Sometimes I considered myself before Him as a poor criminal at the feet of the judge, at other times I beheld Him in my heart as my Father, as my God. I worshiped Him the oftenest that I could, keeping my mind in His holy presence, and recalling it as often as I found it wandered from Him. I found no small pain in this exercise, and yet I continued it, notwithstanding all the difficulties that occurred, without troubling or disquieting myself when my mind had wandered involuntarily. I made this my business as much all the day long as at the appointed times of prayer; for at all times, every hour, every minute, even in the height of my business, I drove away from my mind everything that was capable of interrupting my thought of God. Such has been my common practice ever since I entered in religion; and though I have done it imperfectly, yet I have found great advantages by it. These, I well know, are to be imputed to the mere mercy and goodness of God, because we can do nothing without Him, and *I* still less than any. But when we are faithful to keep ourselves in His holy Presence, and set Him always before us, this not only hinders our offending Him, and doing anything that may displease Him, at least willfully, but it also begets in us a holy freedom, and if I may so speak, a familiarity with God, wherewith we ask, and that successfully, the graces we stand in need of. In fine, by often repeating these acts, they become habitual, and the presence of God is rendered as it were natural to us.

Brother Lawrence, in *The Practice of the Presence of God*

ABOVE THE STORMS AND CLOUDS

No one has ever seen God; the only God,
who is at the Father's side, he has made him known.

(JOHN 1:18)

When by and through Christ we have an access unto the Father, we then behold his glory also, and see his love that he peculiarly bears unto us, and act faith thereon. We are then, I say, to eye it, to believe it, to receive it, as in him; the issues and fruits thereof being made out unto us through Christ alone. Though there be no light for us but in the beams, yet we may by beams see the sun, which is the fountain of it. Though all our refreshment actually lie in the streams, yet by them we are led up unto the fountain. Jesus Christ, in respect of the love of the Father, is but the beam, the stream; wherein though actually all our light, our refreshment lies, yet by him we are led to the fountain, the sun of eternal love itself. Would believers exercise themselves herein, they would find it a matter of no small spiritual improvement in their walking with God.

This is that which is aimed at. Many dark and disturbing thoughts are apt to arise in this thing. Few can carry up their hearts and minds to this height by faith, as to rest their souls in the love of the Father; they live below it, in the troublesome region of hopes and fears, storms and clouds. All here is serene and quiet. But how to attain to this pitch they know not. This is the will of God, that he may always be eyed as benign, kind, tender, loving, and unchangeable therein; and that peculiarly as the Father, as the great fountain and spring of all gracious communications and fruits of love.

JOHN OWEN, IN *OF COMMUNION WITH GOD THE FATHER, SON AND HOLY GHOST*

Definite Prayers, Definite Answers

Whatever you ask in prayer, you will receive, if you have faith.
(Matthew 21:22)

How long is it since you last offered up a definite prayer? People pray for "a blessing" on an address or a meeting or a mission, and some blessing is certain to come, for others are also pleading with God about the matter. You ask for relief from pain or healing of sickness, but Godless people, for whom no one appears to be praying, often recover, and sometimes in a seemingly miraculous way. And we may feel that we might have got better even if no prayer had been offered on our behalf. It seems to me that so many people cannot put their finger upon any really definite and conclusive answer to prayer in their own experience. Most Christians do not give God a chance to show His delight in granting His children's petitions, for their requests are so vague and indefinite. If this is so, it is not surprising that prayer is so often a mere form — and almost mechanical repetition, day by day, of certain phrases, a few minutes' "exercise" morning and evening.

Then there is another point. Have you, when in prayer, ever had the witness borne in upon you that your request was granted? Those who know something of the private life of men of prayer are often amazed at the complete assurance which comes over them at times that their prayers are answered, long before the boon they seek is actually in their possession. Our Lord Himself always had this assurance, and we should ever bear in mind that, although He was God, He lived His earthly life as a perfect Man, depending upon the Holy Spirit of God. When He stood before the opened tomb of Lazarus, before He had actually called upon the dead to come forth, He said, "Father, I thank Thee that Thou hast heard Me. And I know that Thou hearest Me always" (John 11:41-42, kjv).

An Unknown Christian, in *The Kneeling Christian*

Wrapped Up in Divine Love

O God, you are my God; earnestly I seek you; my soul thirsts for you;
my flesh faints for you, as in a dry and weary land where there is no water.

(Psalm 63:1)

Thursday, April 1, 1742. I seem to be declining, with respect to my life and warmth in divine things; had not so free access to God in prayer as usual of late. O that God would humble me deeply in the dust before him! I deserve hell every day, for not loving my Lord more, who has, I trust, loved me, and given himself for me; and every time I am enabled to exercise any grace renewedly, I am renewedly indebted to the God of all grace for special assistance. Where then is boasting? Surely it is excluded, when we think how we are dependent on God for the being and every act of grace. Oh, if ever I get to heaven, it will be because God will, and nothing else; for I never did anything of myself, but get away from God! My soul will be astonished at the unsearchable riches of divine grace, when I arrive at the mansions, which the blessed Savior is gone before to prepare. What are all the storms of this lower world, if Jesus by his Spirit does but come walking on the seas! — Sometime past, I had much pleasure in the prospect of the heathen being brought home to Christ, and desired that the Lord would employ me in that work: — but now, my soul more frequently desires to die, to be with Christ. O that my soul were wrapped up in divine love, and my longing desires after God increased! O that I may be always humble and resigned to God, and that he would cause my soul to be more fixed on himself, that I may be more fitted both for doing and suffering!

Jonathan Edwards, in *The Life and Diary of David Brainerd*

SPIRIT AND TRUTH

Worship the LORD in the splendor of holiness;
tremble before him, all the earth!
(PSALM 96:9)

Among Christians, one still finds the three classes of worshippers. Some in their ignorance hardly know what they're asking for. They pray earnestly, but receive little. There are others having more correct knowledge who try to pray with all their minds and hearts. They often pray most earnestly and yet do not attain the full blessedness of worship in spirit and truth. It is into this third class we must ask our Lord Jesus to take us. He must teach us how to worship in spirit and truth. This alone is spiritual worship; this makes us the kind of worshippers the Father seeks. In prayer, everything will depend on our understanding and practicing worship in spirit and truth. "God is a Spirit, and they that worship Him, must worship Him in spirit and truth." The first thought suggested here by the Master is that there must be harmony between God and His worshippers. This is according to a principle which prevails throughout the universe: correspondence between an object and the organ to which it reveals or yields itself. The eye is receptive to light, the ear to sound. The man who truly wants to worship God — to find, know, possess, and enjoy God — must be in harmony with Him and have the capacity for receiving Him. Because God is Spirit, we must worship in spirit. What does this mean? God is Spirit, not bound by space or time. In His infinite perfection, He is the same always and everywhere. His worship must not be confined by place or form, but be spiritual as God Himself is spiritual. This is a lesson of deep importance.

ANDREW MURRAY, IN *WITH CHRIST IN THE SCHOOL OF PRAYER*

On Praying Ground

He chose us in him before the foundation of the world,
that we should be holy and blameless before him.

(Ephesians 1:4)

As prayer leads up to and brings forth a consecrated full consecration, so prayer entirely impregnates a consecrated life. The prayer life and the consecrated life are intimate companions. They are Siamese twins, inseparable. Prayer enters into every phase of a consecrated life. A prayerless life which claims consecration is a misnomer, false, counterfeit. Consecration is really the setting apart of one's self to a life of prayer. It means not only to pray, but to pray habitually, and to pray more effectually. It is the consecrated man who accomplishes most by his praying. God must hear the man wholly given up to God. God cannot deny the requests of him who has renounced all claims to himself, and who has wholly dedicated himself to God and his service. This act of the consecrated man puts him "on praying ground and pleading terms" with God. It puts him in reach of God in prayer. It places him where he can get hold of God, and where he can influence God to do things which he would not otherwise do. Consecration brings answers to prayer. God can depend upon consecrated men. God can afford to commit himself in prayer to those who have fully committed themselves to God. He who gives all to God will get all from God. Having given all to God, he can claim all that God has for him.

E. M. Bounds, in *The Essentials of Prayer*

Responding to the Shepherd

I lay down my life for the sheep.
(John 10:15)

"My sheep hear my voice and I know them, and they follow me; and I give them eternal life." Notice the sequence of the verbs. My sheep *hear* my voice. They *follow* me. I *give* them eternal life. The first step is to hear His voice and begin to follow the Shepherd, and then He does all the giving. This is a mystery I cannot explain, but in His great eternal knowledge, He knows when to call us. There is no past, present, or future with the Lord. It is all an eternal *now* with Him. It is not easy to turn the controls of your life over to Another when you can't see Him. But when you can know He's there and speak with Him and to Him naturally, the barriers go down. The response of your heart to His initial love for you releases your love for Him. You discover that He has long sought you, called to you, prepared for you, loved you. And now you know the way into the fold: Response to the Shepherd Himself, Jesus Christ.

Have you responded to Him? Have you spoken to Him, simply, naturally, out of the need of your heart? In your own words?

He is there.

If you are interested in Him, you can come. Your very interest proves that you have heard His voice. And He has said: "Everyone who has heard . . . comes to me."

ROSALIND RINKER, IN *PRAYER: CONVERSING WITH GOD*

HE PRAYS FOR US

*I am praying for them. I am not praying for the world
but for those whom you have given me, for they are yours.*

(JOHN 17:9)

When men urge a petition they use such arguments as they believe likely to influence most the parties with whom they plead, and so does Christ in His prayer. He, who was eternally in the Father's bosom, well knew the delight that the Father had in His beloved people; He knew the intense complacency with which He regarded them, the interest He had in them, and that He had given them to Him to be gathered from their wanderings, washed from their sins, have their ignorance instructed, be clothed in the best robe that heaven's wardrobe could provide for them, made members of His own body, and presented by Him without spot or wrinkle, accepted in Himself, to share His kingdom, to live in His life, to share His Joy, to know His peace, and to sit upon His throne forever. He received them as the pledge of His Father's love; "Thine they were, and thou gavest them me." I am glorified in being their High Priest (Hebrews 5:5, KJV). I know their salvation redounds to Thine honour, and fills thee with joy, and shall yet fill heaven and earth with Thy praise. "I pray for them!" They have polluted their souls, but I am their salvation. "I pray for them!" They have been lost, but I am come to seek and to save that which was lost; they have been blind, and naked, and poor, and captives, and in prison, but Thy Spirit is upon Me because Thou hast anointed Me to open the eyes of the blind, to unstop the ears of the deaf, to open the prison doors to them that are bound, to proclaim liberty to the captives, and the acceptable year of the Lord. "I pray for them."

MARCUS RAINSFORD, IN *OUR LORD PRAYS FOR HIS OWN*

AN ENCOUNTER OF WILLS

Trust in the LORD forever, for the LORD GOD is an everlasting rock.
(ISAIAH 26:4)

We may say too soon, "Thy will be done;" and too ready acceptance of a situation as His will often means feebleness or sloth. It may be His will that we surmount His will. It may be His higher will that we resist His lower. Prayer is an act of will much more than of sentiment, and its triumph is more than acquiescence. Let us submit when we must, but let us keep submission in reserve rather than in action, as a ground tone rather than the sole effort. Prayer with us has largely ceased to be *wrestling*. But is that not the dominant scriptural idea? It is not the sole idea, but is it not the dominant? Prayer is not merely the meeting of two moods or two affections, the laying of the head on a divine bosom in trust and surrender. That may have its place in religion, but it is not the nerve and soul of prayer. Nor is it religious reverie. Prayer is an encounter of *wills* — till one will or the other give way. It is not a spiritual exercise merely, but in its maturity it is a cause acting on the course of God's world. It is, indeed, by God's grace that prayer is a real cause, but such it is. And of course there must be in us a faith corresponding to the grace. Of course also there is always, behind all, the readiness to accept God's will without a murmur when it is perfectly evident and final.

P. T. FORSYTH, IN *THE SOUL OF PRAYER*

PROOFS OF HIS LOVE

We felt that we had received the sentence of death. But that was to make us rely not on ourselves but on God who raises the dead.

(2 CORINTHIANS 1:9)

This morning our poverty, which has now lasted more or less for several months, had become exceedingly great. I left my house a few minutes after seven to go to the Orphan-Houses, to see whether there was enough money to take in the milk, which is brought about eight o'clock. On my way it was specially my request that the Lord would be pleased to pity us, even as a father pitieth his children, and that He would not lay more upon us than He would enable us to bear, I especially entreated Him that He would now be pleased to refresh our hearts by sending us help. I likewise reminded Him of the consequences that would result, both in reference to believers and unbelievers, if we should have to give up the work because of want of means, and that He therefore would not permit of its coming to nought. I moreover again confessed before the Lord that I deserved not that He should continue to use me in this work any longer. While I was thus in prayer, about two minutes' walk from the Orphan-Houses, I met a brother who was going at this early hour to his business. After having exchanged a few words with him, I went on; but he presently ran after me, and gave me £1 for the Orphans. Thus the Lord speedily answered my prayer. Truly, it is worth being poor and greatly tried in faith, for the sake of having day by day such precious proofs of the loving interest which our kind Father takes in everything that concerns us. And how should our Father do otherwise?

GEORGE MÜLLER, IN *ANSWERS TO PRAYER*

BEGIN WITH GOD

*Worthy are you, our Lord and God, to receive glory
and honor and power, for you created all things.*
(REVELATION 4:11)

We are right when and only when we stand in a right position relative to God, and we are wrong so far and so long as we stand in any other position. Much of our difficulty as seeking Christians stems from our unwillingness to take God as He is and adjust our lives accordingly. We insist upon trying to modify Him and to bring Him nearer to our own image. The flesh whimpers against the rigor of God's inexorable sentence and begs like Agag for a little mercy, a little indulgence of its carnal ways. It is no use. We can get a right start only by accepting God as He is and learning to love Him for what He is. As we go on to know Him better we shall find it a source of unspeakable joy that God is just what He is. Some of the most rapturous moments we know will be those we spend in reverent admiration of the Godhead. In those holy moments the very thought of change in Him will be too painful to endure. So let us begin with God. Back of all, above all, before all is God; first in sequential order, above in rank and station, exalted in dignity and honor. As the self-existent One He gave being to all things, and all things exist out of Him and for Him. "Thou art worthy, O Lord, to receive glory and honour and power: for thou hast created all things, and for thy pleasure they are and were created." Every soul belongs to God and exists by His pleasure. God being Who and What He is, and we being who and what we are, the only thinkable relation between us is one of full lordship on His part and complete submission on ours. We owe Him every honour that it is in our power to give Him. Our everlasting grief lies in giving Him anything less.

A. W. TOZER, IN *THE PURSUIT OF GOD*

Joining with the Brokenhearted Father

Weeping may tarry for the night, but joy comes with the morning.
(Psalm 30:5)

It will take more than tears to make prayer effective; but a burdened heart, a soul crying out to God, is the very essence of intercession. It is a spiritual crime to be calloused while the world goes to hell. It is spiritually criminal to pray casually, dry-eyed and burdenless, while a world is in sin and pain. It is Christlike for your heart to weep with those who weep (Romans 12:15). It is Christlike for you to be so filled with loving compassion that you pray with tears for those broken, fettered, and destroyed by sin. Prayer is not recreational or arbitrary for the Christian. Prayer is the very business of Christ's kingdom. Prayer is joining with God the broken-hearted Father, Christ the weeping High Priest, and the tender, interceding Holy Spirit by sharing their heartbeat and bearing with them the same burdens which they carry in their loving hearts. To pray with tears is to make an eternal investment. To pray with tears is to sow your tears for eternal harvest. No tear shed in burdened intercession for others is ever forgotten by God, unrecorded, or in vain. Intercession watered with your tears is one of the most powerful forms of prayer known. As surely as God is in heaven, "Those who sow in tears will reap with songs of joy. He who goes out weeping, carrying seed to sow, will return with songs of joy, carrying sheaves with him" (Psalm 126:5-6, NIV).

Quiet Confidence

I have calmed and quieted my soul, like a weaned child
with its mother; like a weaned child is my soul within me.

(Psalm 131:2)

Picture Martha and Mary waiting day after day for Jesus to come, yet not till Lazarus' body had been in the grave four days did Jesus Christ appear on the scene. Days of absolute silence, of awful repose on the heart on the part of God! Is there anything analogous to it in your life? Can God trust you like that, or are you still wanting a visible answer? "Whatsoever we ask, we receive of Him" (1 John 3:22, kjv). If God has given you a silence, praise Him. Think of the things you prayed to God about and tried to hold and, because of His love, He dare not let you hold them and they went. For a time you said, "I asked God to give me bread and He gave me a stone." But He did not, and you found that He gave you the bread of life. You prayed that you might keep the thing that seemed to make your life as a Christian possible. You asked that it might always be preserved by God, and suddenly the whole thing went to pieces. That was God's answer. After the silence, if we are spiritual and can interpret His silence, we always get the trust in God that knows prayers are answered every time, not sometimes. The manifestation of the answer in place and time is a mere matter of God's sovereignty. Be earnest and eager on the line of praying. One wonderful thing about God's stillness in connection with prayers is that He makes us still, makes us perfectly confident. The contagion of Jesus Christ's stillness gets into us — "I know He has heard me" — and His silence is the proof He has heard.

Oswald Chambers, in *If You Will Ask*

BEFORE THE THRONE

Let us then with confidence draw near to the throne of grace,
that we may receive mercy and find grace to help in time of need.
(HEBREWS 4:16)

Consider the place, throne, or seat on which the great God has placed himself to hear the petitions and prayers of poor creatures — and that is the throne of grace of the mercy seat. In these days of the gospel, God has taken up his seat, his abiding-place, in the mercy and forgiveness; and from his throne of grace he intends to hear the sinner and to commune with him. Poor souls! They are very apt to entertain strange thoughts of God and his attitude toward them, and suddenly conclude that God will pay no attention to them. Yet he is upon his mercy seat. He has taken up his place on purpose there, to the end that he may hear and regard the prayers of poor creatures. If he had said, "I will commune with you from my throne of judgment," then indeed you might have trembled and fled from the great and glorious majesty. But when he says that he will hear and commune with souls upon the throne of grace, or upon the mercy seat, this should encourage you and cause you to hope. Come boldly to the throne of grace!

JOHN BUNYAN, IN *PILGRIM'S PRAYER BOOK*

ASKING IS EASY

Your kingdom come, your will be done, on earth as it is in heaven.
(MATTHEW 6:10)

Sometimes intercession is taking man's needs and presenting them to the Father. At other times intercession is taking the Father's desires and praying for those things to be done on earth. The Bible is clear about many of God's desires. As intercessors we should learn to pray in such a way that His desires are being fulfilled on earth.

For instance, in 1 Timothy 2:3-4 Paul says, "This is good, and pleases God our Savior, who wants all men to be saved and to come to a knowledge of the truth." There is a parallel passage in 2 Peter 3:9 that says God does not want "anyone to perish, but everyone to come to repentance." Knowing this is God's desire, how do we pray?

If we say, "Father save the world," then we throw the entire responsibility on God. God wants us to co-labor with Him in intercession. We do this by discovering those things that will *cause* God's desire to be accomplished.

John 17 is a good example. The Father desired that the world would believe His Son was sent by Him. Jesus did *not* pray, "Father make the world believe that You sent me." Such a prayer would have thrown all the responsibility on the Father. What He did pray was "that all of them [His followers] may be one, Father, just as you are in me and I am in you. May they also be in us so that the world may believe that you have sent me" (John 17:21, NIV). He had discovered and prayed that which would *cause* God's desire to be accomplished.

The most difficult part of intercession is taking the time and effort to discover what to pray. Asking is the easy part. An intercessor needs to know what the Scriptures say about God's desires and then prayerfully seek what will cause those desires to happen on earth.

LEE BRASE, IN *PRAYING FROM GOD'S HEART*

FIRST, FORGIVE

Forgive us our debts, as we also have forgiven our debtors.
(MATTHEW 6:12)

When Mr. Alexander and I were holding meetings in Launceston, Tasmania, we had a day of fasting and prayer. There was an active Christian man in the community who had a son-in-law, and he and his wife had some trouble with that son-in-law. They had forbidden his ever coming under their roof again. At the morning service I spoke, as I always did, on the day of fasting and prayer, on hindrances to prayer. When I reached this part of my sermon the man was deeply convicted of that sin. As he went away from the meeting to his home he was wondering whether he ought to speak to his wife about this matter. He went up the steps, reached out his hand to open the door, still thinking about this. Unknown to him, his wife had been at the meeting also, and as he reached out to open the door his wife opened the door from the other side and instantly said, "Telegraph him to come at once." And they did. And power in prayer came into the life of that man and woman.

There are some reading these words who have had no power in prayer for days, or weeks, or months, or it may be for years, simply because of bitterness that they have in their heart toward someone. There is no use whatever of your praying until you let God cast out that bitterness. Listen again to the words of Jesus Christ Himself, "When ye stand praying, forgive, if ye have aught against any; that your Father also which is in heaven may forgive you your trespasses."

R. A. TORREY, IN *THE POWER OF PRAYER*

When We Pray

> *In everything by prayer and supplication with*
> *thanksgiving let your requests be made known to God.*
>
> (Philippians 4:6)

Do we realize that there is nothing the devil dreads so much as prayer? His great concern is to keep us from praying. He loves to see us "up to our eyes" in work—provided we do not pray. He does not fear because we are eager and earnest Bible students—provided we are little in prayer. Someone has wisely said, "Satan laughs at our toiling, mocks at our wisdom, but trembles when we pray." All this is so familiar to us—but do we really pray? If not, then failure must dog our footsteps, whatever signs of apparent success there may be. Let us never forget that the greatest thing we can do for God or for man is to pray. For we can accomplish far more by our prayers than by our work. Prayer is omnipotent; it can do anything that God can do! When we pray, God works. All fruitfulness in service is the outcome of prayer—of the worker's prayers or of those who are holding up holy hands on his behalf. We all know how to pray, but perhaps many of us need to cry as the disciples did of old, "Lord, teach us to pray."

> O Lord, by whom we come to God,
> The Life, the Truth, the Way,
> The path of prayer yourself have trod;
> Lord, teach us how to pray.

An Unknown Christian, in *The Kneeling Christian*

Search Me, O God

> *O Lord, you have searched me and known me!*
>
> (Psalm 139:1)

As one looks at some star-galaxy, and sees it only as a wreath of dimming mist, so one becomes conscious of innumerable unregarded sins, merely by the shadow which they fling upon the face of the heavens. But when one observes through a telescope the nebulous drift, it resolves itself into a cluster of stars, almost infinite in number. And when one examines in the secret place of communion the cloud which darkens the face of God, it is seen to scatter and break into a multitude of sins. If, then, in the hour of prayer we have no living intercourse with God, let us plead with the psalmist, "Search me, O God, and know my heart; try me, and know my thoughts; and see if there be any way of wickedness in me, and lead me in the way everlasting" (Psalm 139:23-24, KJV). He who has engaged to "search Jerusalem with candles" (Zephaniah 1:12, KJV) will examine us through and through, will test us as silver is proved, will sift us as wheat. He will bring up from the unexplored depths of our nature all that is contrary to the mind of Christ, and reduce every thought and imagination to the obedience of his will.

David McIntyre, in *The Hidden Life of Prayer*

A CHILD'S RIGHT

Whoever does not receive the kingdom of God like a child shall not enter it.
(LUKE 18:17)

The Jewish law and the prophets know something of God as a Father. Occasional and imperfect, yet comforting glimpses they had of the great truth of God's Fatherhood, and of our sonship. Christ lays the foundation of prayer deep and strong with this basic principle. The law of prayer, the right to pray, rests on our sonship. "Our Father" brings us into the closest relationship to God. Prayer is the child's approach, the child's plea, the child's right. It is the law of prayer that looks up, that lifts up the eye to "Our Father, who art in heaven." Our Father's house is our home in heaven. Heavenly citizenship and heavenly homesickness are in prayer. Prayer is an appeal from the lowness, from the emptiness, from the need of earth, to the highness, the fullness and to the all-sufficiency of heaven. Prayer turns the eye and the heart heavenward with child's longings, a child's trust and a child's expectancy. To hallow God's name, to speak it with bated breath, to hold it sacredly, this also belongs to prayer. The only way to heaven is by route of prayer, such prayer of the heart which every one is capable of. It is prayer, not of reasonings which are the fruits of study, or of the exercise of the imagination, which fills the mind with wondering objects, but which fails to settle salvation, but the simple, confidential prayer of the child to his Father in heaven.

E. M. BOUNDS, IN *THE REALITY OF PRAYER*

The Work of the Spirit

*The Spirit himself bears witness with
our spirit that we are children of God.*
(Romans 8:16)

Whenever there is mention made of comfort and consolation in the Scripture given to the saints (as there is most frequently), it is the proper consequent of the work of the Holy Ghost towards them. Comfort or consolation in general, is the setting and composing of the soul in rest and contentedness in the midst of or from troubles, by the consideration or presence of some good, wherein it is interested, outweighing the evil, trouble, or perplexity that it hath to wrestle withal. Consolation ariseth from the presence or consideration of a greater good, that outbalances the evil or perplexity wherewith we are to contend. Now, in the effects or acts of the Holy Ghost before mentioned lie all the springs of our consolation. There is no comfort but from them; and there is no trouble that we may not have comfort in and against by them. That a man may have consolation in any condition, nothing is required but the presence of a good, rendering the evil wherewith he is pressed inconsiderable to him. Suppose a man under the greatest calamity that can possibly befall a child of God, or a confluence of all those evils numbered by Paul, Romans 8:35, etc.; let this man have the Holy Ghost performing the works mentioned before towards him, and, in despite of all his evils, his consolations will abound. Suppose him to have a sense of the love of God all the while shed abroad in his heart, a clear witness within that he is a child of God, accepted with him, that he is sealed and marked of God for his own, that he is an heir of all the promises of God, and the like; it is impossible that man should not triumph in all his tribulations.

John Owen, in *Of Communion with God the Father, Son and Holy Ghost*

Be Real with God

When you come to appear before me,
who has required of you this trampling of my courts?
(Isaiah 1:12)

If you may not come to God with the occasions of your private life and affairs, then there is some unreality in the relation between you and Him. If some private crisis absorbs you, some business or family anxiety of little moment to others but of much to you, and if you may not bring that to God in prayer, then one of two things. Either it is not you, in your actual reality, that came to God, but it is you in a pose — you in some role which you are trying with poor success to play before Him. You are trying to pray as another person than you are — a better person, perhaps, as some great apostle, who should have on his worshipping mind nothing but the grand affairs of the Church and Kingdom, and not be worried by common cares. You are praying in court-dress. You are trying to pray as you imagine one should pray to God, as another person than you are, and in other circumstances. You are creating a self and a situation to place before God. Either that or you are not praying to a God who loves, helps, and delivers you in every pinch of life, but only to one who uses you as a pawn for the victory of His great kingdom. You are not praying to Christ's God. You are praying to a God who cares only for great actors in His kingdom, for the heroic people who cherish nothing but the grand style, or for the calm people who do not deeply feel life's trials. The reality of prayer is bound up with the reality and intimacy of life. And its great object is to get home as we are to God as He is, and to win response even when we get no compliance.

P. T. Forsyth, in *The Soul of Prayer*

Audience with God

Guard your steps when you go to the house of God. To draw near
to listen is better than to offer the sacrifice of fools,
for they do not know that they are doing evil.

(Ecclesiastes 5:1)

There was a time when I had wandered far from God, and had definitely decided that I would not accept Jesus Christ; nevertheless, I prayed every night. I had come to a place where I doubted whether the Bible was the Word of God, and whether Jesus Christ was the Son of God, and even doubted whether there were a personal God; nevertheless, I prayed every night. I am glad that I was brought up that way, and that the habit of prayer was so instilled into me that I came back out of the darkness of agnosticism into the clear light of an intelligent faith in God and His Word. Nevertheless, prayer was largely a matter of form. There was little real thought of God, and no real approach to God. And even after I was converted, yes, even after I had entered the ministry, prayer was largely a matter of form. But the day came when I realized what real prayer meant, realized that prayer was having an audience with God, actually coming into the presence of God and asking and getting things from Him. And the realization of that fact transformed my prayer life. Before that, prayer had been a mere duty, and sometimes a very irksome duty, but from that time on prayer has been not merely a duty but a privilege, one of the most highly esteemed privileges of life. Before that the thought I had was, "How much time must I spend in prayer?" The thought that now possesses me is, "How much time may I spend in prayer without neglecting the other privileges and duties of life?"

R. A. Torrey, in *The Power of Prayer*

FEEDING ON HIS PRESENCE

*Jesus answered him, "If anyone loves me, he will keep
my word, and my Father will love him, and we will
come to him and make our home with him."*

(JOHN 14:23)

When, by an act of lively faith, you are placed in the Presence of God, recollect some truth wherein there is substance and food; pause gently and sweetly thereon, not to employ the reason, but merely to calm and fix the mind: for you must observe, that your principal exercise should ever be the Presence of God; your subject, therefore, should rather serve to stay the mind, than exercise the understanding.

From this procedure, it will necessarily follow, that the lively faith in a God immediately present in our inmost soul, will produce an eager and vehement pressing inwardly into ourselves, and a restraining all our senses from wandering abroad: this serves to extricate us speedily from numberless distractions, to remove us far from external objects, and to bring us nigh unto our God, Who is only to be found in our inmost centre, which is the Holy of Holies wherein He dwelleth.

He hath even promised "to come and make his abode with him that doth his will" (John 14:23). Saint Augustine accuses himself of wasting his time, by not having from the first sought God in this manner of prayer.

When we are thus fully introverted, and warmly penetrated throughout with a living sense of the Divine Presence; when the senses are all recollected, and withdrawn from the circumference to the center, and the soul is sweetly and silently employed on the truths we have read, not in reasoning, but in feeding thereon, and in animating the will by affection, rather than fatiguing the understanding by study. In stillness and repose, with respect, confidence and love, swallow the blessed food of which we have tasted: this method is, indeed, highly necessary, and will advance the soul farther in a short time, than any other in a course of years.

JEANNE GUYON, IN *A SHORT AND EASY METHOD OF PRAYER*

PRAYERS RISING FROM GRIEF

*Likewise the Spirit helps us in our weakness. For we do not
know what to pray for as we ought, but the Spirit himself
intercedes for us with groanings too deep for words.*

(ROMANS 8:26)

Prayer is not, as many take it to be, just a few babbling, prating, complimentary expressions, but a sensible feeling in the heart, an awareness of
what God is and what we are. Prayer is sensible of many diverse things.
Sometimes we pray with sense—awareness—of sin, sometimes with a
sense of mercy needed or received, and sometimes with a sense that God is
ready to give us mercy.

Often in prayer there is a sense of the need of mercy by reason of our
understanding the danger of sin. The soul feels, and from feeling it sighs,
groans, and breaks in the heart. Right prayer can bubble up out of the heart
pressed with grief and bitterness. When Hannah prayed for a child, the
Scripture says, "In bitterness of soul Hannah wept much and prayed to the
Lord" (1 Samuel 1:10, NIV). And the Lord heard her prayer and she conceived
and gave birth to the great prophet Samuel.

"I am worn out calling for help; my throat is parched. My eyes fail,
looking for my God," cried David (Psalm 69:3, NIV). David roars, weeps,
faints at heart, and fails at the eyes: "I am feeble and utterly crushed; I
groan in anguish of heart. All my longings lie open before you, O Lord; my
sighing is not hidden from you. My heart pounds, my strength fails me;
even the light has gone from my eyes" (Psalm 38:8-10, NIV). Hezekiah
mourns like a dove: "I cried like a swift or a thrush, I moaned like a mourning dove. My eyes grew weak as I looked at the heavens. I am troubled: O
Lord, come to my aid!" (Isaiah 38:14, NIV). Ephraim moans before the Lord
and the Lord hears his cry: "I have surely heard Ephraim's moaning," God
said to his prophet (Jeremiah 31:18, NIV).

In all these instances mentioned here, and in hundreds more that might
be named from the Scriptures, you may see that prayer carries in it a sensible
feeling disposition, and often it is awareness of the awfulness of sin.

JOHN BUNYAN, IN *PILGRIM'S PRAYER BOOK*

His Holiness

Strive for peace with everyone, and for the holiness
without which no one will see the Lord.
(Hebrews 12:14)

When we see the holiness of God, we shall adore and magnify Him. Moses had to learn the same lesson. God told him to take his shoes from off his feet, for the place whereon he stood was holy ground. When we hear men trying to make out that they are holy, and speaking about their holiness, they make light of the holiness of God. It is His holiness that we need to think and speak about; when we do that, we shall be prostrate in the dust. You remember, also, how it was with Peter. When Christ made Himself known to him, he said, "Depart from me, for I am a sinful man, O Lord!" A sight of God is enough to show us how holy He is, and how unholy we are. We find that Job too, had to be taught the same lesson. "Then Job answered the Lord, and said: Behold I am vile; what shall I answer Thee? I will lay my hand upon my mouth." . . . If we are struggling to live a higher life, and to know something of God's holiness and purity, what we need is to be brought into contact with Him, that He may reveal Himself. Then we shall take our place before Him as those men of old were constrained to do. We shall hallow His Name — as the Master taught His disciples, when He said, "Hallowed be Thy Name." When I think of the irreverence of the present time, it seems to me that we have fallen on evil days. Let us, as Christians, when we draw near to God in prayer, give Him His right place. "Let us have grace whereby we may serve God acceptably, with reverence and Godly fear, for our God is a consuming fire."

D. L. Moody, in *Prevailing Prayer*

A Heart Reaching Out to God

Indeed our fellowship is with the Father and with his Son Jesus Christ.
And we are writing these things so that our joy may be complete.

(1 John 1:3-4)

"The goal of prayer is the ear of God," a goal that can only be reached by patient and continued and continuous waiting upon him, pouring out our hearts to him and permitting him to speak to us. Only by so doing can we expect to know him, and as we come to know him better we shall spend more time in his presence and find presence a constant and ever-increasing delight. *Always* does not mean that we are to neglect the ordinary duties of life; what it means is that the soul which has come into intimate contact with God in the silence of the prayer-chamber is never out of conscious touch with the Father, that the heart is always going out to him in loving communion, and that the moment the mind is released from the task on which it is engaged, it returns naturally to God as the bird does to its nest. What a beautiful conception of prayer we get if we regard it in this light, if we view it as a constant fellowship, an unbroken audience with the king. Prayer then loses every vestige of dread which it may once have possessed; we regard it no longer as a duty which must be performed, but rather as a privilege which is to be enjoyed, a rare delight that is always revealing some new beauty. Thus, when we open our eyes in the morning, our thought instantly mounts heavenward. To many Christians the morning hours are the most precious portion of the day, because they provide the opportunity for the hallowed fellowship that gives the keynote to the day's program. And what better introduction can there be to the never-ceasing glory and wonder of a new day than to spend it alone with God? It is said that Mr. Moody, at a time when no other place was available, kept his morning watch in the coal-shed, pouring out his heart to God, and finding in his precious Bible a true "feast of fat things."

E. M. Bounds, in *Purpose in Prayer*

CONSTANT SUPPLICATION

Blessed be God, because he has not rejected my prayer
or removed his steadfast love from me!
(PSALM 66:20)

In looking back upon the character of our prayers, if we do it honestly, we shall be filled with wonder that God has ever answered them. There may be some who think their prayers worthy of acceptance — as the Pharisee did; but the true Christian, in a more enlightened retrospect, weeps over his prayers, and if he could retrace his steps he would desire to pray more earnestly. Remember, Christian, how cold thy prayers have been. When in thy closet thou shouldst have wrestled as Jacob did; but instead thereof, thy petitions have been faint and few — far removed from that humble, believing, persevering faith, which cries, "I will not let thee go except thou bless me." Yet, wonderful to say, God has heard these cold prayers of thine, and not only heard, but answered them. Reflect also, how infrequent have been thy prayers, unless thou hast been in trouble, and then thou hast gone often to the mercy-seat: but when deliverance has come, where has been thy constant supplication? Yet, notwithstanding thou hast ceased to pray as once thou didst, God has not ceased to bless. When thou hast neglected the mercy-seat, God has not deserted it, but the bright light of the Shekinah has always been visible between the wings of the cherubim. Oh! it is marvellous that the Lord should regard those intermittent spasms of importunity which come and go with our necessities. What a God is he thus to hear the prayers of those who come to him when they have pressing wants, but neglect him when they have received a mercy; who approach him when they are forced to come, but who almost forget to address him when mercies are plentiful and sorrows are few. Let his gracious kindness in hearing such prayers touch our hearts, so that we may henceforth be found "Praying always with all prayer and supplication in the Spirit."

CHARLES SPURGEON, IN *MORNING BY MORNING*

A Prayer Warrior at Work

Let us then with confidence draw near to the throne of grace,
that we may receive mercy and find grace to help in time of need.

(Hebrews 4:16)

We had entered the room about 8 o'clock in the morning, several had gone out, others had come in, but Hyde was on his face on the floor, and had led us in prayer several times. Meals had been forgotten, and my tired feeling had gone, and the revival account and message that I was to deliver and concerning which I had been very anxious had gone out of my mind, until about 3:30 when Hyde got up, and I found we were the only two present. He took me right to the door, then took my hand and said, "Go in and speak, that is *your* work, I shall go back to the Prayer Room to pray for you, that is *my* work. When the service is over, come into the Prayer Room again and we shall praise God together." What a thrill, like an electric shock, passed through me as we parted. It was easy to speak though I was speaking through an interpreter. What I said, I do not know. Before the meeting was through, the Indian translator overcome by his feelings and overpowered by the Spirit of God failed to go on and another had to take his place. I know the Lord spoke that night, He spoke to me, and spoke to many. I realized then the Power of Prayer; how often I had read of blessing in answer to prayer, but it was brought home to me that evening with such force that ever since, I try to enlist prayer warriors to pray for me whenever I stand up to deliver His messages. It was one of the most wonderful services I ever attended, and I know that it was the Praying Saint behind the scenes that brought the blessing down on me.

Captain E. G. Carré, in *A Present-Day Challenge to Prayer*

The Stages of Prayer

He is able to save to the uttermost those who draw near to God
through him, since he always lives to make intercession for them.
(Hebrews 7:25)

This is the inner meaning of prayer. It is more than asking, it is communion, fellowship, cooperation, identification, with God the Father and the Son by the Holy Spirit. Prayer is more than words, for it is mightiest when wordless. It is more than asking, for it reaches its highest glory when it adores and asks nothing. When a child entered his father's study and walked up to him at his desk, the father turned and asked, "What do you want, Sonnie?" The little chap answered, "Nothing, Daddy, I just came to be with you." This mystery of the Spirit is the key to other mysteries. The secret of the Lord is made manifest to those who pray in the fellowship of the Spirit. There are stages of prayer. In one stage we pray and ask Him to help. There is a more wonderful way in which He prays and we assent, and His praying is ours. He makes intercession within the temple of our hearts, and our Lord ever lives to make intercession for us at the right hand of the Father. The Spirit within our spirit prays, working in us to will and to do the will and good pleasure of our Father who is in heaven. He is God the Spirit representing God the Father and God the Son, and the Three are one God. He is the power that worketh in us. He it is that unifies hearts in prayer and makes them an irresistible unity in intercession. The assurance of answered prayer comes from Him, and He it is that makes prayer the mightiest force in the universe of God. The secret of it all is in Him. The power of it all is by Him. The joy of it all is with Him.

Samuel Chadwick, in The Path of Prayer

Praying in Perfect Confidence

From his fullness we have all received, grace upon grace.

(John 1:16)

[Brother Lawrence] told me that all consists in one hearty renunciation of everything which we are sensible does not lead to God. That we might accustom ourselves to a continual conversation with Him, with freedom and in simplicity. That we need only to recognize God intimately present with us, to address ourselves to Him every moment, that we may beg His assistance for knowing His will in things doubtful, and for rightly performing those which we plainly see He requires of us, offering them to Him before we do them, and giving Him thanks when we have done. That in this conversation with God we are also employed in praising, adoring, and loving Him incessantly, for His infinite goodness and perfection. That, without being discouraged on account of our sins, we should pray for His grace with a perfect confidence, as relying upon the infinite merits of our Lord Jesus Christ. That God never failed offering us His grace at each action; that he distinctly perceived it, and never failed of it, unless when his thoughts had wandered from a sense of God's presence, or he had forgotten to ask His assistance. That God always gave us light in our doubts when we had no other design but to please Him. That our sanctification did not depend upon *changing* our works, but in doing that for God's sake which we commonly do for our own. That it is lamentable to see how many people mistook the means for the end, addicting themselves to certain works, which they performed imperfectly, by reason of their human or selfish regards.

Brother Lawrence, in *The Practice of the Presence of God*

BLESSED BE HIS NAME AT ALL TIMES

The Lord disciplines the one he loves, and
chastises every son whom he receives.
(HEBREWS 12:6)

How true is the sentence of Augustine, "Earthly riches are full of poverty."
Rich stores of corn and wine will never satiate a hungry soul. Purple and
fine linen may only mask a threadbare life. The shrill blare of fame's trum-
pet cannot subdue the discords of the spirit. The best night that Jacob ever
spent was that in which a stone was his pillow, and the skies the curtains of
his tent. When Jacob was held in derision by youths whose fathers he would
have disdained to set with the dogs of his flock, he was made a spectacle to
angels, and became the theme of their wonder and joy. The defeat which
Adam sustained in Paradise, the Redeemer retrieved in the desolation of
the desert and the anguish of his passion. The cross we are called to bear
may be heavy, but we have not to carry it far. And when God bids us lay it
down, heaven begins. Chrysostom, on his way to exile, exclaimed, "Thank
God for everything." If we imitate him we shall never have a bad day.
Alexander Simson, a famous Scottish minister of two hundred years ago,
once, when out walking, fell, and broke his leg. He was found "sitting with
his broken leg in his arm, and always crying out, 'Blessed be the Lord;
blessed be his name.'" And truly, seeing that all things work together for
good to those who love God, he was wise. Richard Baxter found reason to
bless God for a discipline of pain which endured for five and thirty years.
And Samuel Rutherford exclaims, "Oh, what owe I to the furnace, the file,
and the hammer of my Lord Jesus!"

DAVID MCINTYRE, IN *THE HIDDEN LIFE OF PRAYER*

In His Name

The glory that you have given me I have given to them,
that they may be one even as we are one.
(John 17:22)

What does it mean when Jesus gives us the power over His name — the free use of it — with the assurance that whatever we ask in it will be given to us? The ordinary comparison of one person giving another, on some special occasion, the liberty to ask something in his name, comes altogether short here. Jesus solemnly gives to *all* His disciples a general and unlimited power to use His Name at *all* times for *everything* they desire. He could not do this if He did not know that He could trust us with His interests and that His honor would be safe in our hands. The free use of someone else's name is always a token of great confidence and close union. Someone who gives his name to another stands aside to let that person act for him. When the Lord Jesus went to heaven, He left His work — the management of His Kingdom on earth — in the hands of His servants. He also gave them His Name to draw all the supplies they needed for the due conduct of His business. Christ's servants have the spiritual power to use the Name of Jesus only insofar as they yield themselves to live only for the interests and the work of the Master. The use of the Name always supposes the surrender of our interests to Him Whom we represent. We are one; we have one life and one Spirit with Him. For this reason we may proceed in His Name. Our power in using that Name, whether with God, men, or devils, *depends on the measure of our spiritual life-union with Christ.* Our use of His Name rests on the unity of our lives with Him.

Andrew Murray, in *With Christ in the School of Prayer*

The Possibilities of Prayer

To Seth also a son was born, and he called his name Enosh.
At that time people began to call upon the name of the Lord.
(Genesis 4:26)

Prayer is direct address to God. Prayer secures blessings, and makes men better because it reaches the ear of God. Prayer is only for the betterment of men when it has affected God and moved him to do something for men. Prayer affects men by affecting God. Prayer moves men because it moves God to move men. Prayer influences men by influencing God to influence them. Prayer moves the hand that moves the world.

> That power is prayer, which soars on high,
> Through Jesus to the throne;
> And moves the hand which moves the world,
> To bring salvation down.

The utmost possibilities of prayer have rarely been realized. The promises of God are so great to those who truly pray, when he puts himself so fully into the hands of the praying ones, that it almost staggers our faith and causes us to hesitate with astonishment. His promise to answer, and to do and to give "all things," "anything," "whatsoever," and "all things whatsoever," is so large, so great, so exceeding broad, that we stand back in amazement and give ourselves to questioning and doubt. We "stagger at the promises through unbelief." Really the answers of God to prayer have been pared down by us to our little faith, and have been brought down to the low level of our narrow notions about God's ability, liberality, and resources. Let us ever keep in mind and never for one moment allow ourselves to doubt the statement that God means what he says in all of his promises. God's promises are his own word. His veracity is at stake in them.

Pray, Then Do

How then will they call on him in whom they have not believed?
And how are they to believe in him of whom they have never heard?

(Romans 10:14)

Another condition of prevailing prayer is the consistent use of means to secure the object prayed for, if means are within our reach and are known by us to be necessary to the securing of the end. To pray for a revival and use no other means is to tempt God. This, I could plainly see, was the case of those who offered prayer in the prayer meeting of which I have spoken. They continued to offer prayer for a revival of religion, but out of meeting they were as silent as death on the subject and opened not their mouths to those around them. They continued this inconsistency until a prominent impenitent man in the community administered to them in my presence a terrible rebuke. He expressed just what I deeply felt. He rose, and with the utmost solemnity and tearfulness said: "Christian people, what can you mean? You continue to pray in these meetings for a revival of religion. You often exhort each other here to wake up and use means to promote a revival. You assure each other, and assure us who are impenitent, that we are on the way to hell; and I believe it. You also insist that if you should wake up, and use the appropriate means, there would be a revival and we should be converted. You tell us of our great danger, and that our souls are worth more than all worlds; and yet you keep busy in your comparatively trifling employments and use no such means. We have no revival and our souls are not saved." Here he broke down and fell, sobbing, back into his seat. This rebuke fell heavily upon that prayer meeting, as I shall ever remember.

Charles Finney, in *Power from on High*

TRULY KNOWING GOD

I count everything as loss because of the surpassing
worth of knowing Christ Jesus my Lord.
(PHILIPPIANS 3:8)

For millions of Christians God is no more real than He is to the non-Christian. They go through life trying to love an ideal and be loyal to a mere principle. Over against all this cloudy vagueness stands the clear scriptural doctrine that God can be known in personal experience. A loving Personality dominates the Bible, walking among the trees of the garden and breathing fragrance over every scene. Always a living Person is present, speaking, pleading, loving, working, and manifesting Himself whenever and wherever His people have the receptivity necessary to receive the manifestation. The Bible assumes as a self-evident fact that men can know God with at least the same degree of immediacy as they know any other person or thing that comes within the field of their experience. The same terms are used to express the knowledge of God as are used to express knowledge of physical things. "O *taste* and see that the Lord is good" (Psalm 34:8, NASB, emphasis added). The whole import of the Scripture is toward this belief. What can all this mean except that we have in our hearts organs by means of which we can know God as certainly as we know material things through our five senses? We apprehend the physical world by exercising the faculties given us for the purpose, and we possess spiritual faculties by means of which we can know God and the spiritual world if we will obey the Spirit's urge and begin to use them. But the very ransomed children of God themselves: why do they know so little of that habitual conscious communion with God which the Scriptures seem to offer? The answer is our chronic unbelief. Faith enables our spiritual sense to function. Where faith is defective the result will be inward insensibility and numbness toward spiritual things. This is the condition of vast numbers of Christians today.

A. W. TOZER, IN *THE PURSUIT OF GOD*

THE WORK OF PRAYER

Being in an agony he prayed more earnestly; and his sweat
became like great drops of blood falling down to the ground.

(LUKE 22:44)

The work of praying is prerequisite to all other work in the kingdom of God, for the simple reason that it is by prayer that we couple the powers of heaven to our helplessness, the powers which can turn water into wine and remove mountains in our own life and in the lives of others, the powers which can awaken those who sleep in sin and raise up the dead, the powers which can capture strongholds and make the impossible possible. There are no doubt many believers who have not given much attention to prayer as work. Prayer is looked upon mainly as a means of sustaining our life in God from day to day in the midst of an atmosphere which is so worldly that it chokes to death our weak, frail, spiritual life. And we pray accordingly. We move in a narrow circle about ourselves and those nearest to us. Now and then we widen the circle a little bit, especially when we gather with the people of God, and the mighty tasks of the kingdom of God at home and abroad are placed before us. But when we get back home into our daily routine, our prayer-circle narrows down again. Only the Spirit of prayer can teach us to labor in prayer, to employ prayer as a means of doing spiritual work. Every time we see how selfish and slothful we are in prayer, we should cry in our helplessness to Him who giveth gladly and upbraideth not. He can create, that is, bring into being that which is not. God be praised! One of the things that the Spirit must teach us about prayer as work is this: to learn to take time to pray. All work takes time. When it becomes clear to us that prayer is a part of our daily program of work, it will also become clear to us that there is time also for this work, just as we set aside time for other necessary things, such as eating and dressing.

OLE HALLESBY, IN *PRAYER*

PRAISE WITH PRAYER

Although they knew God, they did not honor
him as God or give thanks to him.
(ROMANS 1:21)

Gratitude and thanksgiving always looks back at the past though it may also take in the present. But prayer always looks to the future. Thanksgiving deals with things already received. Prayer deals with things desired, asked for and expected. Prayer turns to gratitude and praise when the things asked for have been granted by God. As prayer brings things to us which beget gratitude and thanksgiving, so praise and gratitude promote prayer, and induce more praying and better praying. Gratitude and thanksgiving forever stand opposed to all murmurings at God's dealings with us, and all complainings at our lot. Gratitude and murmuring never abide in the same heart at the same time. An unappreciative spirit has no standing beside gratitude and praise. And true prayer corrects complaining and promotes gratitude and thanksgiving. Dissatisfaction at one's lot, and a disposition to be discontented with things which come to us in the providence of God, are foes to gratitude and enemies to thanksgiving. The murmurers are ungrateful people. Appreciative men and women have neither the time nor disposition to stop and complain. The bane of the wilderness journey of the Israelites on their way to Canaan was their proneness to murmur and complain against God and Moses. For this, God was several times greatly grieved, and it took the strong praying of Moses to avert God's wrath because of these murmurings. The absence of gratitude left no room nor disposition for praise and thanksgiving just as it is so always. But when these same Israelites were brought through the Red Sea dry shod, while their enemies were destroyed, there was a song of praise led by Miriam, the sister of Moses.

E. M. BOUNDS, IN *THE ESSENTIALS OF PRAYER*

ALL THE HEAVEN I WANT

I looked, and behold, on Mount Zion stood the Lamb.

(REVELATION 14:1)

The apostle John was privileged to look within the gates of heaven, and in describing what he saw, he begins by saying, "I looked, and, lo, a Lamb!" This teaches us that the chief object of contemplation in the heavenly state is "the Lamb of God, which taketh away the sins of the world." Nothing else attracted the apostle's attention so much as the person of that Divine Being, who hath redeemed us by his blood. He is the theme of the songs of all glorified spirits and holy angels. Christian, here is joy for thee; thou hast looked, and thou hast seen the Lamb. Through thy tears thine eyes have seen the Lamb of God taking away thy sins. Rejoice, then. In a little while, when thine eyes shall have been wiped from tears, thou wilt see the same Lamb *exalted on his throne.* It is the joy of thy heart to hold daily fellowship with Jesus; thou shalt have the same joy to a higher degree in heaven; thou shalt enjoy the constant vision of his presence; thou shalt dwell with him forever. "I looked, and, lo, a Lamb!" Why, that Lamb is heaven itself; for as good Rutherford says, "Heaven and Christ are the same thing;" to be with Christ is to be in heaven, and to be in heaven is to be with Christ. That prisoner of the Lord very sweetly writes in one of his glowing letters — "O my Lord Jesus Christ, if I could be in heaven without thee, it would be a hell; and if I could be in hell, and have thee still, it would be a heaven to me, for thou art all the heaven I want." It is true, is it not, Christian? Does not thy soul say so?

CHARLES SPURGEON, IN *MORNING BY MORNING*

ABANDONED TO GOD

Humble yourselves, therefore, under the mighty hand of God so that at the proper time he may exalt you, casting all your anxieties on him, because he cares for you.

(1 PETER 5:6-7)

Great faith produces great abandonment: we must confide in God "hoping against hope" (Romans 4:18). Abandonment is the casting off of all selfish care, that we may be altogether at the Divine Disposal. All Christians are exhorted to this resignation: for it is said to all, "Be not anxious for tomorrow, for your Heavenly Father knoweth all that is necessary for you" (Matthew 6:34,32). "In all thy ways acknowledge him, and he shall direct thy paths" (Proverbs 3:6). "Commit thy ways unto the Lord, and thy thoughts shall be established" (Proverbs 16:3). "Commit thy ways unto the Lord, and he himself will bring it to pass" (Psalm 37:5).

Our abandonment then should be as fully applied to external as internal things, giving up all our concerns into the hands of God, forgetting ourselves, and thinking only of Him; by which the heart will remain always disengaged, free, and at peace. It is practiced by continually losing our own will in the will of God; by renouncing every particular inclination as soon as it arises, however good it may appear, that we may stand in indifference with respect to ourselves, and only will that which God from eternity hath willed; by being resigned in all things, whether for soul or body, whether for time or eternity; by leaving what is past in oblivion, what is to come to Providence, and devoting the present moment to God, which brings with itself God's eternal order, and is as infallible a declaration to us of His will as it is inevitable and common to all; by attributing nothing that befalls us to the creature, but regarding all things in God, and looking upon all, excepting only our sins, as infallibly proceeding from Him. Surrender yourselves, then, to be led and disposed of just as God pleaseth, with respect both to your outward and inward state.

JEANNE GUYON, IN *A SHORT AND EASY METHOD OF PRAYER*

THE FATHER OF FAITH

> *By faith Abraham obeyed when he was called to go out*
> *to a place that he was to receive as an inheritance.*
> *And he went out, not knowing where he was going.*
> (HEBREWS 11:8)

Abraham, the friend of God, was a striking illustration of one of the Old Testament saints who believed strongly in prayer. Abraham was not a shadowy figure by any means. In the simplicity and dimness of the patriarchal dispensation, as illustrated by him, we learn the worth of prayer, as well as discover its antiquity. The fact is, prayer reaches back to the first ages of man on earth. We see how the energy of prayer is absolutely required in the simplest as well as in the most complex dispensations of God's grace. When we study Abraham's character, we find that after his call to go out into an unknown country, on his journey with his family and his household servants, wherever he tarried by the way for the night or longer, he always erected an altar, and "called upon the name of the Lord." And this man of faith and prayer was one of the first to erect a family altar, around which to gather his household and offer the sacrifices of worship, of praise and of prayer. These altars built by Abraham were, first of all, essentially altars about which he gathered his household, as distinguished from secret prayer. As God's revelations became fuller and more perfect, Abraham's prayerfulness increased, and it was at one of those spiritual eras that "Abraham fell on his face and God talked with him." On still another occasion we find this man, "the father of the faithful," on his face before God, astonished almost to incredulity at the purposes and revelations of Almighty God to him in promising him a son at his old age, and the wonderful arrangements which God made concerning his promised son. Even Ishmael's destiny is shaped by Abraham's prayer when he prayed, "O that Ishmael might live before thee!" What a remarkable story is that of Abraham's standing before God repeating his intercessions for the wicked city of Sodom, the home of his nephew Lot, doomed by God's decision to destroy it! Sodom's fate was for a while stayed by Abraham's praying, and was almost entirely relieved by the humility and insistence of the praying of this man who believed strongly in prayer and who knew how to pray.

E. M. BOUNDS, IN *PRAYER AND PRAYING MEN*

THE LIFE OF PRAYER

Rejoice always, pray without ceasing, give thanks in all circumstances;
for this is the will of God in Christ Jesus for you.
(1 THESSALONIANS 5:16-18)

"Men ought always to pray, and" — although faintness of spirit attends on prayer like a shadow — "not faint." The soil in which the prayer of faith takes root is a life of unbroken communion with God, a life in which the windows of the soul are always open towards the City of Rest. We do not know the true potency of prayer until our hearts are so steadfastly inclined to God that our thoughts turn to him, as by divine instinct, whenever they are set free from the consideration of earthly things. It has been said of Origen (in his own words) that his life was "one unceasing supplication." By this means above all others the perfect idea of the Christian life is realized. Intercourse between the believer and his Lord ought never to be interrupted.

"The vision of God," says Bishop Westcott, "makes life a continuous prayer." And in that vision all fleeting things resolve themselves, and appear in relation to things unseen. In a broad use of the term, prayer is the sum of all the service that we render to God, so that all fulfillment of duty is, in one sense, the performance of divine service, and the familiar saying, "Work is worship," is justified. "I am prayer," said a Psalmist (Psalm 109:4, KJV). "In everything by prayer and supplication, with thanksgiving," said an Apostle.

In the Old Testament that life which is steeped in prayer is often described as a walk with God. Enoch walked in assurance, Abraham in perfectness, Elijah in fidelity, the sons of Levi in peace and equity. Or it is spoken of as a dwelling with God, even as Joshua departed not from the Tabernacle; or as certain craftsmen of the olden time abode with a king for his work. Again, it is defined as the ascent of the soul into the Sacred Presence; as the planets, "with open face beholding," climb into the light of the sun's countenance, or as a flower, lit with beauty and dipped in fragrance, reaches upwards towards the light.

DAVID MCINTYRE, IN *THE HIDDEN LIFE OF PRAYER*

THE NEED FOR SINCERITY

If I had cherished iniquity in my heart, the Lord would not have listened.
(PSALM 66:18)

When men bear iniquity in their hearts, at the time of their prayers before God, it is as though a great impenetrable wall is separating them from God. You must understand this: you may pray for the preventing of temptation while at the same time you have a secret love for the very thing which you are praying to resist and are asking strength against. This shows the wickedness of man's heart, which will even love and hold fast to that which with the mouth it prays against. Of this sort are those who honor God with their mouths, but their hearts are far from him: "My people come to you, as they usually do, and sit before you to listen to your words, but they do not put them into practice. With their mouths they express devotion, but their hearts are greedy for unjust gain" (Ezekiel 33:31, NIV). How ugly it would be in our eyes if we should see a beggar ask for alms with the intention of throwing it to the dogs! Or think of that man who prays with one breath, "Bestow this upon me," and with the next breath, "I beseech you, do not give it to me!" And thus it is with those people who say with their mouths, "Your will be done," and with their hearts they mean everything else. With their mouths they say, "Hallowed be your name," and with their hearts and lives they delight to dishonor him all the day long. These are the prayers that become sin, and though they are prayed often, the Lord will never answer them.

When men pray for show to be heard, and to be thought a somebody in religion, and the like, these prayers also fall short of God's approbation and are never likely to be answered in reference to eternal life. There are those who seek repute and applause for their eloquent words and who seek more to tickle the ears and heads of their hearers than anything else.

JOHN BUNYAN, IN *PILGRIM'S PRAYER BOOK*

Finding the Heart of God in Prayer

Be imitators of God, as beloved children.

(Ephesians 5:1)

The Holy Spirit can give you eyes to see what others may fail to see. He can help you discern when people are discouraged, sad, or defeated. He can point out to you spiritual neglect, the need for revival, for new vision and greater obedience. He can inspire you to pray for the growth of the church, for the youth about you, for specially used servants of God. His bringing of needs to your attention is His call to you to pray. Satan does not object to your recognizing the needs, but he wants you to criticize and ridicule. The Holy Spirit, as your indwelling Prayer Partner, wants to make you prayerful, not critical. Satan wants you to talk about people and their needs; the Holy Spirit wants you to intercede in prayer for them. God's heart is pained by the sin, the indifference, and the godlessness of our age. Our loving Savior and the tender Holy Spirit plead in interceding prayer for the broken lives, broken homes, and the tragedies of sin and injustice throughout the world. They long for you to join them in daily intercession for the hurting, the broken, the lost, and those being destroyed by sin. God the Father wants someone to intercede for everyone in need. God hears the cry of the orphan, the sob of the brokenhearted, the angry words of the violent, and the screams of their victims. God feels the woes of the prisoners and the refugees, the hunger pangs of those starving for food. He is touched by the sorrow of those who mourn, the helplessness and hopelessness of those chained by habits of sin. He understands the spiritual darkness and the vague but deep dissatisfaction of those who have never received the gospel. The more faithfully and sincerely you pray for these needs, the more deeply the Holy Spirit will be able to burden you with these things which break the heart of God.

Wesley Duewel, in *Touch the World Through Prayer*

THE HEIGHT OF PRAYER

*Blessed be the God and Father of our Lord Jesus Christ, who has blessed
us in Christ with every spiritual blessing in the heavenly places.*

(EPHESIANS 1:3)

If God's will is to be done on earth as it is in heaven, prayer begins with adoration. Of course, it is thanks and petition; but before we give even our prayer we must first receive. The Answerer provides the very prayer. What we do here rests on what God has done. What we offer is drawn from us by what He offers. Our self-oblation stands on His; and the spirit of prayer flows from the gift of the Holy Ghost, the great Intercessor. Hence praise and adoration of His work in itself comes before even our thanksgiving for blessings to us. At the height of prayer, if not at its beginning, we are preoccupied with the great and glorious thing God has done for His own holy name in Redemption, apart from its immediate and particular blessing to us. We are blind for the time to ourselves. We cover our faces with our wings and cry "Holy, holy, holy is the Lord God of hosts; the fullness of the earth is His glory." Our full hearts glorify. We magnify His name. His perfections take precedence of our occasions. We pray for victory in the present war, for instance, and for deliverance from all war, for the sake of God's kingdom—in a spirit of adoration for the deliverance there that is not destroyed, or foiled, even by a devilry like this. If the kingdom of God not only got over the murder of Christ, but made it its great lever, there is nothing that it cannot turn to eternal blessing and to the glory of the holy name. But to the perspective of this faith, and to its vision of values so alien to human standards, we can rise only in prayer.

P. T. FORSYTH, IN *THE SOUL OF PRAYER*

Faith's Answers

Without faith it is impossible to please him, for whoever would draw near
to God must believe that he exists and that he rewards those who seek him.
(Hebrews 11:6)

It is the desire, the wish of the heart, that God delights to hear and to answer. When the centurion wanted Christ to heal his servant, he thought he was not worthy to go and ask the Lord himself, so he sent his friends to make the petition. He sent out messengers to meet the Master, and say, "Do not trouble yourself to come; all you have to do is to speak the word, and the disease will go." Jesus said to the Jews, "I have not found so great faith, no, not in Israel." He marveled at the faith of this centurion; it pleased him, so that he healed the servant then and there. Faith brought the answer. In John we read of a nobleman whose child was sick. The father fell on his knees before the Master, and said, "Come down, ere my child die." Here you have both earnestness and faith; and the Lord answered the prayer at once. The nobleman's son began to amend that very hour. Christ honored the man's faith. In his case there was nothing to rest upon but the bare word of Christ, but this was enough. It is well to bear always in mind, that the object of faith is not the creature, but the Creator; not the instrument, but the Hand that wields it. Richard Sibbes puts it for us thus: "The object in believing is God, and Christ as Mediator. We must have both to found our faith upon. We cannot believe in God, except we believe in Christ. For God must be satisfied by God; and by Him must that satisfaction be applied — the Spirit of God — by working faith in the heart, and for raising it up when it is dejected. All is supernatural in faith."

D. L. Moody, in Prevailing Prayer

Prayer and God's Mercy

Says the Lord God: This also I will let the house of Israel ask
me to do for them: to increase their people like a flock.
(Ezekiel 36:37)

Prayer is the forerunner of mercy. Turn to sacred history, and you will find that scarcely ever did a great mercy come to this world unheralded by supplication. You have found this true in your own personal experience. God has given you many an unsolicited favour, but still great prayer has always been the prelude of great mercy with you. When you first found peace through the blood of the cross, you had been praying much, and earnestly interceding with God that he would remove your doubts, and deliver you from your distresses. Your assurance was the result of prayer. When at any time you have had high and rapturous joys, you have been obliged to look upon them as answers to your prayers. When you have had great deliverances out of sore troubles, and mighty helps in great dangers, you have been able to say, "I sought the Lord, and he heard me, and delivered me from all my fears." Prayer is always the preface to blessing. It goes before the blessing as the blessing's shadow. When the sunlight of God's mercies rises upon our necessities, it casts the shadow of prayer far down upon the plain. Or, to use another illustration, when God piles up a hill of mercies, he himself shines behind them, and he casts on our spirits the shadow of prayer, so that we may rest certain, if we are much in prayer, our pleadings are the shadows of mercy. Prayer is thus connected with the blessing to show us the value of it. If we had the blessings without asking for them, we should think them common things; but prayer makes our mercies more precious than diamonds. The things we ask for are precious, but we do not realize their preciousness until we have sought for them earnestly.

Charles Spurgeon, in *Morning by Morning*

STANDING FIRM BY PRAYER

The weapons of our warfare are not carnal but mighty in God.
(2 CORINTHIANS 10:4, NKJV)

One of the greatest difficulties in war is to find a man who can keep his head when everyone else lost theirs. It is only done by steady practice. "Wherefore take unto you the whole armor of God"—not to fight, but to stand. We are not told to attack, to storm the forts of darkness. We are told to stand, unpanicky and unbudged, more than conquerors. A conqueror is one who fights and wins, a "more than conqueror" is one who easily and powerfully overcomes. The struggle is not against flesh and blood; it is against principalities and powers. We cannot touch them by intellect or organization, by courage or foresight of forethought. We cannot touch them at all unless we are based on redemption.

"Wherefore take unto you the whole armor of God." It is not given, we have to take it; it is there for us to put on, understanding what we are doing. We have the idea that prayer is for special times, but we have to put on the armor of God for the continual practice of prayer, so that any struggling onslaught of the powers of darkness cannot touch the position of prayer. When we pray easily it is because Satan is completely defeated in his onslaughts; when we pray with difficulty it is because Satan is gaining a victory. We have not been continuously practicing; we have not been facing things courageously; we have not been taking our orders from our Lord. Our Lord did not say, "Go" or "Do." He said, "Watch and pray."

OSWALD CHAMBERS, IN *IF YOU WILL ASK*

Save Us from Self

> *Do not fear, Daniel, for from the first day that you set*
> *your heart to understand, and to humble yourself*
> *before your God, your words were heard.*
>
> (Daniel 10:12, NKJV)

Pride prevents prayer, for prayer is a very humbling thing. How hateful pride must be in the sight of God! It is God who gives us all things "richly to enjoy." "What have you that you did not receive?" asks St. Paul (1 Corinthians 4:7, KJV). Surely, surely we are not going to let pride, with its hateful, ugly sister, jealousy, ruin our prayer life? God cannot do great things for us whereby we may be glad if they are going to "turn our heads." Oh, how foolish we can be! Sometimes, when we are insistent, God does give us what we ask at the expense of our holiness. "He gave them their request, but sent leanness into their soul" (Psalm 106:15, KJV). O God, save us from that—save us from self! Again, self asserts itself in criticizing others. Let this thought burn itself into your memory—the more like Jesus Christ a man becomes, the less he judges other people. It is an infallible test. Those who are always criticizing others have drifted away from Christ. They may still be his but have lost his Spirit of love. Beloved reader, if you have a criticizing nature, allow it to dissect yourself and never your neighbor. You will be able to give it full scope, and it will never be unemployed! Is this a harsh remark? Does it betray a tendency to commit the very sin—for it is sin—it condemns? It would do so were it spoken to any one individual. But its object is to pierce armor which is seemingly invulnerable. And no one who, for one month, has kept his tongue "from picking and stealing" the reputation of other people will ever desire to go back again to backbiting. "Love suffers long and is kind" (1 Corinthians 13:4, NKJV). Do we? Are we? We are ourselves no better because we have managed to paint other people in worse colors than ourselves. But, singularly enough, we enhance our own spiritual joy and our own living witness for Christ when we refuse to pass on disparaging information about others, or when we refrain from "judging" the work or lives of other people. It may be hard at first, but it soon brings untold joy and is rewarded by the love of all around.

An Unknown Christian, in *The Kneeling Christian*

THE TRUE LIFE OF FAITH

To me to live is Christ.
(PHILIPPIANS 1:21)

To many a believer, it was a new epoch in his spiritual life when it was revealed to him how truly and entirely Christ was his life, standing responsible for his remaining faithful and obedient. It was then that he really began to live a *life of faith*. No less blessed will be the discovery that Christ is responsible for our prayer-life too. As the center and embodiment of all prayer, it is communicated by Him through the Holy Spirit to His people. "He ever liveth to make intercession" as the Head of the Body. He is the Leader in that new and living way which He has opened up as the Author and the Perfecter of our faith. He provides everything for the life of His redeemed ones by giving His own life in them. He cares for their life of prayer by taking them up into His heavenly prayer-life, giving and maintaining His prayer-life within them. "I have prayed for thee," not to render thy faith needless, but "that thy faith fail not." Our faith and prayer of faith is rooted in His. If we pray with and in the eternal Intercessor, abiding in Him, "ask whatsoever ye will, and it shall be done unto you." The thought of our fellowship in the intercession of Jesus reminds us of what He has taught us more than once before. All these wonderful prayer-promises have the glory of God, in the manifestation of His Kingdom and the salvation of sinners, as their aim. As long as we pray chiefly for ourselves, the promises of the last night must remain a sealed book to us. The promises are given to the fruit-bearing branches of the Vine, to disciples sent into the world to live for perishing men as the Father sent Him, to His faithful servants and intimate friends who take up the work He leaves behind. Like their Lord, they have become seed-corn, losing their lives to multiply them. Let us each find out what our work is, and which souls are entrusted to our special prayers. Let us make our intercession for them our life of fellowship with God.

ANDREW MURRAY, IN *WITH CHRIST IN THE SCHOOL OF PRAYER*

Drawing Near

In him all the fullness of God was pleased to dwell, and through
him to reconcile to himself all things, whether on earth
or in heaven, making peace by the blood of his cross.

(Colossians 1:19-20)

The Voice of God is a friendly Voice. No one need fear to listen to it unless he has already made up his mind to resist it. The blood of Jesus has covered not only the human race but all creation as well. We may safely preach a friendly Heaven. The heavens as well as the earth are filled with the good will of Him that dwelt in the bush. The perfect blood of atonement secures this forever. Whoever will listen will hear the speaking of Heaven. This is definitely not the hour when men take kindly to an exhortation to *listen*, for listening is not today a part of popular religion. We are at the opposite end of the pole from there. Religion has accepted the monstrous heresy that noise, size, activity and bluster make a man dear to God. But we may take heart. To a people caught in the tempest of the last great conflict God says, "Be still, and know that I am God," and still He says it, as if He means to tell us that our strength and safety lie not in noise but in silence. It is important that we get still to wait on God. And it is best that we get alone, preferably with our Bible outspread before us. Then if we will we may draw near to God and begin to hear Him speak to us in our hearts. I think for the average person the progression will be something like this: First a sound as of a Presence walking in the garden. Then a voice, more intelligible, but still far from clear. Then the happy moment when the Spirit begins to illuminate the Scriptures, and that which had been only a sound, or at best a voice, now becomes an intelligible word, warm and intimate and clear as the word of a dear friend. Then will come life and light, and best of all, ability to see and rest in and embrace Jesus Christ as Savior and Lord and All.

A. W. Tozer, in *The Pursuit of God*

Prayer Is Not Easy

I tell you, ask, and it will be given to you; seek, and you
will find; knock, and it will be opened to you.

(Luke 11:9-10)

The parables of the Friend at Midnight and the Unjust Judge are not like Jesus' other parables, for they teach by contrast and not by comparison. God is not like the reluctant friend or the unjust judge. Then why tell these stories? The point in common between them and prayer is that in both *importunity prevails*. If the suppliants were not heard for their much speaking, their persistence had much to do with their prevailing. What place is there for such importunity in the prayers of children to their heavenly Father? Our Lord Himself prayed with intensity and importunity. He rose early to pray. He spent all nights in prayer. The Epistle to the Hebrews (5:7) tells us that He offered up prayers and supplications with strong crying and tears. The awe of Gethsemane is full of mystery. He called upon God as Father, but in His praying there was the sweat and agony of blood. "He kneeled down and prayed, saying, Father, if Thou be willing, remove this cup from Me: nevertheless not My will, but Thine, be done . . . and being in an agony He prayed more earnestly; and His sweat became as it were great drops of blood falling down to the ground" (Luke 22:41-44, kjv). St. Matthew (26:38-46) tells us that He prayed a third time using the same words. He wrought many mighty works in nature and in men, calming the tempest, casting out demons and raising the dead, but in none of them is there any trace of strain or travail. Virtue went out of Him and He wearied in toil, but there was the ease of mastery in all He did; yet of His praying it is said, "As He prayed He sweat." He prayed in agony unto blood. If God be father, why such agony in the praying of His Son? Prayer is not the easy thing that seems to be implied in the simplicity of asking our Heavenly Father for what we want and getting it. There is travail in it. There is work in it. There is entreaty in it. There is importunity in it.

Samuel Chadwick, in *The Path of Prayer*

Worship the Living God

The Lord is the true God; he is the living God and the everlasting King.
(Jeremiah 10:10)

True worship is not conditioned by any religious atmosphere. It is like a well of water springing up from within the heart of the lover for the Beloved. It took a negative form of worship to open my eyes to the meaning of true worship. I was visiting my first Chinese temple in the city of Shanghai. Inside, it was dark and shadowy and lined with double rows of dusty idols on heavy pedestals. At the far end was a tall loft and a giant gilded idol was set among heavy draperies that covered all but its feet. A Chinese woman came in to worship. She burned incense, she waved it before the dumb idol, she prostrated her little self before the huge fifty-foot god and waited for an answer. Was there any? There was none. So that was "worshiping idols." Suddenly I knew that the God I worshiped was alive, that He was a Person who responded to me and to whom I could respond. But did I worship the Ever-Living One? Did I really know what worship meant? Suddenly I wanted to get out of that temple and go home. I wanted to go into my room and close the door and lock it. I wanted to get on my knees with my face to the floor, like that little Chinese woman. But unlike her, I wanted to worship the living God who created and sustains all life, and who has revealed Himself as He is in the Person of Jesus Christ. I wanted to be quiet and let all the love and adoration and worship of my heart go out to Him in a way that I had never done before. Worship to me had meant "Sunday morning worship service." I wonder sometimes now what that means, for I have learned that it is in silence, holy silence, that my heart pours out its best love and worship to my Lord and my God.

ROSALIND RINKER, IN *PRAYER: CONVERSING WITH GOD*

That His Name May Be Glorified

Help us, O God of our salvation, for the glory of your name.
(Psalm 79:9)

Restlessness in prayer comes from striving against the Spirit of prayer. But when we in prayer seek only the glorification of the name of God, then we are in complete harmony with the Spirit of prayer. Then our hearts are at rest both while we pray and after we have prayed. The reason is that we now seek by our prayers only that which will glorify the name of God. Then we can wait for the Lord. We have learned to leave it to Him to decide what will best serve to glorify His name, either an immediate or a delayed answer to our prayer. Permit me to cite an example to show how bold, even importunate, prayer can become when the one who is praying desires nothing but the glorification of the name of God by his supplications. In 1540 Luther's good friend, Frederick Myconius, became deathly sick. He himself and others expected that he would die within a short time. One night he wrote with trembling hand a fond farewell to Luther, whom he loved very much. When Luther received the letter, he sent back the following reply immediately, "I command thee in the name of God to live because I still have need of thee in the work of reforming the church. . . . The Lord will never let me hear that thou art dead, but will permit thee to survive me. For this I am praying, this is my will, and may my will be done, because I seek only to glorify the name of God." Myconius had already lost the faculty of speech when Luther's letter came. But in a short time he was well again. And, true enough, survived Luther by two months! Nothing makes us so bold in prayer as when we can look into the eye of God and say to Him, "Thou knowest that I am not praying for personal advantage, nor to avoid hardship, nor that my own will in any way should be done, but only for this, that Thy name might be glorified."

Ole Hallesby, in *Prayer*

PRAYER IS OBEDIENCE

You are my friends if you do what I command you.
(JOHN 15:14)

True praying, be it remembered, is not mere sentiment, nor poetry, nor eloquent utterance. Nor does it consist of saying in honeyed cadences, "Lord, Lord." Prayer is not a mere form of words; it is not just calling upon a name. Prayer is obedience. It is founded on the adamantine rock of obedience to God. Only those who obey have the right to pray. Behind the praying must be the doing; and it is the constant doing of God's will in daily life which gives prayer its potency, as our Lord plainly taught. No name, however precious and powerful, can protect and give efficiency to prayer which is unaccompanied by the doing of God's will. Neither can the doing, without the praying, protect from divine disapproval. If the will of God does not master the life, the praying will be nothing but sickly sentiment. If prayer does not inspire, sanctify, and direct our work, then self-will enters, to ruin both work and worker. How great and manifold are the misconceptions of the true elements and functionings of prayer! There are many who earnestly desire to obtain an answer to their prayers but who go unrewarded and unblessed. They fix their minds on some promise of God and then endeavour by dint of dogged perseverance, to summon faith sufficient to lay hold upon, and claim it. This fixing of the mind on some great promise may avail in strengthening faith, but, to this holding on to the promise must be added the persistent and importunate prayer that expects and waits till faith grows exceedingly. And who is there that is able and competent to do such praying save the man who readily, cheerfully, and continually *obeys God*? Faith, in its highest form, is the attitude as well as the act of a soul surrendered to God, in whom his Word and his Spirit dwell. It is true that faith must exist in some form, or another, in order to prompt praying; but in its strongest form, and in its largest results, faith is the fruit of prayer.

E. M. BOUNDS, IN *THE NECESSITY OF PRAYER*

Pray with the Heart

Seek the LORD and his strength; seek his presence continually!
(Psalm 105:4)

Prayer is the guide to perfection and the sovereign good; it delivers us from every vice, and obtains us every virtue; for the one great means to become perfect, is to walk in the presence of God: He Himself hath said, "walk in my presence and be ye perfect" (Genesis 17:1). It is by prayer alone that we are brought into this presence, and maintained in it without interruption.

You must then learn a species of prayer, which may be exercised at all times; which doth not obstruct outward employments; and which may be equally practiced by princes, kings, prelates, priests and magistrates, soldiers and children, tradesmen, labourers, women and sick persons: it cannot, therefore, be the prayer of the head, but of the heart; not a prayer of the understanding alone, which is so limited in its operations that it can have but one object at one time; but the prayer of the heart is not interrupted by the exercises of reason: indeed nothing can interrupt this prayer, but irregular and disordered affections: and when once we have tasted of God, and the sweetness of His love, we shall find it impossible to relish aught but Himself.

Nothing is so easily obtained as the possession and enjoyment of God, for "in him we live, move, and have our being;" and He is more desirous to give Himself into us, than we can be to receive Him.

All consists in the manner of seeking Him; and to seek aright, is easier and more natural to us than breathing. Though you think yourselves ever so stupid, dull, and incapable of sublime attainments, yet, by prayer, you may live in God Himself with less difficulty or interruption than you live in the vital air. Will it not then be highly sinful to neglect prayer?

Jeanne Guyon, in *A Short and Easy Method of Prayer*

ETERNAL PRAYERS

When he had taken the scroll, the four living creatures and the twenty-four elders fell down before the Lamb, each holding a harp, and golden bowls full of incense, which are the prayers of the saints.
(REVELATION 5:8)

Praying parents can intercede for their children and grandchildren until, long after the death of the parents, those prayers still convey wonderful blessings. The godly intercessions of church and mission founders and leaders are answered over the decades. Every true intercessor prays many prayers which will not have their full answer before the prayer warrior joins the church in heaven. Prayers prayed in the Spirit never die until they accomplish God's intended purpose. His answer may not be what we expected, or when we expected it, but God often provides much more abundantly than we could think or ask. He interprets our intent and either answers or stores up our prayers (Revelation 8:2-5). Sincere prayers are never lost. Energy, time, love, and longing can be endowments that will never be wasted or go unrewarded. Jesus Christ continues to endow the church with His intercession. Paul endowed the church with prayer. So did innumerable Old and New Testament saints and leaders. The mighty out-pourings of God's Spirit in the Millennium and in the new heaven and the new earth will surely be built upon all those holy intercessions which were not fully answered before. Do not be discouraged when prayers are not immediately answered. You can endow with God's mercies, with the Holy Spirit's ministries, and with the angelic assistance and protection. Pray on and on; prayer is never, never in vain.

WESLEY DUEWEL, IN *TOUCH THE WORLD THROUGH PRAYER*

Beholding Jesus

Do not be conformed to this world, but be transformed by the renewal of your mind.

(Romans 12:2)

One of the most instructive and suggestive passages in the entire Bible, showing the mighty power of prayer to transform us into the likeness of our Lord Jesus Himself, is found in Second Corinthians 3:18: "But we all, with unveiled face beholding as in a mirror the glory of the Lord, are transformed into the same image from glory to glory, even as from the Lord the Spirit." The thought is this, that the Lord is the Sun, you and I are mirrors, and just as a mischievous boy on a bright sunshiny day will catch rays of the sun in a piece of broken looking-glass and reflect them into your eyes and mine with almost blinding power, so we as mirrors, when we commune with God, catch the rays of His moral glory and reflect them out upon the world "from glory to glory." That is, each new time we commune with Him we catch something new of His glory and reflect it out upon the world. You remember the story of Moses. He went up into the Mount and tarried alone for forty days with God, gazing upon that ineffable glory, and caught so much of the glory in his own face that when he came down from the Mount, though he himself knew it not, his face so shone that he had to draw a veil over it to hide the blinding glory of it from his fellow Israelites. Even so we, going up into the mount of prayer, away from the world, alone with God, and remaining long alone with God, catch the rays of His glory. When we come down to our fellow men it is not so much that our faces shine (though I do believe that sometimes even our faces shine), but our characters, with the glory that we have been beholding. And we reflect out upon the world the moral glory of God from "glory to glory," each new time of communion with Him catching something new of His glory to reflect out upon the world. *Oh, here is the secret of becoming much like God, remaining long alone with God.* If you won't stay long with Him, you won't be much like Him.

R. A. Torrey, in *The Power of Prayer*

The Finished Work

When Christ had offered for all time a single sacrifice for sins,
he sat down at the right hand of God.

(Hebrews 10:12)

The house seemed empty, so [Hudson Taylor] took the story he found to a favourite corner in the old warehouse, thinking he would read it. Many miles away, his mother was specially burdened that Saturday afternoon about her only son. Leaving her friends she went alone to plead with God for his salvation. Hour after hour passed while that mother was still upon her knees, until her heart was flooded with a joyful assurance that her prayers were heard and answered. The boy was reading, meanwhile, the booklet he had picked up, and as the story merged into something more serious he was arrested by the words: "The finished work of Christ." Who can explain the mystery of the Holy Spirit's working? Truth long familiar, though neglected, came back to mind and heart. Then came the thought with startling clearness, "If the whole work is finished, the whole debt paid, what is there left for me to do?" The one, the only answer took possession of his soul: "There was nothing in the world for me to do save to fall upon my knees and accepting this Saviour and His salvation to praise Him for evermore." Another surprise awaited him not long after, when, picking up a notebook he thought was his own, he found an entry in his sister's writing to the effect that she would give herself daily to prayer until God should answer in the conversion of her only brother. The young girl had recorded this decision just a month previously:

> Brought up in such a circle and saved under such circumstances, it was perhaps natural that from the very commencement of my Christian life I was led to feel that promises of the Bible are very real, and that prayer is in sober fact transacting business with God, whether on one's behalf or on behalf of those for whom one seeks His blessing.

Dr. and Mrs. Howard Taylor, in *Hudson Taylor's Spiritual Secret*

GOD'S PRESENCE

Draw near to God, and he will draw near to you.
(JAMES 4:8)

The patriarch Jacob, "in the howling wilderness," saw a vision of God and cried out in wonder, "Surely the Lord is in this place; and I knew it not." Jacob had never been for one small division of a moment outside the circle of that all-pervading Presence. But he knew it not. That was his trouble, and it is ours. Men do not know that God is here. What a difference it would make if they knew. The Presence and the manifestation of the Presence are not the same. There can be the one without the other. God is here when we are wholly unaware of it. He is *manifest* only when and as we are aware of His Presence. On our part there must be surrender to the Spirit of God, for His work it is to show us the Father and the Son. If we co-operate with Him in loving obedience God will manifest Himself to us, and that manifestation will be the difference between a nominal Christian life and a life radiant with the light of His face. Always, everywhere God is present, and always He seeks to discover Himself. To each one He would reveal not only that He is, but *what* He is as well. He did not have to be persuaded to discover Himself to Moses. "And the Lord descended in the cloud, and stood with him there, and proclaimed the name of the Lord." He not only made a verbal proclamation of His nature but He revealed His very Self to Moses. It will be a great moment for some of us when we begin to believe that God's promise of self revelation is literally true: that He promised much, but promised no more than He intends to fulfill. Our pursuit of God is successful just because He is forever seeking to manifest Himself to us. The revelation of God to any man is not God coming from a distance upon a time to pay a brief and momentous visit to the man's soul. Thus to think of it is to misunderstand it all.

A. W. TOZER, IN *THE PURSUIT OF GOD*

GROWING YOUR FAITH

According to your faith be it done to you.
(MATTHEW 9:29)

Faith needs a life of prayer for its full growth. In all the different parts of the spiritual life there is a close union between unceasing action and reaction, so that each may be both cause and effect. Thus it is with faith. There can be no true prayer without faith; some measure of faith must precede prayer. And yet prayer is also the way to more faith: There can be no higher degrees of faith except through much prayer. Nothing needs to grow as much as our faith. "Your faith groweth exceedingly" is said of one church. When Jesus spoke the words, "According to your faith be it unto you" (Matthew 9:29, KJV), He announced the law of the Kingdom, which tells us that different people have different degrees of faith, that one person may have varying degrees, and that the amount of faith will always determine the amount of one's power and blessing. If we want to know where and how our faith is to grow, the Master points us to the throne of God. It is in prayer, exercising one's faith in fellowship with the living God, that faith can increase. Faith can only live by feeding on what is Divine, on God Himself. It is in the adoring worship of God — the waiting on Him and for Him in the deep silence of soul that yields itself for God to reveal Himself — that the capacity for knowing and trusting God will be developed. As we take His Word from the Blessed Book and ask Him to speak it to us with His living, loving voice, the power to believe and receive the Word as God's own word to us will emerge in us. It is in prayer, in living contact with God in living faith, that faith will become strong in us. Many Christians cannot understand, nor do they feel the need, of spending hours with God. But the Master says (and the experience of His people has confirmed) that men of strong faith are men of much prayer.

ANDREW MURRAY, IN *WITH CHRIST IN THE SCHOOL OF PRAYER*

Something Else in Store

> *To him who is able to do far more abundantly than all that we*
> *ask or think, according to the power at work within us,*
> *to him be glory in the church and in Christ.*
>
> (Ephesians 3:20-21)

In view of the difficulty of bringing our hearts to this complete submission to the Divine will, we may well adopt Fenelon's prayer: "O God, take my heart, for I cannot give it; and when Thou hast it, keep it, for I cannot keep it for Thee; and save me in spite of myself." Some of the best men the world has ever seen have made great mistakes on this point. Moses could pray for Israel and could prevail with God; but God did not answer his petition for himself. He asked that God would take him over Jordan, that he might see Lebanon; and after the forty years' wandering in the wilderness, he desired to go into the Promised Land; but the Lord did not grant his desire. Was that a sign that God did not love him? By no means. He was a man greatly beloved of God, like Daniel; and yet God did not answer this prayer of his. Moses wished to enter the Promised Land; but the Lord had something else in store for him. As someone has said, God kissed away his soul, and took him home to Himself. "God buried him" — the greatest honor ever paid to mortal man. Fifteen hundred years afterward God answered the prayer of Moses; He allowed him to go into the Promised Land, and to get a glimpse of the coming glory. On the Mount of Transfiguration, with Elijah, the great prophet, and with Peter, James, and John, he heard the voice come from the throne of God. "This is My beloved Son; hear ye Him." That was better than to have gone over Jordan, as Joshua did, and to sojourn for thirty years in the land of Canaan. So when our prayers for earthly things are not answered, let us submit to the will of God, and know that it is all right.

D. L. Moody, in *Prevailing Prayer*

GOD OUR GUIDE

Be still, and know that I am God.
(PSALM 46:10)

If we want to know what to do, we need to know first who will tell us. The best kind of beginning, when we are wanting to know the will of God, is to concentrate first on God himself. I have been told that in one of the China Inland Mission homes in China there was a motto on the wall that said, "The sun stood still. The iron did swim. This God is our God for ever and ever. He will be our guide even unto death." This God, the One who, in answer to the prayer of an ordinary man, stopped the sun in its course, the God who suspended his own law of gravity and made an ax head float, this is the God to whom I come. This is the God whose will and direction I am asking. This God is the One whose promises I am counting on. And can he help me out of my predicament? Whatever my predicament may be, as soon as I compare it with the circumstances surrounding the miracles of the sun and the ax, my doubts seem comical. God knows all about those comical doubts. He knows our frame. He remembers that we are dust, and it is to us, knowing all this better than we know it ourselves, that he made those promises. God is, according to Isaiah 43, our Creator, our Redeemer, the Lord our God, the Holy One of Israel, our Savior. Would we ask him to be anything more than this, before we admit in our hearts that he can be trusted? He is called also El Shaddai, "the God who is Enough." Will we settle for that?

ELISABETH ELLIOT, IN *GOD'S GUIDANCE*

God's Power at Work

> *Let the favor of the Lord our God be upon us,*
> *and establish the work of our hands upon us.*
> (Psalm 90:17)

Paul prays that God by his power may "fulfill every good purpose of yours and every act prompted by your faith" (2 Thessalonians 1:11, NIV). That is simply marvelous. Assuming that Christians will develop such wholesome and spiritually minded purposes, Paul prays that God himself may take these purposes and so work them out as to bring them to fruition, to fulfillment. We may have all kinds of wonderful ideas about what we as Christians might do, yet somehow never get around to doing any of them. Alternatively, we may immediately proceed to organization and administration, and never seek, except in sporadic and accidental ways, the decisive approval and blessing of God on our Christian dreams. The truth is that unless God works in us and through us, unless God empowers these good purposes of ours, they will not engender any enduring spiritual fruit; they will not display any life-transforming, people-changing power. "Unless the Lord builds the house, its builders labor in vain. Unless the Lord watches over the city, the watchmen stand guard in vain" (Psalm 127:1, NIV). And unless the Lord fulfills our good, faith-prompted purposes, they will remain arid, fruitless — either empty dreams or frenetic activity with no life, but in either case spiritually anemic. That means we need to go over our own agendas and priorities, and those of the people and leaders in our churches and missions, and ask again and again, "What are our goals, our purposes? What should we be attempting for Christ's sake?" And as we find answers to such questions, we must intercede with God that he, by his great power, might bring these good purposes, these faith-prompted acts, to bountiful fruitfulness.

D. A. CARSON, IN *A CALL TO SPIRITUAL REFORMATION*

BREAD FROM HEAVEN

Give us this day our daily bread.
(MATTHEW 6:11)

My wife and I never went into debt because we believed it to be unscriptural according to Romans 13:8: "Owe no man anything, but to love one another" (KJV). Therefore, we have no bills with our tailor, butcher, or baker, but we pay for everything in cash. We would rather suffer need than contract debts. Thus, we always know how much we have, and how much we can give away. Many trials come upon the children of God on account of not acting according to Romans 13:8. November 27 was the Lord's day. Our money had been reduced to two pence. Our bread was hardly enough for the day. I brought our need before the Lord several times. When I gave thanks after lunch, I asked Him to give us our daily bread, meaning literally that He would send us bread for the evening. While I was praying, there was a knock at the door. A poor sister came in and brought us some of her dinner and five shillings. Later, she also brought us a large loaf of bread. Thus, the Lord not only gave us bread but also money. At the end of the year, we looked back and realized that all our needs had been met more abundantly than if I had received a regular salary. We are never losers from doing the will of the Lord. I have not served a hard Master, and that is what I delight to show. God was also faithful to heal my physical infirmities. One Saturday afternoon, I broke a blood vessel in my stomach and lost a considerable quantity of blood. Immediately after I prayed, I began to feel better. Do not attempt to imitate me in this matter if you do not have the faith. But if you do, it will most assuredly be honored by God.

GEORGE MÜLLER, IN *THE AUTOBIOGRAPHY OF GEORGE MÜLLER*

MAY HIS NAME BE HOLY

Holy, holy, holy is the LORD of hosts; the whole earth is full of his glory!
(ISAIAH 6:3)

"Hallowed be Your name" (Matthew 6:9, NKJV). We have a tendency to read these words and to conclude that they are part of the address, that they are simply an acknowledgment of an existing truth. That is, we believe we are saying: "Our Father in heaven, Your name is holy." But that's not the format of the prayer. This line of the Lord's Prayer is not simply an assertion that God's name is holy. Rather, it's a petition. Everyone knows what a petition is — it's a piece of paper that people pass around for others to sign in hopes that this written evidence of agreement on an issue will induce the government or the ruling body of some association to change the rules of the game. A petition, then, is a request. For this reason, those specific requests Jesus gave His disciples in the Lord's Prayer are known as the petitions. These are the priorities that Jesus indicated His disciples should ask for in their prayers. And the very first thing that Jesus told them to pray for was that the name of God would be regarded as holy. What does it mean to say that God is holy? It means that He is different from anything that we experience or find in the material universe, that God the Creator differs from all creatures. The primary way in which God differs from all creatures is that He is uncreated and eternal, whereas each of us is created and finite. We are not eternal but temporal. If nothing else separates the Creator from the creature, it is that high, transcendent element of God's own being, so marvelous, so majestic that He is worthy of the adoration of every creature. This line of the Lord's prayer is not just a part of the address but a petition. We must see this if we are to understand what Jesus is teaching us about prayer. Jesus is not saying, "Father, Your name is holy," but, "Father, may Your name be hallowed." That is, He is teaching us to ask that God's name would be regarded as sacred, that it would be treated with reverence, and that it would be seen as holy.

R. C. SPROUL, IN *THE PRAYER OF THE LORD*

PRAYER'S SHAPING POWER

As for me, far be it from me that I should sin against the LORD by ceasing
to pray for you, and I will instruct you in the good and the right way.

(1 SAMUEL 12:23)

When we are in God's presence by prayer we are right, our will is morally right, we are doing His will. However unsure we may be about other acts and efforts to serve Him we know we are right in this. If we ask truly but ask amiss, it is not a sin, and He will in due course set us right in that respect. We are sure that prayer is according to His will, and that we are just where we ought to be. And that is a great matter for the rightness of our thought, and of the aims and desires proposed by our thoughts. It means much both as to their form and their passion. If we realize that prayer is the acme of our right relation to God, if we are sure that we are never so right with Him in anything we do as in prayer, then prayer must have the greatest effect and value for our life, both in its purpose and its fashion, in its spirit and its tenor. What puts us right morally, right with God (as prayer does), must have a great shaping power on every part and every juncture of life. And, of course, especially upon the spirit and tenor of our prayer itself, upon the form and complexion of our petition.

The prayerless spirit saps a people's moral strength because it blunts their thought and conviction of the Holy. It must be so if prayer is such a moral blessing and such a shaping power, if it pass, but its nature, from the vague volume and passion of devotion to formed petition and effort. Prayerlessness is an injustice and a damage to our own soul, and therefore to its history, both in what we do and what we think. The root of all deadly heresy is prayerlessness. Prayer finds our clue in a world otherwise without form and void. And it draws a magic circle round us over which the evil spirits may not pass.

P. T. FORSYTH, IN *THE SOUL OF PRAYER*

The Discipline and Power of Prayer

You saw the affliction of our fathers in Egypt
and heard their cry at the Red Sea.
(Nehemiah 9:9)

A cry brings God. A cry is mightier than the polished phrase. The Pharisee prayed within himself. His prayers revolved on ruts of vanity in his own mind and heart. The publican cried and was heard. It is not of emergency exits of the soul that we are thinking but the sustained habit and experience of the man of prayer. Such prayer comes by training, and there is no discipline so exacting. Coleridge says of such praying that it is the very highest energy of which the human heart is capable, and it calls for the total concentration of all the faculties. The mass of worldly men and learned men he pronounced incapable of prayer. To pray as God would have us pray is the greatest achievement of earth. Such a life of prayer costs. It takes time. Hurried prayers and muttered litanies can never produce souls mighty in prayer. Learners give hours regularly every day that they may become proficient in art and mechanism. Our Lord rose before daybreak that He might pray, and not infrequently He spent all night in prayer. All praying saints have spent hours every day in prayer. In these days there is no time to pray; but without time, and a lot of it, we shall never learn to pray. It ought to be possible to give God one hour out of twenty-four all to Himself. Anyway, let us make a start in the discipline of training in prayer by setting apart a fixed time every day for the exercise of prayer. We must seriously set our hearts to learn how to pray. Believe me, to pray with all your heart and strength, with the reason and the will, to believe vividly that God will listen to your voice through Christ, and verily do the thing He pleaseth thereupon — this is the last, the greatest achievement of the Christian's warfare upon earth.

Samuel Chadwick, in *The Path of Prayer*

SAFE AND SECURE IN CHRIST

Who shall separate us from the love of Christ? Shall tribulation, or distress, or persecution, or famine, or nakedness, or danger, or sword?

(ROMANS 8:35)

God Himself and the fullness of God is our "portion," God is our "rock," God is our "refuge," God is our "high tower," God is our "redeemer," God is our "sanctifier," God is our "preserver," God is our "Father," God is our "husband," God is our "salvation," and "our God for ever and ever." How secure must they be who have believed on His name! We are taught in Scripture that our security flows from three great facts. The Father has *loved us* with an everlasting love — a love that never changes; Christ, who died for our sins, is now at God's right hand in resurrection glory and ever lives to make *intercession for us*, pleading His work finished and accepted; and God the Holy Ghost *dwelleth in* us. "A threefold cord is hard to be broken!" (Ecclesiastes 4:12, KJV). Will God lose those He has loved with an everlasting love? Will Christ forget those for whom He ever lives to intercede? Will God cast off those to whom He has sent the Holy Ghost, to dwell in them, for ever be in them — "and be in them a well of living water springing up unto everlasting life" (John 4:14, KJV), and that they might be built together for His own habitation through the Spirit? If these things be so, we *are safe*, completely safe, and we *ought* to be happy. Only unbelief and distrust can interfere with our abiding happiness. Our peace ought to be as a river, and our righteousness like the waves of the sea. If these things be so, we may well be assured that *all things are working together for our good*. Can it be true that Father, Son, and Holy Ghost are mutually, equally, and alike interested in us, and that anything can go wrong, really wrong with us?

MARCUS RAINSFORD, IN *OUR LORD PRAYS FOR HIS OWN*

EFFECTIVE PRAYER

They do not cry to me from the heart, but they wail upon their beds;
for grain and wine they gash themselves; they rebel against me.
(HOSEA 7:14)

It is an easy thing for men to be very hot for such things as rituals and forms of prayer as they are written in a book. Yet they are altogether forgetful to inquire within themselves whether or not they have the spirit and power of prayer. These people are like painted men, and their prayers are like a false voice. They appear as hypocrites to God, and their prayers are an abomination: "If anyone turns a deaf ear to the law, even his prayers are detestable" (Proverbs 28:9, NIV). When therefore you intend to pray to the Lord of heaven and earth, consider the following particulars:

1. Consider seriously what you want. Do not, as many who in their words only beat the air, ask for such things as indeed you do not desire, nor see that you stand in need of.

2. When you see what you want, keep to that and take heed to pray sensibly.

3. Take heed that your heart as well as your mouth speaks to God. Let not your mouth go any further than you strive to draw out your heart along with it. David would lift his heart and soul to the Lord; and for good reason, for so far as a man's mouth goes along without his heart, so far his prayer is but lip-labor only. If you have in mind to enlarge in prayer before God, see to it that it be with your heart.

4. Avoid just affecting expressions and pleasing yourself with their use, because you can quickly forget the real life of prayer.

Real prayer is a serious concern, for we are speaking to the Sovereign Lord of all the universe, who is willing to move heaven and earth in answer to sincere and reasonable prayer. Prayer is not a mechanical duty, but a wonderful opportunity to develop a loving and caring relationship with the most important Person in our lives.

JOHN BUNYAN, IN *PILGRIM'S PRAYER BOOK*

LIFTED ABOVE THE WORLD

Pray earnestly to the Lord of the harvest
to send out laborers into his harvest.
(MATTHEW 9:38)

Monday, April 12. This morning the Lord was pleased to lift up the light of his countenance upon me in secret prayer, and made the season very precious to my soul. And though I have been so depressed of late, respecting my hopes of future serviceableness in the cause of God; yet now I had much encouragement respecting that matter. I was especially assisted to intercede and plead for pour souls, and for the enlargement of Christ's kingdom in the world, and for special grace for myself, to fit me for special services. I felt exceedingly calm, and quite resigned to God, respecting my future employment, when and where he pleased. My faith lifted me above the world, and removed all those mountains, that I could not look over of late. I wanted not the favor of man to lean upon; for I knew Christ's favor was infinitely better, and that it was not matter of when, nor where, nor how Christ should send me, nor what trials he should still exercise me with, if I might be prepared for his work and will. I now found revived, in my mind, the wonderful discovery of infinite wisdom in all the dispensations of God towards me, which I had a little before I met with my great trial at college; everything appeared full of divine wisdom. Blessed be the Lord, he is never unmindful of me, but always sends me needed supplies; and, from time to time when I am like one dead, he raises me to life. O that I may never distrust infinite goodness! O there is a sweet day coming, wherein the weary will be at rest! My soul has enjoyed much sweetness this day in hopes of its speedy arrival. I know I long for God, and a conformity to his will, in inward purity and holiness, ten thousand times more than for anything here below.

JONATHAN EDWARDS, IN *THE LIFE AND DIARY OF DAVID BRAINERD*

Persevering in Prayer

Keep alert with all perseverance, making supplication for all the saints.
(Ephesians 6:18)

Why do most of us fail so miserably in prayer? I have pondered this question nearly ever since I, by the grace of God, began to pray. I think we will all admit, both to ourselves and to others, without any question, that to pray is difficult for all of us. The difficulty lies in the very act of praying. To pray, really to pray, is what is difficult for us. It feels like too much of an effort. That the natural man feels that prayer is an effort is not strange in the least. He "receiveth not the things of the Spirit of God; for they are foolishness unto him" (1 Corinthians 2:14, KJV). "The mind of the flesh is enmity against God" (Romans 8:7, KJV). The natural man may, of course, feel a desire to pray at times. He may feel a desire to pray when he is in danger, for instance, or when he is in religious frame of mind. But he can never become reconciled to daily and regular prayer. He feels that it is unreasonable on the part of God to be so particular about this matter of praying. That this is the natural man's view of prayer does not surprise us. It cannot help but surprise us, however, when we find that this view is prevalent also among believing Christians, at least among many of us. At conversion we were led into a life of earnest, diligent prayer. Our seasons of prayer were the happiest time of the day. But after a longer or shorter period of time, we began to encounter difficulties in our prayer life. Prayer which was once the free, happy, grateful communion of a redeemed soul with God had begun to become a matter of duty. Without practice no Christian will become a real man or woman of prayer. And practice cannot be attained without perseverance. But to move in prayer as though one were in one's element, to pray daily with a willing spirit, with joy, with gratitude and with adoration is something which is far beyond our human capacities and abilities. A miracle of God is necessary every day for this.

Ole Hallesby, in *Prayer*

Following One Master

Blessed are the pure in heart, for they shall see God.

(Matthew 5:8)

The true disciple has a single eye. "Purity of heart," wrote Kierkegaard, "is to will one thing." The glory of God is to be our primary motive. It should not surprise us then if what looked like a very simple thing (I don't ask very much, do I?) turns out to be a spiritual matter, an object that reveals my heart's direction. "The Lord alone did lead him," was written about Israel. You can follow only one person at a time. Rushing off in all directions at once, trying to serve two masters, will ruin us. The sooner we make up our minds to take up the cross and follow one Lord and one Master, the sooner we will be shown the right road, the path of righteousness. It is not reasonable to ask for guidance in one matter if we have rejected the guidance already given. Let us first go back, if possible, to where we turned away. If this is no longer possible, let us confess our sin. It may often be a "small" thing in which we see we have been disobedient, while it is a "big" decision we are asking guidance for, but it is a big thing that has stopped us, brought us to attention, and forced us back to God. If he asks us then about something smaller, we are given the chance to correct it. All our problems are theological ones, William Temple said. All of them have to do with our relationship to God and his to us, and this is precisely why it makes sense to come to God with them.

Elisabeth Elliot, in *God's Guidance*

Rest in His Presence

The Lord will fight for you, and you have only to be silent.
(Exodus 14:14)

As soon as the soul by faith places itself in the Presence of God, and becomes recollected before Him, let it remain thus for a little time in a profound and respectful silence.

But if, at the beginning, in forming the act of faith, it feels some little pleasing sense of the Divine Presence; let it remain there without being troubled for a subject, and proceed no farther, but carefully cherish this sensation while it continues: as soon as it abates, the will may be excited by some tender affection; and if by the first moving thereof, it finds itself reinstated in sweet peace, let it there remain: the smothered fire must be gently fanned; but as soon as it is kindled, we must cease that effort, lest we extinguish it by our own activity.

I would warmly recommend it to all, never to finish prayer, without remaining some little time after in a respectful silence. It is also of the greatest importance for the soul to go to prayer with courage, and such a pure and disinterested love, as seeks nothing from God, but the ability to please Him, and to do His will: for a servant who only proportions his diligence to his hope of reward, renders himself unworthy of all reward.

Go then to prayer, not that ye may enjoy spiritual delights, but that ye may be either full or empty, just as it pleaseth God: this will preserve you in an evenness of spirit, in desertion as well as in consolation, and prevent your being surprised at aridity or the apparent repulses of God.

Jeanne Guyon, in *A Short and Easy Method of Prayer*

Lifting Up Your Soul

Hear the voice of my pleas for mercy, when I cry to you for help,
when I lift up my hands toward your most holy sanctuary.
(Psalm 28:2)

The word "prayer" really means "a wish directed toward" — that is, toward God. All that true prayer seeks is God himself, for with him we get all we need. Prayer is simply "the turning of the soul to God." David describes it as the lifting up of the living soul to the living God. "Unto you, O Lord, do I lift up my soul" (Psalm 25:1, KJV). What a beautiful description of prayer that is! When we desire that the beauty of holiness may be upon us. When we lift up our souls to God in prayer, it gives God an opportunity to do what he will in us and with us. It is putting ourselves at God's disposal. God is always on our side. When man prays, it is God's opportunity. The poet James Montgomery says:

> Prayer is the soul's sincere desire,
> Uttered or unexpressed,
> The motion of a hidden fire
> That trembles in the breast.

"Prayer," says an old Jewish mystic, "is the moment when heaven and earth kiss each other." Prayer, then, is certainly not persuading God to do what we want God to do. It is not bending the will of a reluctant God to our will. It does not change his purpose, although it may release his power. "We must not conceive of prayer as overcoming God's reluctance," says Archbishop Richard Chenevix Trench, "but as laying hold of his highest willingness." For God always purposes our greatest good. Even the prayer offered in ignorance and blindness cannot swerve him from that, although when we persistently pray for some harmful thing, our willfulness may bring it about, and we suffer accordingly. "He gave them their request," says the Psalmist, "but sent leanness into their soul" (Psalm 106:15, KJV). They brought this "leanness" upon themselves. They were "cursed with the burden of a granted prayer."

An Unknown Christian, in *The Kneeling Christian*

GOD'S PROVIDENCE

Give me neither poverty nor riches;
feed me with the food that is needful for me.

(PROVERBS 30:8)

Jesus didn't teach us to pray that God would sell us our daily bread or render it to us in exchange for our service; instead, in this petition, we manifestly ask God to give us something. We ask Him to give us daily bread. We are so needy as to be destitute, but He owns "the cattle on a thousand hills" (Psalm 50:10, NKJV), so we go to Him as beggars asking for His charity. Scripture assures us that we can depend on Him to respond to such requests, for He is a giving God: "Every good and every perfect gift is from above, and comes down from the Father of lights" (James 1:17, NKJV). God gives His gifts in order to provide for the needs of His people, for He is a God of providence. Providence is about God's provision. An integral element of that providence is His provision for our ultimate need of salvation — He provided Jesus, the Lamb without blemish, who was crucified for us. The God of providence is also concerned about our mundane, everyday needs, such as food to eat, water to drink, clothes to wear, and shelter for our bodies. Therefore, in His providence, He makes the crops grow, He makes the rains fall, and He provides what we need for clothing and homes. He gives us what we need for daily life.

David wrote, "I have been young, and now am old; yet I have not seen the righteous forsaken, nor his descendants begging bread" (Psalm 37:25, NKJV). That's a tremendous testimony to the constancy with which God answers the prayers of His people when they bring their needs to Him.

R. C. SPROUL, IN *THE PRAYER OF THE LORD*

Speaking to Him

I cried aloud to the Lord, and he answered me from his holy hill. Selah
(Psalm 3:4)

Me pray aloud? In front of all those people? When I was the only teenager present? Probably no one even knew I was there. Faster and faster went my heart. The person who had been praying for some time stopped. There was silence. No. No. No! I couldn't break it! Let someone else do it. Cautiously I asked myself, who am I arguing with about this thing? Myself? Could it be that God was asking me to pray aloud in front of all these people? What difference could it make to God if I did or if I didn't? While I was still struggling with my thoughts and my objections, an older lady began to pray. I sighed with temporary relief. Why, I said to myself, she can't even speak English! No one can understand a word she is saying, and here she is praying where people can hear her. I listened some more. A sentence or two in German, then a smattering of English, then more German. I withheld further judgment and listened again. Suddenly I felt my heart was being held in God's hand. The old German lady was crying! And she wasn't ashamed to be praying or crying. And the tenderness in her voice told me that her tears were not those of frustration, but of real love for her Lord. She was speaking *to Him. Not to us.* And He was there. I knew it. *He was there.* The rapid conversation in my heart went on: And *you* can speak English and *you* belong to God in a new way since last June and are *you* still afraid? That was enough. I recognized the voice of Jesus, Lover that He is. I would pray aloud, and I would speak straight to Him. I would not be afraid and I would not care if there were tears, and I would not care if my words got tangled up and I would not care if my prayer was like the other or if it wasn't. I would forget all those people and just think about Him.

Rosalind Rinker, in *Prayer: Conversing with God*

GLORY TO GOD

I give thanks to you, O Lord my God, with my whole heart,
and I will glorify your name forever.
(PSALM 86:12)

"That the Father may be glorified in the Son." It is to this end that Jesus on His throne in glory will do everything we ask in His name. Every answer to prayer He gives will have this as its object. When there is no prospect of this object being obtained, He will not answer. It follows as a matter of course that with us, as with Jesus, this must be the essential element in our petitions. The glory of the Father must be the aim — the very soul and life — of our prayer. This was Jesus' goal when He was on earth: "I seek not mine own honor: I seek the honor of Him that sent me." In such words we have the keynote of His life. The first words of His High-Priestly prayer voice it: "Father glorify Thy Son, that Thy Son may glorify Thee on earth: glorify me with Thyself" (John 17:1, 5, KJV). His reason for being taken up into the glory He had with the Father is a twofold one: He has glorified Him on earth; He will still glorify Him in heaven. All He asks is to be able to glorify the Father more. As we begin to share Jesus' feeling on this point, gratifying Him by making the Father's glory our chief object in prayer, too, our prayer cannot fail to get an answer. The Beloved Son has said that nothing glorifies the Father more than His doing what we ask. Therefore, Jesus won't miss any opportunity to do what we request. Let us make His aim ours! Let the glory of the Father be the link between our asking and His doing!

ANDREW MURRAY, IN *WITH CHRIST IN THE SCHOOL OF PRAYER*

THE TORRENT OF HIS GRACES

Do not grieve the Holy Spirit of God,
by whom you were sealed for the day of redemption.
(EPHESIANS 4:30)

Judge by this what content and satisfaction [Brother Lawrence] enjoys: While he continually finds in himself so great a treasure he is no longer in an anxious search after it, but has it open before him, and may take what he pleases of it.

He complains much of our blindness; and cries often that we are to be pitied who content ourselves with so little while God has infinite treasure to bestow. Blind as we are, we hinder God and stop the current of His graces. But when He finds a soul penetrated with a lively faith, He pours into it His graces and favors plentifully; there they flow like a torrent which, after being forcibly stopped against its ordinary course, when it has found a passage, spreads itself with impetuosity and abundance. Yes, we often stop this torrent by the little value we set upon it. But let us stop it no more; let us enter into ourselves and break down the bank that hinders it. Let us make way for grace; let us redeem the lost time, for perhaps we have little left. Death follows us close; let us be well prepared for it; for we die but once, and a miscarriage *there* is irretrievable. I say again, let us enter into ourselves. The time presses, there is no room for delay; our souls are at stake. I believe you have taken such effectual measures that you will not be surprised. I commend you for it; it is the one thing necessary. We must, nevertheless, always work at it, because not to advance in the spiritual life is to go back. But those who have the gale of the Holy Spirit go forward even in sleep. If the vessel of our soul is still tossed with winds and storms, let us awake the Lord, who reposes in it, and He will quickly calm the sea.

BROTHER LAWRENCE, IN *THE PRACTICE OF THE PRESENCE OF GOD*

THANKING GOD FOR HIS WORK AMONG CHRISTIANS

Because I have heard of your faith in the Lord Jesus and
your love toward all the saints, I do not cease to give
thanks for you, remembering you in my prayers.
(EPHESIANS 1:15-16)

In the same way that we give thanks to God when we recognize his quiet and effective work in our lives, so we thank God when we hear of his work in others. If we hear of substantial numbers of people in another city or country who have been genuinely transformed by the gospel, we would not think of going to them to thank them for becoming Christians. Instead, we thank God for so working in them that they have become Christians. That is what Paul is doing [in Ephesians 1:15-23]. So if we intend to imitate the prayers of Paul, we will be attentive to reports of the progress of the gospel, not only in circles immediately around us, but also from places we have never visited. We may subscribe to a missionary organization's newsletter; we may receive the prayer letters of some who are working abroad; we may glance at the news reports found in some Christian magazines. When we find reliable reports of people who have by God's grace become Christians, we will learn to respond as Paul does; we immediately turn to the God whose grace has sovereignly intervened in their lives, with such happy result, and offer him praise and thanksgiving. If even the angels of heaven rejoice over a single sinner who repents, it does not seem too much to ask the people of God to offer thanksgiving at the same news. When was the last time you offered such thanksgiving to God? Is it conceivable that we could hear the news of people coming to Christ without expressing our gratitude to God?

D. A. CARSON, IN *A CALL TO SPIRITUAL REFORMATION*

THE COMPASSION OF CHRIST

From his fullness we have all received, grace upon grace.
(JOHN 1:16)

"We have," saith the apostle, "such an high priest as can, and consequently doth, suffer with us, endure our infirmities." And in what respect he suffers with us in regard of our infirmities, or hath a fellow-feeling with us in them, he declares in the next words, "He was tempted like as we are," v. 15. It is as to our infirmities, our temptations, spiritual weakness; therein, in particular, hath he a compassionate sympathy and fellow-feeling with us. Whatever be our infirmities, so far as they are our temptations, he doth suffer with us under them, and compassionates us. There are two ways of expressing a fellow-feeling and suffering with another, both are eminent in Christ:

1. He *grieves and labours* with us. Zech. 1:12, "The angel of the Lord answered and said, O Lord of hosts, how long wilt thou not have mercy on Jerusalem?" He speaks as one intimately affected with the state and condition of poor Jerusalem; and therefore he hath bid all the world take notice that what is done to them is done to him, 2:8-9; yea, to "the apple of his eye."

2. In the second he abounds. Isa. 40:11, "He shall feed his flock like a shepherd, he shall gather the lambs with his arm, and carry them in his bosom, and gently lead them that are with young." Yea, we have both here together, *tender compassionateness and assistance.* The whole frame wherein he is here described is a frame of the greatest tenderness, compassion, condescension that can be imagined. His people are set forth under many infirmities; some are lambs, some great with young, some very tender, some burdened with temptations, nothing in any of them all strong or comely. To them all Christ is a shepherd, that feeds his own sheep, and drives them out to pleasant pasture; where, if he sees a poor weak lamb, he doth not thrust him on, but takes him into his bosom, where he both easeth and refresheth him: he leads him gently and tenderly.

JOHN OWEN, IN *OF COMMUNION WITH GOD THE FATHER, SON AND HOLY GHOST*

LABORING IN PRAYER

I desire then that in every place the men should pray, lifting holy hands.
(1 TIMOTHY 2:8)

Prayer is hard work and more. There are wonderful times of refreshing in prayer, but there are also times of hard, unglamorous, unspectacular labor in intercession. Prayer is realism. Mountains are to be moved; demons are to be routed. The superficial Christian resents prayer that is work, wrestling, warfare. Then suddenly there is a tragic accident, terminal illness, or imminent death. Then the superficial Christian pleads for the prayer of those who know how to prevail. Suddenly he wants nothing less than importunate praying. Prayer is wrestling, like Jacob at Jabbok. The wrestling may be quietly wrought, but it will be in an agony of earnestness. The word in Colossians 4:12 concerning Epaphras was that he was agonizing in prayer: "He is always wrestling [literally 'agonizing'] in prayer for you, that you may stand firm in all the will of God, mature and fully assured." Is that an accurate description of your prayer for your friends, for your church, for your nation? Paul pleaded for this kind of agonizing importunity on his own behalf: "I urge you, brothers, by our Lord Jesus Christ and by the love of the Spirit, to join me in my struggle by praying to God for me" [literally, "to agonize with me in prayer"] (Romans 15:30). When Moses stood in the gap for Israel, he engaged in agonizing importunity. It was such agonizing importunity in Gethsemane when Christ's prayer perspiration turned to great clots of blood, falling down on the ground (Luke 22:44). You can learn to prevail in prayer. You can learn to prevail over yourself and over Satan until God sees and sends His angels to hasten the answer.

WESLEY DUEWEL, IN *TOUCH THE WORLD THROUGH PRAYER*

CASTING BURDENS ON HIM

The LORD bless you and keep you; the LORD make
his face to shine upon you and be gracious to you.
(NUMBERS 6:24-25)

Then with the heat of summer came added perplexities. Not from his own Committee, but in a roundabout way Hudson Taylor learned that the Scotch physician who was to be his colleague had already sailed from England with wife and children. No instructions had reached him as to providing accommodation for the family, and as the weeks went by he realized that unless he took steps in the matter they would be left without a roof over their heads. Criticism was already too current in the community as to the management of the society he represented; so he had to keep his troubles to himself, as far as possible, and seek to cast his burden upon the Lord.

One who is really leaning on the Beloved finds it always possible to say, "I will fear no evil, for thou art with me." But I am so apt, like Peter, to take my eyes off the One to be trusted and look at the winds and waves. . . . Oh for more stability! The reading of the Word and meditation on the promises have been increasingly precious to me of late. At first I allowed my desire to acquire the language speedily to have undue prominence and a deadening effect on my soul. But now, in the grace that passes all understanding, the Lord has again caused His face to shine upon me.

And to his sister he added:

I have been puzzling my brains again about a house, etc., but to no effect. So I have made it a matter of prayer, and have given it entirely into the Lord's hands, and now I feel quite at peace about it. He will provide and be my God in this and every perplexing step.

It must have seemed almost too good to be true when, only two days after the above was written, Hudson Taylor heard of premises that could be rented.

DR. AND MRS. HOWARD TAYLOR, IN *HUDSON TAYLOR'S SPIRITUAL SECRET*

Let Christ Reign in Prayer

Seek the LORD while he may be found; call upon him while he is near.
(ISAIAH 55:6)

Prayer is the supreme instance of the hidden character of the Christian life. It is the antithesis of self-display. When men pray, they have ceased to know themselves, and know only God whom they call upon. Prayer does not aim at any direct effect on the world; it is addressed to God alone, and is therefore the perfect example of undemonstrative action. Of course there is danger even here. Prayer of this kind can seek self-display, it can seek to bring to light that which is hidden. This may happen in public prayer, which sometimes (though not often nowadays) degenerates into an empty noise. But there is no difference; it is even more pernicious if I turn myself into a spectator of my own prayer performance, if I am giving a show for my own benefit. I may enjoy myself like a pleased spectator or I may catch myself praying and feel strange and ashamed. The publicity of the market place affords only a more naive form than the publicity which I am providing for myself. Where is the innermost chamber Jesus is thinking of where I can hide, if I cannot be sure of myself? How can I lock it so well that no audience spoils the anonymity of prayer and thus robs me of the reward of hidden prayer? How are we to be protected from ourselves, and our own premeditations? How are we to drive out reflection by reflecting? The only way is by mortifying our own wills which are always obtruding themselves. And the only way to do this is by letting Christ alone reign in our hearts, by surrendering our wills completely to him, by living in fellowship with Jesus and by following him. Then we can pray that his will may be done, the will of him who knows our needs before we ask. Only then is our prayer certain, strong and pure.

DIETRICH BONHOEFFER, IN *THE COST OF DISCIPLESHIP*

HUMILITY IN PRAYER

I proclaimed a fast there, at the river Ahava, that we might humble ourselves before our God, to seek from him a safe journey for ourselves, our children, and all our goods.

(EZRA 8:21)

God puts a great price on humility of heart. It is good to be clothed with humility as with a garment. It is written, "God resisteth the proud, but giveth grace to the humble." That which brings the praying soul near to God is humility of heart. That which gives wings to prayer is lowliness of mind. That which gives ready access to the throne of grace is self-depreciation. Pride, self-esteem, and self-praise effectually shut the door of prayer. He who would come to God must approach Him with self hid from his eyes. He must not be puffed-up with self-conceit, nor be possessed with an over-estimate of his virtues and good works.

Humility is a rare Christian grace, of great price in the courts of heaven, entering into and being an inseparable condition of effectual praying. It gives access to God when other qualities fail. It takes many descriptions to describe it, and many definitions to define it. It is a rare and retiring grace. Its full portrait is found only in the Lord Jesus Christ. Our prayers must be set low before they can ever rise high. Our prayers must have much of the dust on them before they can ever have much of the glory of the skies in them. In our Lord's teaching, humility has such prominence in His system of religion, and is such a distinguishing feature of His character, that to leave it out of His lesson on prayer would be very unseemly, would not comport with His character, and would not fit into His religious system.

E. M. BOUNDS, IN *THE ESSENTIALS OF PRAYER*

TRIED BY GOD

Prove me, O LORD, and try me; test my heart and my mind.
(PSALM 26:2)

Let me call attention to that prayer of David, in which he says: "Search me, O, God, and know my heart; try me, and know my thoughts, and see if there be any wicked way in me, and lead me in the way everlasting!" I wish all my readers would commit these verses to memory. If we should all honestly make this prayer once every day there would be a good deal of change in our lives.

"Search me." — not my neighbor. It is so easy to pray for other people, but so hard to get home to ourselves. I am afraid that we who are busy in the Lord's work are very often in danger of neglecting our vineyard. In this Psalm, David got home to himself. There is a difference between God searching me and my searching myself. I may search my heart, and pronounce it all right, but when God searches me as with a lighted candle, a good many things will come to light that perhaps I knew nothing about.

"Try me." David was tried when he fell by taking his eye off from the God of his father Abraham. "Know my thoughts." God looks at the thoughts. Are our thoughts pure? Have we in our hearts thoughts against God or against His people — against any one in the world? If we have, we are not right in the sight of God. Oh, may God search us, everyone!

I do not know any better prayer that we can make than this prayer of David. One of the most solemn things in the Scripture history is that when holy men — better men than we are — were tested and tried, they were found to be as weak as water away from God. Let us be sure that we are right.

D. L. MOODY, IN *PREVAILING PRAYER*

Right Prayer

I cry out to God Most High, to God who fulfills his purpose for me.
(Psalm 57:2)

If the grace of God is in you, it will be natural for you to groan out your condition to God, as natural as it is for a nursing child to cry out for the breast of his mother. Genuine prayer is one of the first things to reveal that a man is a Christian. But yet, if it be the right kind of prayer it will be as follows:

1. Right prayer must desire God in Christ, for himself; for his holiness, love, wisdom, and glory. Right prayer will run to God only through Christ, so that it will center on God and on God alone. As the psalmist has prayed: "Whom have I in heaven but you? And being with you, I desire nothing on earth" (Psalm 73:25, NIV).

2. Right prayer must enjoy continually communion with him, both here and hereafter. "In righteousness I will see your face; when I awake, I will be satisfied with seeing your likeness" (Psalm 17:15, NIV). And as Paul wrote, "For while we are still in this tent, we groan, being burdened — not that we would be unclothed, but that we would be further clothed, so that what is mortal may be swallowed up by life" (2 Corinthians 5:2-4, NIV).

3. Right prayer is accompanied with a continual labor after that which is prayed for. "My soul waits for the Lord more than the watchmen wait for the morning" (Psalm 130:6, NIV). For note, I beseech you, there are two things that provoke to prayer. The one is detestation of sin and the things of this life; the other is a burning desire for communion with God, in a holy and undefiled state and inheritance. To pray rightly we must pray knowing every good thing comes from God. But we must also work hard so the Spirit of God can very often achieve his purpose through us.

John Bunyan, in *Pilgrim's Prayer Book*

THE ESSENTIAL WORK

The men took some of their provisions,
but did not ask counsel from the LORD.
(JOSHUA 9:14)

The great difficulty in intercession is myself, nothing less or more. The first thing I have to do is to take myself to school. My first duty is not to assert freedom, but to find an absolute Master. We think that to be without a master is the sign of a high type of life. Insurgent, impertinent human beings have no master, noble beings have. I must learn not to take myself too seriously. Myself is apt to be my master, I pray to myself.

We are all Pharisees until we are willing to learn to intercede. We must go into heaven backward; we must grow into doing some definite thing by praying, not by seeing. To learn this lesson of handling a thing by prayer properly is to enter a very severe school. A Christian's duty is not to himself or to others, but to Christ. We think of prayer as a preparation for work, or a calm after having done work, whereas prayer is the essential work. It is the supreme activity of everything that is noblest in our personality. We won't bring down to earth what we see in vision about our Master, we move around it in devotional speculations, but we won't bring it straight down to earth and work it out in actualities. . . . If we make our own discernment the judge, we are wrong. We base it all on an abstract truth divorced from God. We pin our faith on what God has done and not on the God who did it, and when the case begins to go wrong again, we do not intercede, we begin to scold God. We get fanatical. We upset the court of heaven by saying, "I must do this thing." That is not intercession, that is rushing where angels fear to tread. It is the fanatical frenzy, storming the throne of God and refusing to see His character while sticking true to our assertions of what He said He would do. Beware of making God fit the mold of His own precedent.

OSWALD CHAMBERS, IN *IF YOU WILL ASK*

WORK LESS, PRAY MORE

Provide yourselves with moneybags that do not grow old,
with a treasure in the heavens that does not fail.

(LUKE 12:33)

I had constantly cases brought before me, which proved that one of the especial things which the children of God needed in our day was to have their faith strengthened. I might visit a brother who worked fourteen or even sixteen hours a day at his trade, the necessary result of which was, that not only his body suffered, but his soul was lean, and he had no enjoyment in God. I might point out to him that he ought to work less, in order that his bodily health might not suffer, and that he might gather strength for his inner man, by reading the word of God, by meditation over it, and by prayer. The reply, however, I generally found to be something like this: "But if I work less, I do not earn enough for the support of my family. Even now, whilst I work so much, I have scarcely enough." There was no trust in God, no real belief in the truth of that word, "Seek ye first the kingdom of God, and his righteousness, and all these things shall be added unto you." I might reply something like this: "My dear brother, it is not your work which supports your family, but the Lord; and he who has fed you and your family when you could not work at all, on account of illness, would surely provide for you and yours; if, for the sake of obtaining food for your inner man, you were to work only for so many hours a day as would allow you proper time for retirement. And is it not the case now that you begin the work of the day after having had only a few hurried moments for prayer; and when you leave off your work in the evening, and mean then to read a little of the word of God, are you not too much worn out in body and mind to enjoy it, and do you not often fall asleep whilst reading the Scriptures, or whilst on your knees in prayer?"

GEORGE MÜLLER, IN *THE AUTOBIOGRAPHY OF GEORGE MÜLLER*

LINGERING IN PRAYER

Seek the LORD and his strength; seek his presence continually!
(1 CHRONICLES 16:11)

Crowds were thronging and pressing Him; great multitudes came together to hear and to be healed of their infirmities; and He had no leisure so much as to eat. But He found time to pray. And this one who sought retirement with so much solitude was the Son of God, having no sin to confess, no shortcoming to deplore, no unbelief to subdue, no languor of love to overcome. Nor are we to imagine that His prayers were merely peaceful meditations, or rapturous acts of communion. They were strenuous and warlike, from that hour in the wilderness when angels came to minister to the prostrate Man of Sorrows, on to that awful "agony" in which His sweat was, as it were, great drops of blood. His prayers were sacrifices, offered up with strong crying and tears.

Now, if it was part of the sacred discipline of the Incarnate Son that He should observe frequent seasons of retirement, how much more is it incumbent on us, broken as we are and disabled by manifold sin, to be diligent in the exercise of private prayer! To hurry over this duty would be to rob ourselves of the benefits which proceed from it. We know, of course, that prayer cannot be measured by divisions of time. But the advantages to be derived from secret prayer are not to be obtained unless we enter on it with deliberation. We must "shut the door," enclosing and securing a sufficient portion of time for the fitting discharge of the engagement before us.

In the morning we should look forward to the duties of the day, anticipating those situations in which temptation may lurk, and preparing ourselves to embrace such opportunities of usefulness as may be presented to us. In the evening we ought to remark upon the providences which have befallen us, consider our attainment in holiness, and endeavor to profit by the lessons which God would have us learn. All this cannot be pressed into a few crowded moments. We must be at leisure when we enter the secret place.

DAVID MCINTYRE, IN *THE HIDDEN LIFE OF PRAYER*

Prayer Changes Us

Will any teach God knowledge,
seeing that he judges those who are on high?
(Job 21:22)

After warning His disciples against hypocritical prayer and pagan prayer, Jesus went on to say, "Therefore do not be like them. For your Father knows the things you have need of before you ask Him" (Matthew 6:8, NKJV). With these words, Jesus echoed the thoughts of David, who wrote: "O Lord, You have searched me and known me. You know my sitting down and my rising up; You understand my thought afar off. You comprehend my path and my lying down, and are acquainted with all my ways. For there is not a word on my tongue, but behold, O Lord, You know it altogether" (Psalm 139:1-4, NKJV). Jesus is simply seconding the psalmist's affirmation that the Lord knows what we need before we ask it.

One of the most frequently asked questions in the theology of prayer is, "Does prayer change things?" The answer is evident. The New Testament makes it clear that prayer changes all kinds of things. The next question that comes is, "Does prayer change God's mind?" What would induce God to change His mind? Perhaps new information, some knowledge He lacks until we communicate it to Him for His consideration. However, the Bible tells us that when we come to our King in prayer, He already knows what we are going to ask for and He knows what we need better than we do. We have to remember that this One we're talking to is omniscient. He doesn't learn anything new. No prayer of any human being ever uttered in history ever changed the mind of God in the slightest, because His mind doesn't ever need to be changed. The most important thing it changes is us. As we engage in communion with God more deeply and come to know the One with whom we are speaking more intimately, that growing knowledge of God reveals to us all the more brilliantly who we are and our need to change in conformity to Him. Prayer changes us profoundly.

R. C. Sproul, in *The Prayer of the Lord*

WHEN YOU YOURSELF ARE A PRAYER

Come to me, all who labor and are heavy laden, and I will give you rest.
(MATTHEW 11:28)

We can spend time in silence together with people whom we know real well. That we cannot do with others. We must converse with them, entertain them either with interesting or profound things as the case may be. But with our own dear ones we can speak freely about common and insignificant things. In their presence, too, we can be silent.

It is not necessary to maintain a conversation when we are in the presence of God. We can come into His presence and rest our weary souls in quiet contemplation of Him. Our groanings, which cannot be uttered, rise to Him and tell Him better than words how dependent we are upon Him.

As evening drew nigh, and our little fellow had played until he was tired, I noticed that he drew closer and closer to his mother. At last he found the place he was longing for, mother's lap. He did not have a great deal to say then either. He simply lay there, and let his mother caress him into sleep.

We, too, become tired, deathly tired, of ourselves, of others, of the world, of life, of everything! Then it is blessed to know of a place where we can lay our tired head and heart, our heavenly Father's arms, and say to Him, "I can do no more. And I have nothing to tell you. May I lie here a while and rest? Everything will soon be well again if I can only rest in your arms a while." You yourself are a prayer to God at this moment. All that is within you cries out to Him. And He hears all the pleas that your suffering soul and body are making to Him with groanings which cannot be uttered. But if you should have an occasional restful moment, thank God that you already have been reconciled to Him, and that you are now resting in the everlasting arms.

OLE HALLESBY, IN *PRAYER*

PASSING STRANGERS

Beloved, I urge you as sojourners and exiles to abstain from the passions of the flesh, which wage war against your soul.

(1 PETER 2:11)

It is written, "Be not conformed to this world." Are we conformed to it? Do we go its way? Are its tastes, its pleasures, its pursuits, its companions ours? Or, have we been transformed by the renewing of our minds? Has light from God fallen down upon us, and in His light do we see light? And having seen light doth the world's light around us seem to be darkness? Are we thanking God "who hath called us out of darkness into His marvelous light"?

"Strangers and pilgrims" are travelers! Are we merely passing through the world, using it, and not abusing it? "Strangers and pilgrims" never think of building, or settling down in the country where they sojourn. Their thoughts are upon the loved ones at home, upon the green fields and sunny smiles at home; home is the thought that fills their eyes, their hopes, their hearts, as they travel through the strangers' far-off land. How is it with ourselves?

"Strangers and pilgrims" are known by their language in the country through which they are passing. It is different from that which is spoken around them — the tone is quite different. Aye, and the dress too, therefore they are oftentimes a gazing stock to those among whom, for a short period, their lot is cast. Their manners too are different, you at once perceive it, it strikes you immediately, you would never take them for inhabitants of the land in which they are strangers and pilgrims — never! They could not be mistaken for a single instant. How is it with ourselves? Are we strangers and pilgrims in this world? Is our language different, our manner different, our attire different? Is it impossible for us to associate with the men of the world without their finding out that while we are in the world we are not of it? This is a very solemn question. If it is otherwise with us, then we are ashamed of the cross, we are ensnared by the world where we ought to be but as passing strangers.

MARCUS RAINSFORD, IN *OUR LORD PRAYS FOR HIS OWN*

THE CREATIVE POWER OF PRAYER

Blessed are those whose strength is in you, in whose heart are the highways
to Zion. As they go through the Valley of Baca they make it a place
of springs; the early rain also covers it with pools. They go from
strength to strength; each one appears before God in Zion.

(PSALM 84:5-7)

Prayer brings with it, as food does, a new sense of power and health. We are driven to it by hunger, and, having eaten, we are refreshed and strengthened for the battle which even our physical life involves. For heart and flesh cry out for the living God. God's gift is free; it is, therefore, a gift to our freedom, i.e. renewal to our moral strength, to what makes men of us. Without this gift always renewed, our very freedom can enslave us. The life of every organism is but the constant victory of a higher energy, constantly fed, over lower and more elementary forces. Prayer is the assimilation of a holy God's moral strength.

We must work for this living. To feed the soul we must toil at prayer. And what a labour it is! Our cooperation with God is our receptivity; but it is an active, a laborious receptivity, an importunity that drains our strength away if we do not tap the sources of the Strength Eternal. We work, we slave, at receiving. To him that hath this laborious expectancy it shall be given. Prayer is the powerful appropriation of power, of divine power. It is therefore creative.

Prayer is not mere wishing. It is asking — with a will. Our will goes into it. We turn to an active Giver; therefore we go into action. For we could not pray without knowing and meeting Him in kind. If God has a controversy with Israel, Israel must wrestle with God. Moreover, He is the Giver not only of the answer, but first of the prayer itself. His gift provokes ours. He beseeches us, which makes us beseech Him. And what we ask for chiefly is the power to ask more and to ask better. We pray for more prayer.

P. T. FORSYTH, IN *THE SOUL OF PRAYER*

THE LORD HAS HEARD ME

I call upon you, for you will answer me,
O God; incline your ear to me; hear my words.

(PSALM 17:6)

One day the burden of prayer for the Europeans of the station had fallen on Hyde; for two or three days he never went to bed nor did he go down to meals, and the food sent up to his room was generally carried down again untouched. How often he came and knelt by my bed that I might try to help him to bear the burden. On the Saturday night he was in great agony, McCheyne Paterson and myself remained with him, oh how he prayed and pleaded for the Europeans of the station. It was a vision to me of real agonizing intercession of old, "I will not let thee go," and yet in the determination there was such deep humility, such loving pleading. At 2 o'clock in the morning there was a knock at the door, and Mr. McCheyne Paterson quietly whispered to me, "I am sure that is my wife reminding me that we ought to go to bed," but it was not so, it was a letter from a lady staying at the largest hotel in the place, asking us to have a service for Europeans in the drawing room of the hotel. Hyde heard us reading the letter and he jumped up from his knees and said, "That is the answer to my prayers, I know now that the Lord has heard me." The servant who was entrusted with the message had gone miles in another direction, and had to come back, and found it very difficult at night to get anyone to direct him to us, hence his appearance at 2 o'clock in the morning. He had been told that the message was urgent and a reply absolutely necessary. Hyde's face was just full of peace and joy, and he almost commanded us to accept the invitation and arrange for the service, which we did.

CAPTAIN E. G. CARRÉ, IN *A PRESENT-DAY CHALLENGE TO PRAYER*

PERSONAL PRAYER

> *This is eternal life, that they know you the only true God,*
> *and Jesus Christ whom you have sent.*
> (JOHN 17:3)

Why has God shown Himself to us in three Persons? God is the great Eternal Being, and we are so limited in all our spiritual concepts that He has given us three different glimpses of Himself, through three different Personalities, but the three are One. I believe that God must have anticipated this human confusion of ours about Himself. This is surely one of the reasons He visited this earth in the Person of Jesus Christ. As we study Christ's life, death and resurrection, we find ourselves being overcome by the certain knowledge of God's true character. It is important for us to be able to think of our God as a Person, not an idea, or a principle or even a spiritual concept. It must follow that whatever name we use for Him, that name must have some real meaning for us. There are literally hundreds of names for God in both the Old and New Testament. How many names do you have for the person most beloved on earth to you? Does one mean any more than another? The reason is usually a significant one. We neither offend Him nor pacify Him by the name we choose to use when we speak to Him. His love is unchanging. It is not at all dependent on us or the phrase we happen to use. I know Jesus taught us to "Pray to your Father who is in secret." When He was on earth, He prayed to His Father. He taught us to say, "Our Father, which art in heaven." Most of the time He was concealing His own personal glory and identity, both of which have now been revealed. During His earthly days He voluntarily became dependent upon His Father, though from eternity they have been equal. Jesus invited us to pray in His Name. He assured us that He alone has power to give us eternal life. Is Jesus Christ God? Your answer to this question will determine your attitude toward Him. Is the deity of the Son of God actual? Is it Scriptural? A positive answer to these questions has meant the beginning of a personal relationship with Jesus Christ to many inquiring hearts.

ROSALIND RINKER, IN *PRAYER: CONVERSING WITH GOD*

Prayer and Forgiveness

As the Lord has forgiven you, so you also must forgive.

(Colossians 3:13)

Unlove in the heart is possibly the greatest hindrance to prayer. A loving spirit is a condition of believing prayer. We cannot be wrong with man and right with God. The spirit of prayer is essentially the spirit of love. Intercession is simply love at prayer.

> He prayeth best who loveth best
> All things both great and small;
> For the great God Who loveth us,
> He made and loveth all.

Dare we hate or dislike those whom God loves? If we do, can we really possess the Spirit of Christ? We really must face these elementary facts in our faith if prayer is to be anything more than a mere form. Our Lord not only says, "And pray for those that persecute you; that ye may be sons of your Father who is in heaven" (Matthew 5:44-45, kjv).

We venture to think that large numbers of so-called Christians have never faced this question. To hear how many Christian workers — and prominent ones, too — speak of others from whom they disagree, one must charitably suppose they have never heard that command of our Lord!

Our daily life in the world is the best indication of our power in prayer. God deals with my prayers not according to the spirit and tone which I exhibit when I am praying in public or private, but according to the spirit I show in my daily life.

Hot-tempered people can make only frigid prayers. If we do not obey our Lord's command and love one another, our prayers are well-nigh worthless. If we harbor an unforgiving spirit it is almost wasted time to pray. Christ taught us to say "Forgive us as we forgive." And He goes farther than this. He declares, "If ye forgive not men their trespasses, neither will your heavenly Father forgive your trespasses" (Matthew 6:15, kjv). May we ever exhibit the Spirit of Christ, and not forfeit our own much-needed forgiveness.

An Unknown Christian, in *The Kneeling Christian*

THE SPEAKING BOOK

Open my eyes, that I may behold wondrous things out of your law.
I am a sojourner on the earth; hide not your commandments from me!
(PSALM 119:18-19)

I believe that much of our religious unbelief is due to a wrong conception of and a wrong feeling for the Scriptures of Truth. A silent God suddenly began to speak in a book and when the book was finished lapsed back into silence again forever. Now we read the book as the record of what God said when He was for a brief time in a speaking mood. With notions like that in our heads how can we believe? The facts are that God is not silent, has never been silent. It is the nature of God to speak. The second Person of the Holy Trinity is called the Word. The Bible is the inevitable outcome of God's continuous speech. It is the infallible declaration of His mind for us put into our familiar human words.

I think a new world will arise out of the religious mists when we approach our Bible with the idea that it is not only a book which was once spoken, but a book which is now speaking. The prophets habitually said, "Thus saith the Lord." They meant their hearers to understand that God's speaking is in the continuous present. We may use the past tense properly to indicate that at a certain time a certain word of God was spoken, but a word of God once spoken continues to be spoken, as a child once born continues to be alive, or a world once created continues to exist. And those are but imperfect illustrations, for children die and worlds burn out, but the Word of our God endureth forever.

If you would follow on to know the Lord, come at once to the open Bible expecting it to speak to you. Do not come with the notion that it is a thing which you may push around at your convenience. It is more than a thing, it is a voice, a word, the very Word of the living God.

A. W. TOZER, IN *THE PURSUIT OF GOD*

A TWOFOLD INTERCESSION

He raised him from the dead and seated
him at his right hand in the heavenly places.
(EPHESIANS 1:20)

Prayer is central in heaven. The interpretation of the mystery of interces-sion begins there. It is fellowship in the ministry of our Great High Priest at the right hand of God. "He ever liveth to make intercession" (Hebrews 7:25, KJV). That our Lord should need to pray in the days of His flesh is a mystery of humiliation; that He should need to make intercession in heaven is a mystery of glory. It is a light that transcends our vision. The "why" and the "how" are beyond our understanding, but it is because He so lives to make intercession that He is able to save to the uttermost all who come to God by Him. The truth revealed is explicit, and its effect in experience assures its certainty. The ascended Christ is the Priest-King at the right hand of God. As High Priest He represents man to God; as King He repre-sents God to man. He entered in by the one offering of Himself as a Sacrifice for sin. Having entered by His own blood, He is the One Mediator between God and man, and humanity's Advocate with the Father. He intercedes for men (Hebrews 7:25-27; 9:24). Prayer finds its expression and availableness in terms of Christ and His finished work. He takes the prayers of the earthly altar and adds to them the fires of the heavenly, and they become accept-able and effective through His name (Hebrews 13:15; Revelation 5:8; 8:3). There is a twofold intercession. The High Priest intercedes for us in heaven, and the Holy Spirit intercedes within the temple of the consecrated soul. "The Spirit also helpeth our infirmities: for we know not what we should pray for; but the Spirit itself maketh intercession for us with groanings which cannot be uttered; and he that searcheth the hearts knoweth what is the mind of the Spirit, because he maketh intercession for the saints accord-ing to the will of God" (Romans 8:26-27, KJV). There is such unity of purpose and harmony of method in the two intercessions that the two are one, and what is prayed by the intercessor on earth is prayed by the Intercessor in heaven.

SAMUEL CHADWICK, IN *THE PATH OF PRAYER*

GREATER WORKS THROUGH PRAYER

We are his workmanship, created in Christ Jesus for good works,
which God prepared beforehand, that we should walk in them.

(EPHESIANS 2:10)

If men will not believe, and act upon, our Lord's promises and commands, how can we expect them to be persuaded by any mere human exhortations? Do you remember that our Lord, when speaking to His disciples, asked them to believe that He was in the Father and the Father in Him? Then He added: "If you cannot believe My bare word about this, believe Me for the very works' sake" (John 14:11, KJV). It was as if He said, "If My Person, My sanctified life, and My wonderful words do not elicit belief in Me, then look at My works: surely they are sufficient to compel belief? Believe Me because of what I do." Then He went on to promise that if they would believe, they should do greater works than these. It was after this utterance that He gave the first of those six wonderful promises in regard to prayer. The inference surely is that those "greater works" are to be done only as the outcome of prayer.

May the disciple therefore follow the Master's method? Fellow-worker, if you fail to grasp, fail to trust our Lord's astounding promises regarding prayer, will you not believe them "for the very works' sake"? That is, because of those "greater works" which men and women are performing today — or, rather, the works which the Lord Jesus is doing, through their prayerful cooperation?

What are we "out for"? What is our real aim in life? Surely we desire most of all to be abundantly fruitful in the Master's service. We seek not position, or prominence, or power. But we do long to be fruitful servants. Then we must be much in prayer. God can do more through our prayers than through our preaching. A. J. Gordon once said, "You can do more than pray, after you have prayed, but you can never do more than pray until you have prayed." If only we would believe this!

AN UNKNOWN CHRISTIAN, IN *THE KNEELING CHRISTIAN*

TAKE HIS HAND

The steps of a man are established by
the LORD, when he delights in his way.
(PSALM 37:23)

I would rather have a guide than the best advice or the clearest set of directions. When I lived in Ecuador, I usually traveled on foot. Except for one occasion when I went off alone (and quickly learned what a bad mistake that was), I always had with me a guide who knew the way or knew much better than I did how to find it. Trails often led through streams and rivers that we had to wade, but sometimes there was a log laid high above the water we had to cross.

I dreaded those logs and was always tempted to take the steep, hard way down into the ravine and up the other side. But the Indians would say, "Just walk across, señorita," and over they would go, confident and light-footed. I was barefoot as they were, but it was not enough. On the log, I couldn't keep from looking down at the river below. I knew I would slip. I had never been any good at balancing myself on the tops of walls and things, and the log looked impossible. So my guide would stretch out a hand, and the touch of it was all I needed. I stopped worrying about slipping. I stopped looking down at the river or even at the log and looked at the guide, who held my hand with only the lightest touch. The lesson the Indians taught me was that of trust. The only thing I really needed, the touch of a steady hand, they could provide. If I had been inclined to come to a halt in the middle of the log and raise nasty questions or argue about their ability to keep me from falling, my trust would have collapsed and so would I.

I have found in the Bible plenty of evidence that God has guided people. I find, too, assurance that he is willing to guide me. He has been at it for a long time. His hand reaches toward me. I have only to take it.

ELISABETH ELLIOT, IN *GOD'S GUIDANCE*

GIVING YOURSELF TO JESUS

Standing behind him at his feet, weeping, she began to wet his feet with her tears and wiped them with the hair of her head and kissed his feet and anointed them with the ointment.

(LUKE 7:38)

We should, indeed, surrender our whole being unto Christ Jesus: and cease to live any longer in ourselves, that He may become our life; "that being dead, our life may be hid with Christ in God" (Colossians 3:3). [When] we leave and forsake ourselves, that we may be lost in Him; and this can be effected only by annihilation; which being the true prayer of adoration, renders unto God alone, all "Blessing, honour, glory and power, for ever and ever" (Revelation 5:13).

This is the prayer of truth; "It is worshipping God in spirit and in truth" (John 4:23). "In spirit," because we enter into the purity of that Spirit which prayeth within us, and are drawn forth and freed from our own carnal and corrupt manner of praying; "In truth" because we are thereby placed in the great Truth of the All of God, and the Nothing of the creature.

There are but these two truths, the All, and the Nothing; everything else is falsehood. We can pay due honour to the All of God, only in our own annihilation, which is no sooner accomplished, than He, who never suffers a void in nature, instantly fills us with Himself.

Did we but know the virtue and the blessings which the soul derives from this prayer, we should willingly be employed therein without ceasing. "It is the pearl of great price: it is the hidden treasure" (Matthew 13:44-45), which, whoever findeth, selleth freely all that he hath to purchase it: "It is the well of living water, which springeth up unto everlasting life": It is the adoration of God "in spirit and in truth" (John 4:14-23), and it is the full performance of the purest evangelical precepts.

JEANNE GUYON, IN *A SHORT AND EASY METHOD OF PRAYER*

True Joy

Be blameless and innocent, children of God without blemish
in the midst of a crooked and twisted generation,
among whom you shine as lights in the world.

(Philippians 2:15)

Christians should live so far above the world as not to need or seek its pleasures, and thus recommend religion to the world as a source of the highest and purest happiness. The peaceful look, the joyful countenance, the spiritual serenity and cheerfulness of a living Christian recommend religion to the unconverted. Their satisfaction in God, their holy joy, their living above and shunning the ways and amusements of worldly minds, impress the unconverted with a sense of the necessity and desirableness of a Christian life. Their own interests and their own pleasure are regarded as nothing as compared with the interests and good pleasure of God. They, therefore, cannot seek amusements unless they believe themselves called of God to do so. By a law of our nature we seek to please those whom we supremely love. Also, by a law of our nature, we find our highest happiness in pleasing those whom we supremely love; and we supremely please ourselves when we seek not at all to please ourselves, but to please the object of our supreme affection. Therefore, Christians find their highest enjoyment and their truest pleasure in pleasing God and in seeking the good of their fellow-men; and they enjoy this service all the more because enjoyment is not what they seek, but what they inevitably experience by a law of their nature.

This is a fact of Christian consciousness. The highest and purest of all amusements is found in doing the will of God. Mere worldly amusements are cold and insipid and not worthy of naming in comparison with the enjoyment we find in doing the will of God. To one who loves God supremely it is natural to seek amusements, and everything else that we do seek, with supreme reference to the glory of God.

Charles Finney, in *Power from on High*

LISTENING IN SILENCE

The LORD will fight for you, and you have only to be silent.
(EXODUS 14:14)

Waiting in silence gives God an opportunity to give His thoughts to us. Psalm 62 closes with two thoughts that God spoke to David during his silence: "Power belongs to God" and "Lovingkindness is Thine, O Lord." David could not have been assured of this had he not taken time to listen to God.

In Jeremiah 42:1-4 we read that the remnant of Judah came to Jeremiah saying, "Pray that the Lord your God will tell us where we should go and what we should do." And Jeremiah responded, "I will certainly pray to the Lord your God as you have requested; I will tell you everything the Lord says and will keep nothing back from you." Note that Jeremiah prayed to listen to God. If God is going to be central in our praying, we must learn to listen as well as talk to Him.

When we listen to God, we can be sure what is spoken will never contradict the Scriptures. In fact, most of what God speaks to us will be pure Scripture. He may remind us of a passage or a thought from Scripture, or He may take us to a passage we had never thought of before. Before leaving the earth, Jesus said the Holy Spirit would come and "remind you of everything I have said to you" (John 14:26, NIV).

If you have never practiced the discipline of silence before God, you will have to grow in this discipline. Tell God about a situation or need, then ask Him to speak. At first, wait in silence for one minute. As you are able, extend the time of silence to two or three minutes, or even more.

We are not talking about Eastern religion here. Most Eastern meditation puts the mind in neutral and lets any thoughts come. When the Bible talks about silence before God or biblical meditation, it speaks of a focal point that is either God Himself or the Scriptures. In that setting God's voice can best be heard.

LEE BRASE, IN *PRAYING FROM GOD'S HEART*

PRAYER AND GOD'S PURPOSES

The LORD will fulfill his purpose for me;
your steadfast love, O LORD, endures forever.
(PSALM 138:8)

Prayer is God's business to which men can attend. Prayer is God's necessary business, which men only can do, and that men must do. Men who
belong to God are obliged to pray. They are not obliged to grow rich, nor to
make money. They are not obliged to have large success in business. These
are incidental, occasional, merely nominal, as far as integrity to Heaven
and loyalty to God are concerned. Material successes are immaterial to
God. Men are neither better nor worse with those things or without them.
They are not sources of reputation nor elements of character in the heavenly estimates. But to pray, to really pray, is the source of revenue, the basis
of reputation, and the element of character in the estimation of God. Men
are obliged to pray as they are obliged to be religious. Prayer is loyalty to
God. Non-praying is to reject Christ and to abandon Heaven. A life of
prayer is the only life which Heaven counts.

God is vitally concerned that men should pray. Men are bettered by
prayer, and the world is bettered by praying. God does His best work for the
world through prayer. God's greatest glory and man's highest good are
secured by prayer. Prayer forms the godliest men and makes the godliest
world.

God's promises lie like giant corpses without life, only for decay and
dust unless men appropriate and vivify these promises by earnest and
prevailing prayer. Promise is like the unsown seed, the germ of life in it, but
the soil and culture of prayer are necessary to germinate and culture the
seed. Prayer is God's life-giving breath. God's purposes move along the
pathway made by prayer to their glorious designs. God's purposes are
always moving to their high and benignant ends, but the movement is
along the way marked by unceasing prayer. The breath of prayer in man is
from God.

E. M. BOUNDS, IN *THE REALITY OF PRAYER*

THE SURE PROMISES

We have the prophetic word more fully confirmed, to which you
will do well to pay attention as to a lamp shining in a dark place.

(2 PETER 1:19)

The Bible was given to us from the specific purpose of revealing to us the will of God, and when we find that anything is definitely promised in the Word of God we know that that is His will, for He has said so in so many words. And when we who believe on the name of the Son of God go to God and ask Him for anything that is definitely promised in His Word, we may know with absolute certainty that God has heard our prayer and that the thing which we have asked of God is granted. We do not have to feel it — *God says so, and that is enough.* When you have a definite promise in God's Word you do not need to put any "ifs" before it. All the promises of God are yea and amen in Christ Jesus (2 Corinthians 1:20). They are absolutely sure, and if you plead any plain promise in God's Word you need not put any "ifs" in your petition. You may know that you are asking something that is according to God's will, and it is your privilege to know that God has heard you; and it is your privilege to know that you have the thing you have asked; it is your privilege to get up from prayer with the same absolute certainty that that thing is yours that you will afterward have when you actually see it in your hand. Why should we put any "ifs" in when we take to God any promise of His own? Does God ever lie? There are many cases in which we do not know His will, for the dearest of anything to the true child of God is God's will, but there is no need to put any "ifs" in when He has revealed His will. To put in an "if" in such a case as that is to doubt God, to doubt His Word, and really is to "make God a liar."

R. A. TORREY, IN *THE POWER OF PRAYER*

Heaven on Earth

They who wait for the LORD shall renew their strength;
they shall mount up with wings like eagles; they shall
run and not be weary; they shall walk and not faint.

(ISAIAH 40:31)

Friday, Jan. 6. Feeling and considering my extreme weakness, and want of grace, the pollution of my soul, and danger of temptations on every side, I set apart this day for fasting and prayer, neither eating nor drinking from evening to evening, beseeching God to have mercy on me. My soul intensely longed, that the dreadful spots and stains of sin might be washed away from it. Saw something of the power and all-sufficiency of God. My soul seemed to rest on his power and grace; longed for resignation to his will, and mortification to all things here below. My mind was greatly fixed on divine things: my resolutions for a life of mortification, continual watchfulness, self-denial, seriousness, and devotion, were strong and fixed; my desires ardent and intense; my conscience tender, and afraid of every appearance of evil. My soul grieved with reflection on past levity, and want of resolution for God. I solemnly renewed my dedication of myself to God, and longed for grace to enable me always to keep covenant with him. Time appeared very short, eternity near; and great name, either in or after life, together with all earthly pleasures and profits, but an empty bubble, a deluding dream. Was grieved that I could do so little for God before my bodily strength failed. In the evening, though tired, was enabled to continue instant in prayer for some time. Spent the time in reading, meditation, and prayer, till the evening was far spent: was grieved to think that I could not *watch unto prayer* the whole night. But blessed be God, heaven is a place of continual and incessant devotion, though the earth is dull. It was then my happiness, to continue instant in prayer, and was enabled to continue in it for nearly an hour. My soul was then "strong in the Lord, and in the power of his might." Longed exceedingly for angelic holiness and purity, and to have all my thoughts, at all times, employed in divine and heavenly things. O how blessed is a heavenly temper!

JONATHAN EDWARDS, IN *THE LIFE AND DIARY OF DAVID BRAINERD*

WALKING IN THE VISION

Even though I walk through the valley of the shadow
of death, I will fear no evil, for you are with me.
(PSALM 23:4)

It is so easy when we see things in vision to start out and do them. We are caught up into the seventh heaven, far above all the grubby things of earth. It is magnificent for a time, but we have got to come down. After the Mount of Transfiguration comes the place where we have to live, namely, the demon-possessed valley. The test of reality is our life in the valley, not that we fly up among the golden peaks of the early morning. Peter had his triumphant minute, but he had to go through the mill after it; he went through a tremendous heartbreak before he was fit to hear Jesus say, "Feed my sheep." Peter would have done anything for his Lord — the spirit was willing, but the flesh was weak. We make allowances for the flesh, but we have no business to; we have to make manifest in the flesh the visions of the spirit. Thank God we are going to heaven when we die; but thank God we are not going before we die. We get glimpses of heaven, then we are brought down instantly into actual circumstances. Do not go too long in the light of undisciplined vision. Thank God for the triumphant minute, but we have to walk on earth according to what we saw in vision. After seeing Jesus for that moment on the Mount, we see Him standing after the resurrection on the seashore in the early morning with "a fire of coals there, and fish laid thereon, and bread" (John 21:9, KJV). Thank God for seeing Jesus transfigured, and for the almightiness of the visions He does give, but remember that the vision is to be made real in actual circumstances; the glory is to be manifested in earthen vessels. It has to be exhibited through fingertips, through eyes and hands and feet; wherever Jesus exhibited it.

OSWALD CHAMBERS, IN *IF YOU WILL ASK*

HIS GLORY, NOT OUR PERFECTIONISM

You were bought with a price. So glorify God.
(1 CORINTHIANS 6:20)

Paul prays for "what is best," and understands that this best must issue in "the fruit of righteousness that comes through Jesus Christ," and then carefully adds that all of this is to the glory and praise of God (Philippians 1:11, NIV). This is the ultimate test: it is the test of our motives. Some of us pursue what is excellent, even in the spiritual arena, simply because we find it hard to do anything else. Our perfectionist natures are upset when there is inferior discipline, inferior preaching, inferior witness, inferior praying, inferior teaching. If we are concerned over these things because we sense in them a church that has sunk into contentment with lukewarmness and spiritual mediocrity, if we try to change these things because in our heart of hearts we are zealous for the glory of Christ and the good of his people, that is one thing; if on the other hand our concern over these matters is driven primarily by our own high, perfectionist standards, we will be less inclined to help, and more inclined to belittle. Our own service will become a source of secret pride, precisely because it is more competent than much of what we see around us. And sadly, much of this ostensible concern for quality may be nothing more than self-worship, the ugliest idolatry of them all. Paul has in fact already tried to quash pursuit of this kind of excellence. By praying that the love of the Philippian believers might abound more and more, as a precondition and a means to discerning and approving what is best, he establishes the nature of the excellence that interests him. Love is essentially self-denying; it seeks God's interests, our fellow-believer's good. Now Paul gives his prayer the sharpest focus; the apostle intercedes with God along these lines to the end that God himself might be glorified and praised.

D. A. CARSON, IN *A CALL TO SPIRITUAL REFORMATION*

CHRIST'S GLORY

The LORD said to me, "You are my Son; today I have begotten you.
Ask of me, and I will make the nations your heritage,
and the ends of the earth your possession."

(PSALM 2:7-8)

Oh, if we could enter more fully into the thoughts of God as to the real nature, character, and consequences of sin; and His boundless love for sinners, manifested in the gift of His own Son — descended from heaven into our nature in order to effect our salvation, to vindicate the character of the broken law, and to declare the righteousness of God, that He might be just, and at the same time the Justifier of him who believeth on Jesus, then should we understand what a glorious position Christ did really occupy, and what a marvelous grace Jehovah bestowed upon Him in appointing Him to be the manifestation and incarnation of His Everlasting Love, and the "daysman, to lay his hand upon both."

> Behold my servant, whom I uphold; mine elect, in whom my soul delighteth; I have put my spirit upon him: he shall bring forth judgment to the Gentiles. . . . I the Lord have called thee in righteousness, and will hold thine hand, and will keep thee, and give thee for a covenant of the people, for a light of the Gentiles; to open the blind eyes, to bring out the prisoners from the prison, and them that sit in darkness out of the prison house. I am the Lord: that is my name; and *my glory will I not give to another.* (Isaiah 42:1,6-8, KJV)

This was the work Christ was about to accomplish; and to finish it was in His estimation *to be glorified.* Satan, also, the enemy of God and man, was to be overthrown; the Goliath who had defied the armies of the living God was to be trampled under foot: and the Son of Man was to do it. Death, the wages of sin, was to be fully paid; and through death Christ was to "destroy him that had the power of death" and rise again, to die no more; but with authority to impart His own risen life to His people.

MARCUS RAINSFORD, IN *OUR LORD PRAYS FOR HIS OWN*

ATTUNED TO GOD

> *The Lord answered her, "Martha, Martha, you are anxious*
> *and troubled about many things, but one thing is necessary."*
> (LUKE 10:41-42)

Not until we have come apart from those things which divert our attention to outward things, are our souls free to engage in inward activity. Or perhaps we should speak first of that inward, passive state known as the devotional attitude. As soon as outward things lose their distracting influence over our soul, God Himself attunes our distracted, worldly and earthly-minded souls to prayer.

Many who pray are not aware of this. As soon as they enter into their secret chamber they begin at once to speak with God. Do not do that, my friend. Take plenty of time before you begin to speak. Let quietude wield its influence upon you. Let the fact that you are alone assert itself. Give your soul time to get released from the many outward things. Give God time to play the prelude to prayer for the benefit of your distracted soul. Let the devotional attitude, the attitude of holy passivity, open all the doors of the soul leading into the realm of eternal things.

We are on the whole disposed to emphasize activity in prayer too much. From the time we begin and until we have finished, we are busily engaged in speaking with God. And we feel almost as though there is something wrong or something lacking in our prayer if we do not talk continuously to God.

There is activity in prayer, of course, and it includes speaking with God. But that should not be all. In the quiet and holy hour of prayer we should also be still and permit ourselves to be examined by the Physician of our souls. We should submit to scrutiny under the holy and penetrating light of God and be thoroughly examined in order to ascertain just where our trouble lies.

OLE HALLESBY, IN *PRAYER*

HE IS SUFFICIENT

Submit yourselves therefore to God.
Resist the devil, and he will flee from you.
(JAMES 4:7)

We ought not to doubt that those prayers which are according to the Will of God shall have a full answer, for with regard to them we rest our confidence on the Word and Name of Christ. But there are many requests concerning which we do not easily come to full assurance — they do not stand so clearly in the Divine will as to yield us certainty. And with regard to many of them our prayers seem to return empty.

Moses desired to pass over Jordan with the tribes; but Jehovah said to him, "Speak no more unto Me of this matter." Paul besought the Lord thrice that the thorn which rankled in his flesh might be withdrawn, but the only response assured was, "My grace is sufficient for thee." John, the beloved disciple, encourages us to pray for the salvation of our brethren, but even as we address ourselves to this holy duty he reminds us that "there is a sin unto death," in the face of which, apparently, prayer will not prevail.

We may indeed be sure that "Whatsoever is good for God's children they shall have it; for all is theirs to help them towards heaven; therefore if poverty be good they shall have it; if disgrace or crosses be good they shall have them; for all is ours to promote our greatest prosperity."

When we pray for temporal blessings, we are sometimes conscious of the special aid of the Spirit of intercession. This is, so far, a warrant to believe that our prayer is well-pleasing to God. But we must be careful not to confound the yearnings of nature with the promptings of the Spirit. Only those whose eye is single, and whose whole body, therefore, is full of light, can safely distinguish between the impulses of the flesh and of the Spirit.

DAVID MCINTYRE, IN *THE HIDDEN LIFE OF PRAYER*

The Reward of Patient Prayer

Put your trust in the Lord. There are many who say, "Who will show us some good? Lift up the light of your face upon us, O Lord!" You have put more joy in my heart than they have when their grain and wine abound.

(PSALM 4:5-7)

The natural mind is ever prone to reason, when we ought to believe; to be at work, when we ought to be quiet; to go our own way, when we ought steadily to walk on in God's ways, however trying to nature. When I was first converted, I should have said, What harm can there be to take some of the money which has been put by for the building fund? God will help me again after some time with means for the orphans, and then I can replace it. Or, there is this money due for the legacy of one hundred pounds. This money is quite sure; may I not, therefore, on the strength of it, take some of the money from the building fund, and, when the legacy is paid, replace the money which I have taken? From what I have seen of believers, I know that many would act thus. But how does it work, when we thus anticipate God, by going our own way? We bring, in many instances, guilt on our conscience; but if not, we certainly weaken faith instead of increasing it; and each time we work thus a deliverance of our own we find it more and more difficult to trust in God, till at last we give way entirely to our natural fallen reason, and unbelief prevails. How different, if one is enabled to wait God's own time, and to look alone to him for help and deliverance! When at last help comes, after many seasons of prayer it may be, and after much exercise of faith and patience it may be, how sweet it is, and what a present recompense does the soul at once receive for trusting in God, and waiting patiently for his deliverance! Dear Christian reader, if you have never walked in this path of obedience before, do so now, and you will then know experimentally the sweetness of the joy which results from it.

GEORGE MÜLLER, IN *THE AUTOBIOGRAPHY OF GEORGE MÜLLER*

Being a Blessing

Do not be slothful in zeal, be fervent in spirit, serve the Lord.
Rejoice in hope, be patient in tribulation, be constant in prayer.
(Romans 12:11-12)

The God of the Bible is a God who blesses. His Word is full of multiplied promises that He will do just that. We can be assured that, except in cases where God must discipline or punish, it is always His will to bless people, especially His obedient children. "Jesus went around doing good" (Acts 10:38, NIV). Like Him, we are to go through life blessing everyone we can. We, His disciples, are to be known for our good deeds of blessing to others (Matthew 5:16; Ephesians 2:10). We are to be rich in good deeds (1 Timothy 6:18). We are to be "thoroughly equipped for every good work" (2 Timothy 3:17, NIV).

The greatest way in which Christians can mediate blessing is through prayer. We have the opportunity to pray for those we can contact in no other way. From the leaders of our nation and the leaders of the church to the poor, the needy, and the suffering — we can bring blessing to all through prayer. From our family and closest friends whom we see often, to those we may meet but once or only hear about — we can be God's agents of blessing. The often-repeated request, "Pray for me," is really a plea for blessing and help.

As a Christian, you should go through life blessing others. You can bring streams of blessing, refreshment, and encouragement wherever you go just by punctuating your days with unceasing prayer for others. As time and opportunity permit, you should bless in every possible way as many as you can (Galatians 6:10). Your presence should always be a blessing. But this will be most true if you are faithfully asking for God's blessing on all [those] about you. You can find opportunities to fill your day with prayers of blessing if you are observant.

Wesley Duewel, in *Touch the World Through Prayer*

Vertical and Horizontal

Turn away from evil and do good; let him seek peace and pursue it. For the eyes of the Lord are on the righteous, and his ears are open to their prayer.

(1 Peter 3:11-12)

Jesus said we are to forgive our brothers "seventy times seven" (Matthew 18:22, NKJV) if they sin against us that many times. If they keep repenting over and over again, we have to keep forgiving over and over again, because that's the basic relationship we have with God.

It is terrifying to pray, "O God, please forgive me proportionately to the way in which I forgive people who have offended me." That scares me because I know I have not been anywhere near as gracious in dealing with people who have offended me as God has been in dealing with me, nor am I capable of being so gracious. I will be in deep trouble if God provides forgiveness for me only to the degree that I am willing to provide it to others.

This petition, then, reminds us of the depth of our sinfulness, our need for daily confession, and our need for forgiveness, but also of our Christian duty in our interpersonal relationships on the human level. We are to keep short accounts not just in our vertical relationship with God, but in our horizontal relationships with others.

Yes, my sins have all been paid for, once and for all, on the cross. But Jesus taught us to pray for forgiveness as part of our ongoing communion with God. We need a fresh understanding, a fresh experience, of His grace and of His forgiveness every day. There is no greater state than to get up from your knees knowing that in God's sight you are clean, that He has forgiven every sin you've ever committed. Without that grace, without that forgiveness, I don't think I could live in this world for another sixty seconds. This is something we all desperately need, and we have but to ask for it.

R. C. Sproul, in *The Prayer of the Lord*

THE ROYAL POWER OF THE CHILD OF GOD

Live in harmony with one another. Do not be haughty,
but associate with the lowly. Never be wise in your own sight.
(ROMANS 12:16)

Let us confine ourselves to the chief thought: prayer as an appeal to the friendship of God; and we shall find that two lessons are specially suggested. The one, that if we are God's friends, and come as such to Him, we must prove ourselves the friends of the needy; God's friendship to us and ours to others go hand in hand. The other, that when we come thus we may use the utmost liberty in claiming an answer.

There is a twofold use of prayer: the one, to obtain strength and blessing for our own life; the other, the higher, the true glory of prayer, for which Christ has taken us into His fellowship and teaching, is intercession, where prayer is the royal power a child of God exercises in heaven on behalf of others and even of the kingdom. We see it in Scripture, how it was in intercession for others that Abraham and Moses, Samuel and Elijah, with all the holy men of old, proved that they had power with God and prevailed. It is when we give ourselves to be a blessing that we can specially count on the blessing of God. It is when we draw near to God as the friend of the poor and the perishing that we may count on His friendliness; the righteous man who is the friend of the poor is very specially the friend of God. This gives wonderful liberty in prayer. Lord! I have a needy friend whom I must help. As a friend I have undertaken to help him. In Thee I have a Friend, whose kindness and riches I know to be infinite: I am sure Thou wilt give me what I ask. If I, being evil, am ready to do for my friend what I can, how much more wilt Thou, O my heavenly Friend, now do for Thy friend what he asks?

ANDREW MURRAY, IN *WITH CHRIST IN THE SCHOOL OF PRAYER*

PRAYER AND HEALING

Heal me, O LORD, and I shall be healed; save me,
and I shall be saved, for you are my praise.

(JEREMIAH 17:14)

God's general will for mankind is physical and mental health, but it is not always God's will to heal in a specific situation. God's grace is built even into our genes and chromosomes. God does not delight in any suffering, whether it be physical illness, cruelty, persecution, or deprivation. He is pleased when mankind seeks to discover the medical and surgical procedures that benefit life. We should use great boldness in prayer for the physical, emotional, and mental healing of ourselves and others. We have every right to plead God's promises in holy persistence until God checks us or suggests that healing is not His will. Undoubtedly it would please God if our faith for healing were much stronger.

Divine healing for physical and mental affliction is common on the mission fields. Christ must prove that He is the living, prayer-answering God in contrast to the impotent false gods and religions of pagan nations. It glorifies Christ to answer prayer. Perhaps we who have shared such full gospel light do not need so many evidences of the supernatural. On the other hand, God is just the same today as He has been in the past or will be in the future (Hebrews 13:8). This means He is the same in wisdom, compassion, love, power, and readiness to answer prayer.

There are occasions when suffering can bring blessing to the person who suffers and to others who observe the grace God gives to the sufferer. Sickness is sometimes permitted by God because, through it, He will gain the glory (John 11:4). Most commentators believe that Paul's thorn in the flesh (2 Corinthians 12:7-10) was physical illness of some kind, probably eye trouble. Interestingly enough, it was because of illness that Paul was able to found the church in Galatia (Galatians 4:13). The Galatian Christians loved Paul so much they would gladly have plucked out their own eyes and given them to him if that had been possible (verses 14-15).

WESLEY DUEWEL, IN *TOUCH THE WORLD THROUGH PRAYER*

HE IS THE ONE

She said, "If I touch even his garments, I will be made well."
(MARK 5:28)

What shall we ask for? And is there any special way of asking which will bring a sure answer? [Consider] the sick woman in Mark 5. Did *she* have any difficulty in knowing what to ask? Certainly not. Well, you might argue, she didn't really ask, she just came up behind Jesus and touched His clothes. Yes, but coming and touching were her ways of asking. In Mark 5 the woman's asking was commensurate to her need. For twelve years she had suffered as much at the hands of primitive doctors as from her hemorrhage. Her life was intolerable. She was on her way to an early grave. Then "she heard the reports about Jesus." I love that verse. "She heard the reports about Jesus." What reports? That whoever came to Him was healed! Look back or think back into the gospel records. When was anyone refused who came to Jesus for help of any kind? There was no one. Everyone who came received the help he asked for. Lepers were cleansed, blind eyes were made to see, demons were cast out and personalities restored. The lame walked, the deaf heard, the dead lived again.

This sick woman heard what Jesus had done and although her malady was not listed among the others, she was so desperate she decided within herself that if He could heal all those diseases, He could heal hers, too. *He* could do it. No one else. She was sure now that *He was the one.* Her own desperate need drew her to Him, and if she could only get to Him, she would be well.

It was a glorious moment when I began to see that the power and authority of Jesus Christ were most often used when individuals, not crowds, asked for help. There were only a few whom He healed who did not ask personally. This, too, shows His willingness and His knowledge of our needs.

What shall we ask for?

The simple answer is, *ask for what you need.*

ROSALIND RINKER, IN *PRAYER: CONVERSING WITH GOD*

NO GOOD THING WITHHELD

Father of the fatherless and protector of
widows is God in his holy habitation.

(PSALM 68:5)

In Scotland, a good many years ago, there lived a man with his wife and three children — two girls and a boy. He was in the habit of getting drunk, and thus losing his situation. At last, he said he would take Johnnie, and go off to America, where he would be away from his old associates, and where he could commence life over again. He took the little fellow, seven years old, and went away. Soon after he arrived in America, he went into a saloon and got drunk. He got separated from his boy in the streets, and he has never been seen by his friends since. The little fellow was placed in an institution, and afterward apprenticed in Massachusetts. After he had been there some time he became discontented, and went off to sea; finally, he came to Chicago to work on the lakes. He had been a roving spirit, had gone over sea and land, and now he was in Chicago. When the vessel came into port, one time, he was invited to a Gospel meeting. The joyful sound of the Gospel reached him, and he became a Christian.

After he had been a Christian a little while, he became very anxious to find his mother. He wrote to different places in Scotland, but could not find out where she was. One day he read in the Psalms — "No good thing will He withhold from them that walk uprightly." He closed his Bible, got down on his knees, and said: "O God, I have been trying to walk uprightly for months past; help me to find my mother." It came into his mind to write back to the place in Massachusetts from which he had run away years before. It turned out that a letter from Scotland had been waiting for him there for seven years. He wrote at once to the place in Scotland, and found that his mother was still living; the answer came back immediately. All the nineteen years he had been away, his mother had prayed to God day and night that he might be saved, and that she might live to know what had become of him, and see him — once more.

D. L. MOODY, IN *PREVAILING PRAYER*

Faith to Pray

All that the Father gives me will come to me,
and whoever comes to me I will never cast out.

(John 6:37)

"If we confess our sins, he is faithful and righteous to forgive us our sins, and to cleanse us from all unrighteousness" (1 John 1:9, KJV). That was just what those folk did who came to Christ and heard from Him these words before they departed, "Thy faith hath saved thee." All they did was to come to Jesus and plead their distress before Him, whether it was physical or spiritual or both.

Notice the simple, but unmistakable, mark of a living faith. Such a faith as this sees its own need, acknowledges its own helplessness, goes to Jesus, tells Him just how bad things are and leaves everything with Him.

You and I can now tell how much faith we need in order to pray. We have faith enough when we in our helplessness turn to Jesus.

This shows us clearly that true prayer is a fruit of helplessness and faith. Helplessness becomes prayer the moment that you go to Jesus and speak candidly and confidently with Him about your needs. This is to believe.

The reason that more faith than this is not necessary in order to pray lies in the very nature of prayer. We have seen above that prayer is nothing more involved than to open the door when Jesus knocks and give Him access to our distress and helplessness with all His miracle-working powers.

It is not intended that our faith should help Jesus to fulfill our supplications. He does not need any help; all He needs is access. Neither is it intended that our faith should draw Jesus into our distress, or make Him interested in us, or solicitous on our behalf. He has long since cared for us.

Ole Hallesby, in *Prayer*

Mastery by Prayer

> *If anyone cleanses himself from what is dishonorable,*
> *he will be a vessel for honorable use, set apart as holy,*
> *useful to the master of the house, ready for every good work.*
>
> (2 Timothy 2:21)

By prayers we are set to tasks sometimes which (at first, at least) may add to life's burden. Our eyes being opened, we see problems to which before we were blind, and we hear calls that no more let us alone. And I have said that we are shown ourselves at times in a way to dishearten us, and take effective dogmatism out of us. We lose effect on those people who take others at their own emphatic valuation, who do not try the spirits, and who have acquired no skill to discern the Lord in the apostle. True searching prayer is incompatible with spiritual dullness or self-complacency. And, therefore, such stupidity is not a mere defect, but a vice. It grew upon us because we did not court the searching light, nor haunt the vicinity of the great white Throne. We are chargeable with it because of our neglect of what cures it. Faith is a quickening spirit, it has insight; and religious density betrays its absence. It is not at all the effect of ignorance. Many ignorant people escape it by the exercise of themselves unto godliness; and they not only show wonderful spiritual acumen, but they turn it upon themselves; with a result, often, of great but vigilant humility. We can feel in them the discipline of the Spirit. We can read much habitual prayer between their lines. They have risen far above religion. They are in the Spirit, and live in a long Lord's day. We know that they are not trying to serve Christ with the mere lustiness of natural religion, nor expecting to do the Spirit's work with the force of native temperament turned pious. "The secret of the Lord is with them that fear Him, and He will show them His covenant." The deeper we go into things the more do we enter a world where the mastery and the career is not due to talent but to prayer.

P. T. Forsyth, in *The Soul of Prayer*

OUR GREAT GOD

You have multiplied, O LORD my God, your wondrous deeds
and your thoughts toward us; none can compare with you!
(PSALM 40:5)

The world is perishing for lack of the knowledge of God and the Church is famishing for want of His Presence. The instant cure of most of our religious ills would be to enter the Presence in spiritual experience, to become suddenly aware that we are in God and that God is in us. This would lift us out of our pitiful narrowness and cause our hearts to be enlarged. This would burn away the impurities from our lives as the bugs and fungi were burned away by the fire that dwelt in the bush.

What a broad world to roam in, what a sea to swim in is this God and Father of our Lord Jesus Christ. He is eternal, which means that He antedates time and is wholly independent of it. Time began in Him and will end in Him. To it He pays no tribute and from it He suffers no change. He is immutable, which means that He has never changed and can never change in any smallest measure. To change He would need to go from better to worse or from worse to better. He cannot do either, for being perfect He cannot become more perfect, and if He were to become less perfect He would be less than God. He is omniscient, which means that He knows in one free and effortless act all matter, all spirit, all relationships, all events. He has no past and He has no future. He is, and none of the limiting and qualifying terms used of creatures can apply to Him. Love and mercy and righteousness are His, and holiness so ineffable that no comparisons or figures will avail to express it. Only fire can give even a remote conception of it. In fire He appeared at the burning bush; in the pillar of fire He dwelt through all the long wilderness journey. The fire that glowed between the wings of the cherubim in the holy place was called the "shekinah," the Presence, through the years of Israel's glory, and when the Old had given place to the New, He came at Pentecost as a fiery flame and rested upon each disciple.

A. W. TOZER, IN *THE PURSUIT OF GOD*

THE LORD OUR SHEPHERD

As a shepherd seeks out his flock when he is among his sheep that have been scattered, so will I seek out my sheep, and I will rescue them.

(EZEKIEL 34:12)

We know what we need — a yes or no answer, please, to a simple question. Or perhaps a road sign. Something quick and easy to point the way. But what we really ought to have is the Guide himself. Maps, road signs, a few useful phrases are good things, but infinitely better is someone who has been there before and knows the way.

The Lord is my Shepherd. He can see to everything if we are willing to turn it all over (even the equipment, even the route), but we will not do this unless we believe he means what he says. Can his word be trusted? He has made countless promises. Is he going to fulfill them?

To say yes to these questions is to have faith. It is to start following. The sheep, trusting the shepherd, trots after him down the trail.

But the picture of the Eastern shepherd with his robes and staff, the flock of sheep, the stony path through the ravine, the dark valley, and the grassy place with the quiet pool are so remote from our lives as to seem no more than a romantic painting from another country and another age. We live in towns and cities and suburbs. Our days are full of perplexities far removed from the things that bother rams and ewes and lambs. We muddle along through the thousand decisions of an ordinary day. When we are aware of the need for help in one of them, it is not one relating to good pasturage or a water supply. Time and money fill our minds: how to get them, how to use them, how to save them. But the God of the pastures is, let us not forget, the God of everywhere else. He knows just as much about suburbia or the inner city. He is not at a loss to know what to do with us, no matter where we are or what we are anxious about. Every last thing that enters our heads is known to him.

ELISABETH ELLIOT, IN *GOD'S GUIDANCE*

God's Cause in Prayer

Pray for us, that the word of the Lord may speed ahead and be honored.

(2 Thessalonians 3:1)

To no other energy is the promise of God committed as to that of prayer. Upon no other force are the purposes of God so dependent as this one of prayer. The Word of God dilates on the results and necessity of prayer. The work of God stays or advances as prayer puts forth its strength. Prophets and apostles have urged the utility, force and necessity of prayer. Prayer, with its antecedents and attendants, is the one and only condition of the final triumph of the Gospel. It is the one and only condition which honours the Father and glorifies the Son. Little and poor praying has weakened Christ's power on earth, postponed the glorious results of His reign, and retired God from His sovereignty.

Prayer puts God's work in His hands, and keeps it there. It looks to Him constantly and depends on Him implicitly to further His own cause. Prayer is but faith resting in, acting with, and leaning on and obeying God. This is why God loves it so well, why He puts all power into its hands. Every movement for the advancement of the Gospel must be created by and inspired by prayer. In all these movements of God, prayer precedes and attends as an invariable and necessary condition. In this relation, God makes prayer identical in force and power with Himself and says to those on earth who pray: "You are on the earth to carry on My cause. I am in heaven, the Lord of all, the Maker of all, the Holy One of all. Now whatever you need for My cause, ask Me and I will do it. Shape the future by your prayers, and all that you need for present supplies, command Me. I made heaven and earth, and all things in them. Ask largely. Open thy mouth wide, and I will fill it. It is My work which you are doing. It concerns My cause. Be prompt and full in praying. Do not abate your asking, and I will not wince nor abate in My giving."

E. M. Bounds, in *The Weapon of Prayer*

LEARNING TO KNOW HIM

He disciplines us for our good, that we may share his holiness.
(HEBREWS 12:10)

If the word taught me anything, it taught me to have no connection with debt. I could not think that God was poor, that he was short of resources, or unwilling to supply any want of whatever work was really his. It seemed to me that if there were a lack of funds to carry on work, then to that degree, in that special development, or at that time, it could not be the work of God. To satisfy my conscience I was therefore compelled to resign my connection with the society. The step we had taken was not a little trying to faith. I was not at all sure what God would have me do or whether he would so meet my need as to enable me to continue working as before. But God blessed and prospered me, and how glad and thankful I felt when the separation was really effected! I could look right up into my Father's face with a satisfied heart, ready by his grace to do the next thing as he might teach me, and feeling very sure of his loving care. And how blessedly he did lead me I can never, never tell. It was like a continuation of some of my earlier experiences at home. My faith was not untried; it often, often failed, and I was so sorry and ashamed of the failure to trust such a Father. But oh! I was learning to know him. I would not ever then have missed the trial. He became so near, so real, so intimate! The occasional difficulty about funds never came from an insufficient supply for personal needs, but in consequence of ministering to the wants of scores of the hungry and dying around us. And trials far more searching in other ways quite eclipsed these difficulties and being deeper brought forth in consequence richer fruits.

DR. AND MRS. HOWARD TAYLOR, IN *HUDSON TAYLOR'S SPIRITUAL SECRET*

IN THE GRIP OF THE PEACE OF GOD

May the God of peace himself sanctify you completely,
and may your whole spirit and soul and body be kept
blameless at the coming of our Lord Jesus Christ.
(1 THESSALONIANS 5:23)

It is wonderful that by the guidance of the Holy Spirit, Paul puts the subsiding of suspicion in the first place. The very nature of the old disposition is an incurable suspicion that Jesus Christ cannot do what He came to do. Have you the tiniest suspicion that God cannot sanctify you in His Almighty way? Then you need to let the God of peace slip His great calm all through your insidious unbelief till all is quiet and there is one thing only — God and your soul; not the peace of a conscience at rest only, but the very peace of God which will keep you rightly related to God. "My peace I give unto you," said Jesus. When once you let the God of peace grip you by salvation and squeeze the suspicion out of you till you are quiet before Him, the believing attitude is born, there is no more suspicion, you are in moral agreement with God about everything He wants to do.

One of the things which we need to be cured of by the God of peace is the petulant struggle of doing things for ourselves — "I can sanctify myself; if I cut off this and that and the other I shall be all right." No, Paul says "the very God of peace sanctify you wholly." Has the God of peace brought you into a calm, or is there a clamor and a struggle still? Are you still hanging on to some obstinate conviction of your own? — still struggling with some particular line of things you want? "The God of peace Himself sanctify you wholly." If we are to be sanctified, it must be by the God of peace Himself. The power that makes the life of the saint does not come from our efforts at all, it comes from the heart of the God of peace.

OSWALD CHAMBERS, IN *IF YOU WILL ASK*

PRAY WITH UNDERSTANDING

I will sing praise with my spirit, but I will sing with my mind also.

(1 CORINTHIANS 14:15)

To pray with the understanding — the mind — is to pray while being instructed by the Spirit regarding those things you are to pray for. Though you are in much need of pardon for sin and deliverance from the wrath to come, if you do not understand this, you will either not desire these things or else you will be so lukewarm in your desires after them that God will loathe your asking for them. Thus it was with the church of Laodicea. They lacked knowledge or spiritual understanding; they did not know that they were so poor, wretched, blind, and naked. Their lack of spiritual understanding made them and all their services so loathsome to Christ that he threatened to spew them out of his mouth (Revelation 3:16-17).

Men without understanding may say the same words in prayer as others do, but if there is understanding in one man and none in the other, there is a mighty difference in speaking the same words! The one speaking from a spiritual understanding will know far more in the receiving or in the denying of his desires than the other who prays in words only without the understanding.

Spiritual understanding should see in the heart of God a readiness and a willingness to give those things to the soul that the soul stands in need of. David by spiritual understanding could comprehend the very thoughts of God toward him. And thus it was with the Canaanite woman: she did by faith and a right understanding discern, beyond the seemingly harsh words of Christ to her, tenderness and willingness in his heart to save her daughter. This understanding caused her to be earnest and restless until she could enjoy the mercy she stood in need of (Matthew 15:22-28).

Spiritual understanding, understanding the willingness that is in the heart of God to save sinners, will press the soul to seek after God.

JOHN BUNYAN, IN *PILGRIM'S PRAYER BOOK*

Give Him Praise

Praise the Lord! Oh give thanks to the Lord,
for he is good, for his steadfast love endures forever!
(Psalm 106:1)

Praise is as important as prayer. We must enter into His gates with thanksgiving, and into His courts with praise, and give thanks unto Him and bless His name (Psalm 100:4). At one time in his life Praying Hyde was led to ask for four souls a day to be brought into the fold by his ministry. If on any day the number fell short of this, there would be such a weight on his heart that it was positively painful, and he could neither eat nor sleep. Then in prayer he would ask the Lord to show him what was the obstacle in himself. He invariably found that it was the want of praise in his life. He would confess his sinfulness and pray for a spirit of praise. He said that as he praised God seeking souls would come to him. We do not imply that we, too, should limit God to definite numbers or ways of working; but we do cry: "Rejoice! Praise God with heart and mind and soul."

It is not by accident that we are so often bidden to "rejoice in the Lord." God does not want miserable children; and none of His children has cause for misery. St. Paul, the most persecuted of men, was a man of song. Hymns of praise came from his lips in prison and out of prison: day and night he praised His Savior. The very order of his exhortations is significant.

"Rejoice evermore; pray without ceasing; in everything give thanks: for this is the will of God in Christ Jesus to you" (1 Thessalonians 5:16-18, KJV).

The will of God. Get that thought into your mind. It is not an optional thing.

REJOICE: PRAY: GIVE THANKS

That is the order, according to the will of God — for you, and for me. Nothing so pleases God as our praises — and nothing so blesses the man who prays as the praises he offers!

An Unknown Christian, in *The Kneeling Christian*

LEARNING TO PRAY

*I love the LORD, because he has heard my voice and
my pleas for mercy. Because he inclined his ear to me,
therefore I will call on him as long as I live.*

(PSALM 116:1-2)

There is no way to learn to pray but by praying. No reasoned philosophy of prayer ever taught a soul to pray. The subject is beset with problems, but there are no problems of prayer to the man who prays. They are all met in the fact of answered prayer and the joy of fellowship with God. We know not what we should pray for as we ought, and if prayer waits for understanding, it will never begin. We live by faith. We walk by faith. Edison wrote in 1921: "We don't know the millionth part of one percent about anything. We don't know what water is. We don't know what light is. We don't know what gravitation is. We don't know what enables us to keep on our feet when we stand up. We don't know what electricity is. We don't know what heat is. We don't know anything about magnetism. We have a lot of hypotheses about these things, but that is all. But we do not let our ignorance about all these things deprive us of their use." We discover by using. We learn by practice. Though a man should have all knowledge about prayer, and though he understand all mysteries about prayer, unless he prays he will never learn to pray.

There have been souls that were mighty in prayer, and they learned to pray. There was a period in their lives when they were as others in the matter of prayer, but they became mighty with God and prevailed. In every instance there was a crisis of grace, but it was in the discipline of grace that they discovered the secret of power. They were known as men of God, because they were men of prayer.

SAMUEL CHADWICK, IN *THE PATH OF PRAYER*

PRAYING AGAIN

Leaving them again, he went away and prayed
for the third time, saying the same words again.
(MATTHEW 26:44)

Many people call it submission to the will of God when God does not grant them their requests at the first or second asking, and they say:

"Well, perhaps it is not God's will."

As a rule this is not submission, but spiritual laziness. We do not call it submission to the will of God when we give up after one or two efforts to obtain things by action; we call it lack of strength of character. When the strong man of action starts out to accomplish a thing, if he does not accomplish it the first, or second or one hundredth time, he keeps hammering away until he does accomplish it; and the strong man of prayer when he starts to pray for a thing keeps on praying until he prays it through, and obtains what he seeks. We should be careful about what we ask from God, but when we do begin to pray for a thing we should never give up praying for it until we get it, or until God makes it very clear and very definite to us that it is not His will to give it.

Some would have us believe that it shows unbelief to pray twice for the same thing, that we ought to "take it" the first time that we ask. Doubtless there are times when we are able through faith in the Word or the leading of the Holy Spirit to claim the first time that which we have asked of God; but beyond question there are other times when we must pray again and again and again for the same thing before we get our answer. Those who have gotten beyond praying twice for the same thing have gotten beyond their Master. One of the great needs of the present day is men and women who will not only start out to pray for things, but pray on and on and on until they obtain that which they seek from the Lord.

R. A. TORREY, IN *HOW TO PRAY*

Reconcile First

Men, you are brothers. Why do you wrong each other?

(ACTS 7:26)

If there is someone who has aught against you, go at once, and be reconciled. I remember being in the inquiry room some years ago; I was in one corner of the room, talking to a young lady. There seemed to be something in the way, but I could not find out what it was. At last I said, "Is there not someone you do not forgive?" She looked up at me, and said, "What made you ask that? Has anyone told you about me?" "No," I said; "but I thought perhaps that might be the case, as you have not received forgiveness yourself." "Well," she said, pointing to another corner of the room, where there was a young lady sitting, "I have had trouble with that young lady; we have not spoken to each other for a long time." "Oh," I said, "It is all plain to me now; you cannot be forgiven until you are willing to forgive her." It was a great struggle. But then you know, the greater the cross the greater the blessing. It is human to err, but it is Christlike to forgive and be forgiven. At last this young lady said: "I will go and forgive her." Strange to say, the same conflict was going on in the mind of the lady in the other part of the room. They both came to their right mind about the same time. They met each other in the middle of the floor. The one tried to say that she forgave the other, but they could not finish; so they rushed into each other's arms. Then the four of us — the two seekers and the two workers — got down on our knees together, and we had a grand meeting. These two went away rejoicing.

Dear friend, is this the reason why your prayers are not answered? Is there some friend, some member of your family, someone in the church, you have not forgiven? We sometimes hear of members of the same church who have not spoken to each other for years. How can we expect God to forgive when this is the case?

D. L. Moody, in *Prevailing Prayer*

UNITED WITH CHRIST

When Christ who is your life appears,
then you also will appear with him in glory.
(COLOSSIANS 3:4)

In all Jehovah's dealings with His people in grace and in glory, the divine rule is to begin with the Lord Jesus Christ; to do unto Him, and with Him, what in His purpose of grace and love He intends to do with us, and thus make Him the fountain-head and source of all our blessings. Thus, God in the first instance unites Christ to Himself, and then in Christ unites Himself to His people, making His own union with Christ the ground, reason, and means of His union with us. Thus again,

Christ is "the first begotten among many brethren," and then we are begotten in Him.

Christ is the "most blessed for evermore," and we are "blessed in Him with all spiritual blessings."

First, the Father gave to Christ "to have life in Himself," and then He gave us life in Him.

Christ is first filled with "all the fullness" of God, and then we out "of His fullness have received, and grace for grace."

Christ was first manifested and declared to be the Son of the Father, then we in Him.

Christ crucified for sin, and we "crucified with Him."

Christ risen, we "raised up together with Him."

Christ more than conqueror, we "more than conquerors through Him."

Christ set down at the right hand of the Majesty in the heavens, we "sitting at God's right hand in the heavenly places in Christ Jesus."

The Holy Spirit descending without measure upon Him, that as "the anointing oil upon the head of Aaron went down upon his beard even to the skirts of his raiment," so we might, through the anointing of our High Priest, enjoy His unction and inherit His blessing.

MARCUS RAINSFORD, IN *OUR LORD PRAYS FOR HIS OWN*

CHRISTLIKE PRAYER

"Who has understood the mind of the Lord so as to instruct him?" But we have the mind of Christ.

(1 CORINTHIANS 2:16)

The prayer of faith, like some plant rooted in a fruitful soil, draws its virtue from a disposition which has been brought into conformity with the mind of Christ.

1. It is subject to the Divine will — "This is the confidence that we have in Him, that, if we ask anything according to His will, He heareth us" (1 John 5:14, KJV).

2. It is restrained within the interest of Christ — "Whatsoever ye shall ask in My name, that will I do, that the Father may be glorified in the Son" (John 14:13, KJV).

3. It is instructed in the truth — "If ye abide in Me, and My words abide in you, ye shall ask what ye will, and it shall be done unto you" (John 15:7, KJV).

4. It is energized by the Spirit — "Able to do exceeding abundantly above all that we ask or think, according to the power that worketh in us" (Ephesians 3:20, KJV).

5. It is interwoven with love and mercy — "And when ye stand praying, forgive, if ye have ought against any; that your Father also which is in heaven may forgive you your trespasses" (Mark 11:25, KJV).

6. It is accompanied with obedience — "Whatsoever we ask, we receive of Him, because we keep His commandments, and do those things that are pleasing in His sight" (1 John 3:22, KJV).

7. It is so earnest that it will not accept denial — "Ask, and it shall be given you; seek, and ye shall find; knock, and it shall be opened unto you" (Luke 11:9, KJV).

8. It goes out to look for, and to hasten its answer — "The effectual fervent prayer of a righteous man availeth much" (James 5:16, KJV).

DAVID MCINTYRE, IN *THE HIDDEN LIFE OF PRAYER*

Put Sin Away

Behold, the LORD's hand is not shortened, that it cannot save,
or his ear dull, that it cannot hear; but your iniquities
have made a separation between you and your God, and your
sins have hidden his face from you so that he does not hear.

(Isaiah 59:1-2)

Many and many a man is crying to God in vain, simply because of sin in his life. It may be some sin in the past that has been unconfessed and unjudged, it may be some sin in the present that is cherished, very likely it is not even looked upon as sin, but there the sin is, hidden away somewhere in the heart or in the life, and God "will not hear."

Any one who finds his prayers ineffective should not conclude that the thing which he asks of God is not according to His will, but should go alone with God with the Psalmist's prayer, "Search me, O God, and know my heart: try me, and know my thoughts: and see if there be any wicked way in me" (Psalm 139:23-24, KJV), and wait before Him until He puts His finger upon the thing that is displeasing in His sight. Then this sin should be confessed and put away. Sin is an awful thing, and one of the most awful things about it is the way it hinders prayer, the way it severs the connection between us and the source of all grace and power and blessing. Any one who would have power in prayer must be merciless in dealing with his own sins. "If I regard iniquity in my heart, the Lord will not hear me"(Psalm 66:18, KJV). So long as we hold on to sin or have any controversy with God, we cannot expect Him to heed our prayers. If there is anything that is constantly coming up in your moments of close communion with God, that is the thing that hinders prayer: put it away.

R. A. TORREY, IN *The Power of Prayer*

Think and Pray According to the Word

My people are destroyed for lack of knowledge.

(Hosea 4:6)

Paul prays that they may be filled with knowledge of the will of God, a knowledge that consists of wisdom and understanding of all kinds, at the spiritual level. How else will they withstand the pressures of their surrounding pagan culture, pressures that are as subtle as they are endemic? How else will they think Christianly, and genuinely bring their minds and hearts and conduct into conformity with God's will? Is there anything that our own generation more urgently needs than this? Some of us have chased every fad, scrambled aboard every bandwagon, adopted every gimmick, pursued every encounter with media. Others of us have rigidly cherished every tradition, determined to change as little as possible, worshiped what is aged simply because it is aged. But where are the men and women whose knowledge of God is as fresh as it is profound, whose delight in thinking God's thoughts after him ensures that their study of Scripture is never merely intellectual and self-distancing, whose desire to please God easily outstrips residual and corrupting desires to shine in public?

People cannot live by bread and Jacuzzis alone. We desperately need meditative and reflective dependence on every word that proceeds from the mouth of God (Deuteronomy 8:3; Matthew 4:4). The need takes on painful urgency when we discover that even within our churches, let alone the nation at large, there are rapidly declining standards of the most basic Bible knowledge. True, basic Bible knowledge does not ensure the kind of knowledge of God's will that Paul has in mind. But ignorance of the Bible, the focal place where God has so generously disclosed his will, pretty well ensures that we will not be filled with this knowledge of God's will, this knowledge that consists in all spiritual wisdom and understanding.

Small wonder, then, that this is something for which we must constantly pray.

D. A. Carson, in *A Call to Spiritual Reformation*

Overcoming by Faith

By grace you have been saved through faith.
And this is not your own doing; it is the gift of God.
(Ephesians 2:8)

We may suppress this or that expression or manifestation of selfishness by resolving not to do this or that, and praying and struggling against it. We may resolve upon an outward obedience, and work ourselves up to the letter of an obedience to God's commandments. But to eradicate selfishness from the breast by resolution is an absurdity. So the effort to obey the commandments of God in spirit — in other words, to attempt to love as the law of God requires by force of resolution — is an absurdity. . . . We may abstain from the gratification of a particular desire by the force of resolution. We may go further, and abstain from the gratification of desire generally in the outward life. But this is not to secure the love of God, which constitutes obedience. All our battling with sin in the outward life, by the force of resolution, only ends in making us whited sepulchres. All our battling with desire by the force of resolution is of no avail; for in all this, however successful the effort to suppress sin may be, in the outward life or in the inward desire, it will only end in delusion, for by force of resolution we cannot love.

All such efforts to overcome sin are utterly futile, and as unscriptural as they are futile. The Bible expressly teaches us that sin is overcome by faith in Christ. "He is made unto us wisdom, righteousness, sanctification, and redemption." "He is the way, the truth, and the life." Christians are said to "purify their hearts by faith" (Acts 15:9, KJV). And in Acts 26:18 it is affirmed that the saints are sanctified by faith in Christ. In Romans 9:31-32 it is affirmed that the Jews attained not to righteousness "because they sought it not by faith, but as it were by the works of the law." The doctrine of the Bible is that Christ saves His people from sin through faith; that Christ's Spirit is received by faith to dwell in the heart. It is faith that works by love. Love is wrought and sustained by faith.

Charles Finney, in *Power from on High*

One Step at a Time

How beautiful upon the mountains are the feet of him who brings good news.

(Isaiah 52:7)

A married couple who moved into a new neighborhood. One of the first requests Mary and Jack made was, "Lord, we'd like to get acquainted with our neighbors, and if they don't know You personally as their Savior, we'd like to introduce them to You."

"Lord," prayed Jack, "I'd like to meet the fellow living next door in some casual way and begin to get acquainted with him. I'd like to begin today, and I believe You can arrange it for me. Thank you, Lord."

The morning had scarcely turned to afternoon when the answer came. Their children got into a quarrel over a tricycle with the neighbor's children. Both fathers rushed to the scene. Jack took all the blame for his children, and put out his hand, "I'm Jack, just moved in, glad to meet you." The first request had been answered. The first step had been taken.

The second step: "Lord, I'd like to know what that man is interested in, so we could become friends." The answer came within two days. He was interested in football.

The third step: "Lord, I need two complimentary football tickets, and could I have them by this weekend, please." The tickets came. The friendship grew.

The fourth step: "Lord, I'd like to invite this new friend to the Bible class I teach a few miles from here. Would You put it into his heart to accept when I ask him to go with me tonight?" He accepted. All the way over as they drove, they talked about football. All the way home they talked about Jesus Christ, and what it meant for Him to become one of us. . . . God became a Man.

The fifth step: "Lord, Mary and I would like to invite my friend and his wife to our home some evening this week and have a little talk and Bible reading together." The friends came, and they read and talked quietly together.

The sixth step: "Lord, next week when I ask them over again, will You prepare their hearts, so that they will be ready to accept You as their Saviour? I believe this is the time to ask for this, and I thank You for all You'll be doing in the meantime to draw them to Yourself." When the next week came, the neighbors willingly and gladly accepted Jesus Christ.

Rosalind Rinker, in *Prayer: Conversing with God*

HUNGERING FOR GOD

You will seek the LORD your God and you will find him, if you
search after him with all your heart and with all your soul.

(DEUTERONOMY 4:29)

David did not yearn for everything; nor did he allow his desires to spread out everywhere and hit nothing. Here is the way his desires ran and found expression:

"One thing have I desired of the Lord, that will I seek after; that I may dwell in the house of the Lord all the days of my life, to behold the beauty of the Lord, and to enquire in His temple."

It is this singleness of desire, this definiteness of yearning, which counts in praying, and which drives prayer directly to core and center of supply.

In the Beatitudes Jesus voiced the words which directly bear upon the innate desires of a renewed soul, and the promise that they will be granted: "Blessed are they that do hunger and thirst after righteousness, for they shall be filled."

This, then, is the basis of prayer which compels an answer — that strong inward desire has entered into the spiritual appetite, and clamors to be satisfied. Alas for us! It is altogether too true and frequent, that our prayers operate in the arid region of a mere wish, or in the leafless area of a memorized prayer. Sometimes, indeed, our prayers are merely stereotyped expressions of set phrases, and conventional proportions, the freshness and life of which have departed long years ago.

Without desire, there is no burden of soul, no sense of need, no ardency, no vision, no strength, no glow of faith. There is no mighty pressure, no holding on to God, with a deathless, despairing grasp — "I will not let Thee go, except Thou bless me." There is no utter self-abandonment, as there was with Moses, when, lost in the throes of a desperate, pertinacious, and all-consuming plea he cried: "Yet now, if Thou wilt forgive their sin; if not, blot me, I pray Thee, out of Thy book." Or, as there was with John Knox when he pleaded: "Give me Scotland, or I die!"

E. M. BOUNDS, *THE NECESSITY OF PRAYER*

The Cost of Prayer

Christ also suffered once for sins, the righteous
for the unrighteous, that he might bring us to God.

(1 Peter 3:18)

We ought to give much more time than we do — a great deal more time than we do — to brooding on the fundamental truths on which the Spirit of God works the simplicity of our Christian experience. The fundamental truths are — Redemption and the personal presence of the Holy Ghost, and these two are focused in one mighty Personality, the Lord Jesus Christ.

Remember, what makes prayer easy is not our wits or our understanding, but the tremendous agony of God in Redemption. A thing is worth just what it costs. Prayer is not what it costs us, but what it cost God to enable us to pray. It cost God so much that a little child can pray. It cost God Almighty so much that anyone can pray. But it is time those of us who name His Name knew the secret of the cost, and the secret is here, "My soul is exceeding sorrowful, even unto death." These words open the door to the autobiography of our Lord's agony. We find the real key to Gethsemane in Matthew 4, which records the temptations of our Lord. Here they come again in a deeper and more appalling manner than ever before. We are not looking here (as we do when we deal with the temptations) at the type of temptation we have to go through; we are dealing here with the grappling of God as Man in the last reaches of historic Redemption. Is it not time we paid more attention to what it cost God to make it possible for us to live a holy life? We talk about the difficulty of living a holy life; there is the absolute simple ease of Almighty God in living a holy life because it cost Him so much to make it possible.

Oswald Chambers, in *If You Will Ask*

GOD'S ENCORE

I have this against you, that you have abandoned the love you had at first.
(REVELATION 2:4)

I am beginning to feel that we need a preliminary act of submission not only towards possible future afflictions but also towards possible future blessings. I know it sounds fantastic; but think it over. It seems to me that we often, almost sulkily, reject the good that God offers us because, at that moment, we expected some other good. Do you know what I mean? On every level of our life — in our religious experience, in our gastronomic, erotic, aesthetic, and social experience — we are always harking back to some occasion which seemed to us to reach perfection, setting that up as a norm, and depreciating all other occasions by comparison. But these other occasions, I now suspect, are often full of their own new blessing, if only we would lay ourselves open to it. God shows us a new facet of the glory and we refuse to look at it because we're still looking for the old one. This applies especially to the devotional life. Many religious people lament that the first fervors of their conversion have died away. They think — sometimes rightly, but not, I believe, always — that their sins account for this. They may even try by pitiful efforts of the will to revive what now seem to have been the golden days. But were those fervours — the operative word is *those* — ever intended to last?

It would be rash to say that there is any prayer which God *never* grants. But the strongest candidate is the prayer we might express in the single word *encore*. And how should the Infinite repeat Himself? All space and time are too little for Him to utter Himself in them *once*.

C. S. LEWIS, IN *LETTERS TO MALCOLM*

HOW LONG?

O LORD, how long shall I cry, and thou wilt not hear!
(HABAKKUK 1:2, KJV)

Throughout history, the saints who have seen the greatest works of God have had to wait on God. Abraham was promised a son through whom God would bless all nations. It took twenty-five years before that son was born. Jacob was blessed by his father Isaac. Twenty years passed before he began to see God's blessing on his life. Joseph had a dream from God but it was years later, after enslavement and imprisonment, that the dream came true. Hannah went to the temple "year after year" pleading for a child. Ten years passed after David was anointed as king before he was crowned.

George Müller said that once he knew something was God's will he never quit praying daily for it until God gave it. We are told that he prayed daily for two of his non-Christian friends for over fifty years before they were saved. It is always too soon to quit. Our God acts on behalf of those who wait for Him, who cling to Him, who will not let go of Him.

One of the greatest acts of faith is not to give up on God. During those years of waiting God often seems very inactive. But we are assured in Isaiah 30:18,

> Yet the Lord longs to be gracious to you;
> he rises to show you compassion.
> For the Lord is a God of justice.
> Blessed are all who wait for him!

Jesus "told his disciples a parable to show them that they should always pray and not give up" (Luke 18:1). That parable was about a widow who kept going back to a judge until he gave her her request.

To maintain God-focused or God-centered praying, we need to develop the discipline of clinging to God when nothing seems to be happening. Let God know you will not let go of Him.

LEE BRASE, IN *PRAYING FROM GOD'S HEART*

ALL THROUGH THE SPIRIT

Whoever believes in me, as the Scripture has said,
"Out of his heart will flow rivers of living water."
(JOHN 7:38)

If we but yield ourselves entirely to the disposal of the Spirit, and let Him have His way with us, He will manifest the life of Christ within us. He will do this with a Divine power, maintaining the life of Christ in us in uninterrupted continuity. Surely, if there is one prayer that should draw us to the Father's throne and keep us there, it is this: for the Holy Spirit, whom we as children have received, to stream into us and out from us in greater fullness.

In the variety of the gifts which the Spirit has to dispense, He meets the believer's every need. Just think of the names He bears. The Spirit of grace, to reveal and impart all of grace there is in Jesus. The Spirit of faith, teaching us to begin and go on and increase in ever believing. The Spirit of adoption and assurance, who witnesses that we are God's children, and inspires the confiding and confident Abba, Father! The Spirit of truth, to lead into all truth, to make each word of God ours in deed and in truth. The Spirit of prayer, through whom we speak with the Father; prayer that must be heard. The Spirit of judgment and burning, to search the heart, and convince of sin. The Spirit of holiness, manifesting and communicating the Father's holy presence within us. The Spirit of power, through whom we are strong to testify boldly and work effectually in the Father's service. The Spirit of glory, the pledge of our inheritance, the preparation and the foretaste of the glory to come. Surely the child of God needs but one thing to be able really to live as a child: it is, to be filled with this Spirit.

ANDREW MURRAY, IN *WITH CHRIST IN THE SCHOOL OF PRAYER*

WRESTLING IN PRAYER

Because you are sons, God has sent the Spirit of
his Son into our hearts, crying, "Abba! Father!"
(GALATIANS 4:6)

Let us look at Hyde in the Prayer Room. Some of the seats have been moved aside and a carpet covers this open space. Sometimes there are hundreds of people there, at other times only two or three. Right on his face on the ground is Praying Hyde — this was his favorite attitude for prayer. Listen! he is praying, he utters a petition, and then waits, in a little time, he repeats it, and then waits, and this many times until we all feel that that petition has penetrated into every fiber of our nature, and we feel assured that God has heard and without a doubt He will answer. How well I remember him praying that we might "open our mouth wide that He might fill it" (Psalm 81:10, KJV). I think he repeated the word "wide" scores of times with long pauses between, "wide, Lord," "wide," "open wide," "wide." How effectual it was to hear him address God, "Oh, Father! Father!" Even before he asked anything I always felt that the Father knew what he was going to ask for.

When he finishes his prayer, perhaps half-a-dozen are sobbing, Hyde goes to one of them, and others who are present go to the others. Hyde's arm is round the neck of the one that he is going to deal with; he speaks but little but his well-worn Bible is used and before long he stands up with a smile and the man with him, and he begins to sing, "'Tis done, the great transaction's done," and he is so full of joy that his whole body begins to move, he claps his hands and then his feet begin to move, and look, he begins to dance for joy and others join him until the whole place rings with God's praises.

Sometimes he wants to be alone and I heard of him climbing into the belfry; there, in the dark, high above the others, he pours out his soul to God, men hear the echo of his voice and realize that he must not be disturbed for he is wrestling with God.

CAPTAIN E. G. CARRÉ, IN *A PRESENT-DAY CHALLENGE TO PRAYER*

THE LOVE OF CHRIST

You are precious in my eyes, and honored, and I love you.
(ISAIAH 43:4)

For their sakes he so humbled and emptied himself, in taking flesh, as to become therein a *servant*, in the eyes of the world of no esteem nor account; and a true and real servant unto the Father. For their sakes he humbled himself, and became obedient. All that he did and suffered in his life comes under this consideration. He took on him, for their sakes, a life and course pointed to, Hebrews 5:7-8, a life of prayers, tears, fears, obedience, suffering; and all this with cheerfulness and delight, calling his employment his "meat and drink," and still professing that the law of this obedience was in his heart, that he was content to do this will of God. He that will sorely revenge the least opposition that is or shall be made to him by others, was content to undergo any thing, all things, for believers.

For their sakes he becomes *obedient to death*, the death of the cross. So he professeth to his Father, John 17:19, "For their sakes I sanctify myself;" — "I dedicate myself as an offering, as a sacrifice, to be killed and slain." This was his aim in all the former, that he might die; he was born, and lived, that he might die. He valued them above his life. And if we might stay to consider a little what was in this death that he underwent for them, we should perceive what a price indeed he put upon them. *The curse of the law* was in it, the *wrath of God* was in it, the *loss of God's presence* was in it. It was a fearful cup that he tasted of, and drank of, that they might never taste of it. A man would not for ten thousand worlds be willing to undergo that which Christ underwent for us in that one thing of desertion from God, were it attended with no more distress but what a mere creature might possibly emerge from under. And what thoughts we should have of this himself tells us, John 15:13, "Greater love hath no man than this, that a man lay down his life for his friends." It is impossible there should be any greater demonstration or evidence of love than this.

JOHN OWEN, IN *OF COMMUNION WITH GOD THE FATHER, SON AND HOLY GHOST*

DIFFICULTIES OF PRAYER

The spirit indeed is willing, but the flesh is weak.

(MATTHEW 26:41)

The lack of keeping your heart at rest with God in prayer is what God complains of. Men draw nigh to him with their mouths, and honor him with their lips, but their hearts are far from him. "The Lord says: 'These people come near to me with their mouth and honor me with their lips, but their hearts are far from me. Their worship of me is made up only of rules taught by men'" (Isaiah 29:13, NIV). In Matthew 15:7-9, Jesus called the people who pray in such a way "hypocrites."

May I speak of my own experience, and tell you the difficulty of praying to God as I ought? When I go to pray, I find my heart is disinclined to stay with him. Many times I am forced in my prayers to beg God to take my heart and set it upon himself in Christ. And I beg that, when it is there, he would keep it there. Many times I know not what to pray for, I am so blind. At times I know not how to pray, I am so ignorant. But the Spirit helps us in our weakness: "Teach me your way, O Lord, and I will walk in your truth; give me an undivided heart, that I may fear your name. I will praise you, O Lord my God, with all my heart; I will glorify your name forever" (Psalm 86:11-12, NIV).

The difficulties that the heart has in the time of prayer! No one knows how many byways and back lanes the heart has in which to slip away from the presence of God. How much pride the heart has, if enabled with expressive language to pray to him! How much hypocrisy, if praying before others! And how little consciousness is there of prayer between God and the soul in secret, unless the Spirit of supplication is there to help!

JOHN BUNYAN, IN *PILGRIM'S PRAYER BOOK*

ASK IN HIS NAME

In that day you will ask nothing of me. Truly, truly, I say to you,
whatever you ask of the Father in my name, he will give it
to you. Until now you have asked nothing in my name.
Ask, and you will receive, that your joy may be full.
(JOHN 16:23-24)

Never before had our Lord laid such stress on any promise or command — never! This truly marvelous promise is given us six times over. Six times, almost in the same breath, our Savior commands us to ask whatsoever we will. This is the greatest — the most wonderful — promise ever made to man. Yet most men — Christian men — practically ignore it! Is it not so?

So our blessed Master gives the final exhortation, before He is seized, and bound, and scourged, before His gracious lips are silenced on the cross, "Ye shall ask in My name for the Father Himself loveth you" (John 16:26-27, KJV). We have often spent much time in reflecting upon our Lord's seven words from the cross. And it is well we should do so. Have we ever spent one hour in meditating upon this, our Savior's sevenfold invitation to pray?

Today He sits on the throne of His Majesty on high, and He holds out to us the sceptre of His power. Shall we touch it and tell Him our desires? He bids us take of His treasures. He yearns to grant us "according to the riches of His glory," that we may "be strengthened with power through His Spirit in the inner man." He tells us that our strength and our fruitfulness depend upon our prayers. He reminds us that our very joy depends upon answered prayer (John 16:24).

And yet we allow the devil to persuade us to neglect prayer! He makes us believe that we can do more by our own efforts than by our prayers — by our intercourse with men than by our intercession with God.

AN UNKNOWN CHRISTIAN, IN *THE KNEELING CHRISTIAN*

REVEL IN THE LOVE OF GOD

The love of Christ controls us, because we have concluded this:
that one has died for all, therefore all have died.

(2 CORINTHIANS 5:14)

It takes nothing less than the power of God to enable us to grasp the love of Christ. Part of our deep "me-ism" is manifested in such independence that we do not really want to get so close to God that we feel dependent upon him, swamped by his love. Just as in a marriage a spouse may flee relationships that are too intimate, judging them to be a kind of invasion of privacy when in reality such a reaction is a sign of intense immaturity and selfishness, so also in the spiritual arena: when we are drawn a little closer to the living God, many of us want to back off and stake out our own turf. We want to experience power so that we can be in control; Paul prays for power so that we will be controlled by God himself. Our deep and pathetic self-centeredness is precisely why it takes the power of God to transform us, if we are to know the love of Christ that surpasses knowledge and grow to the maturity the Scriptures hold out before us.

It is wonderful to revel in the love of God. Truly to experience that love, to live in the warmth of its glow, invests all of life with new meaning and purpose. The brotherhood of the saints takes on new depth; "fellowship" becomes precious, not the artificially arranged shaking of hands in a service or the shared pot of tea or coffee. Forgiving others becomes almost natural, because we ourselves, thanks to God's immeasurably rich love, have been forgiven so much. Others may despise us, but that makes little difference if God loves us. How shall trouble or sorrow or bereavement drive us into macabre despair, when we can say, with Paul, "Who shall separate us from the love of Christ?" (Romans 8:35, NIV). Our speech, our thoughts, our actions, our reactions, our relationships, our goals, our values — all are transformed if only we live in the self-conscious enjoyment of the love of Christ.

D. A. CARSON, IN *A CALL TO SPIRITUAL REFORMATION*

Following Christ Daily

I discipline my body and keep it under control,
lest after preaching to others I myself should be disqualified.
(1 Corinthians 9:27)

The Christian needs to observe a strict exterior discipline. But we are not to imagine that that alone will crush the will of the flesh, or that there is any way of mortifying our old man other than by faith in Jesus. The real difference in the believer who follows Christ and has mortified his will and died after the old man in Christ is that he is more clearly aware than other men of the rebelliousness and perennial pride of the flesh, he is conscious of his sloth and self-indulgence and knows that his arrogance must be eradicated. Hence there is a need for daily self-discipline. It is always true of the disciple that the spirit is willing but the flesh is weak, and he must therefore "watch and pray." The spirit knows the right way, and desires to follow it, but the flesh lacks courage and finds it too hard, too hazardous and wearisome, and so it stifles the voice of the spirit. The spirit assents when Jesus bids us love our enemies, but flesh and blood are too strong and prevent our carrying it out. Therefore we have to practice strictest daily discipline; only so can the flesh learn the painful lesson that it has no rights of its own. Regular daily prayer is a great help here, and so is daily meditation on the Word of God, and every kind of bodily discipline and asceticism.

The flesh resists this daily humiliation, first by a frontal attack, and later by hiding itself under the words of the spirit (i.e. in the name of "evangelical liberty"). We claim liberty from all legal compulsion, from self-martyrdom and mortification, and play this off against the proper evangelical use of discipline and asceticism; we thus excuse our self-indulgence and irregularity in prayer, in meditation and in our bodily life. But the contrast between our behavior and the word of Jesus is all too painfully evident.

Dietrich Bonhoeffer, in *The Cost of Discipleship*

Alphabet Prayer

> *Be not rash with your mouth, nor let your heart be hasty*
> *to utter a word before God, for God is in heaven and*
> *you are on earth. Therefore let your words be few.*
>
> (Ecclesiastes 5:2)

I remember hearing of a boy brought up in an English almshouse. He had never learned to read or write, except that he could read the letters of the alphabet. One day a man of God came there, and told the children that if they prayed to God in their trouble, He would send them help. After a time, this boy was apprenticed to a farmer. One day he was sent out into the fields to look after some sheep. He was having rather a hard time; so he remembered what the preacher had said, and he thought he would pray to God about it. Someone going by the field heard a voice behind the hedge. They looked to see whose it was, and saw the little fellow on his knees, saying, "A, B, C, D," and so on. The man said, "My boy, what are you doing?" He looked up, and said he was praying. "Why, that is not praying; it is only saying the alphabet." He said he did not know just how to pray, but a man once came to the poorhouse, who told them that if they called upon God, He would help them. So he thought that if he named over the letters of the alphabet, God would take them and put them together into a prayer, and give him what he wanted. The little fellow was really praying. Sometimes, when your child talks, your friends cannot understand what he says; but the mother understands very well. So if our prayer comes right from the heart, God understands our language. It is a delusion of the devil to think we cannot pray; we can, if we really want anything. It is not the most beautiful or the most eloquent language that brings down the answer; it is the cry that goes up from a burdened heart.

D. L. Moody, in *Prevailing Prayer*

OUR LIFE TRADE

*To him who is able to do far more abundantly than all that
we ask or think, according to the power at work within
us, to him be glory in the church and in Christ Jesus
throughout all generations, forever and ever. Amen.*
(EPHESIANS 3:20-21)

There can be no substitute, no rival for prayer; it stands alone as the great spiritual force, and this force must be imminent and acting. It cannot be dispensed with during one generation, nor held in abeyance for the advance of any great movement — it must be continuous and particular, always, everywhere, and in everything. We cannot run our spiritual operations on the prayers of the past generation. Many persons believe in the efficacy of prayer, but not many pray. Prayer is the easiest and hardest of all things; the simplest and the sublimest; the weakest and the most powerful; its results lie outside the range of human possibilities — they are limited only by the omnipotence of God.

Few Christians have anything but a vague idea of the power of prayer; fewer still have any experience of that power. The Church seems almost wholly unaware of the power God puts into her hand; this spiritual *carte blanche* on the infinite resources of God's wisdom and power is rarely, if ever, used — never used to the full measure of honoring God. It is astounding how poor the use, how little the benefits. Prayer is our most formidable weapon, but the one in which we are the least skilled, the most averse to its use. We do everything else for the heathen save the thing God wants us to do; the only thing which does any good — makes all else we do efficient.

To graduate in the school of prayer is to master the whole course of a religious life. The first and last stages of holy living are crowned with praying. It is a life trade. The hindrances of prayer are the hindrances in a holy life. The conditions of praying are the conditions of righteousness, holiness and salvation. A cobbler in the trade of praying is a bungler in the trade of salvation.

E. M. BOUNDS, IN *PURPOSE IN PRAYER*

PRAISE OPENS THE DOOR

Enter his gates with thanksgiving, and his courts
with praise! Give thanks to him; bless his name!
(PSALM 100:4)

You would be amazed to know how much prayer is hindered by the self-life of Christians. Carnality keeps thousands of prayers from rising higher than the ceiling. "If I had cherished sin in my heart, the Lord would not have listened" (Psalm 66:18, NIV). Sinful thoughts, carnal attitudes, and self-centeredness destroy the power of prayer. These close God's ear to our words and desires.

Scripture often speaks of people prayers and God not hearing. According to James, our relation to God must be true and our motive pure before God will hear us (4:3). Pride cancels many prayers (verse 6). A critical attitude, unforgiveness, and bitterness hidden in the heart block prayer. If you want your prayers to be answered, let the Holy Spirit purify you (verses 6-10).

You can be preserved in purity by the spirit of praise. When Satan comes with such suggestions to your mind, cleanse your thoughts by praise. Praise turns your eyes away from yourself to Jesus. Praise washes away negativism, self-pity, self-centeredness, and the beginnings of self-idolatry. Praise makes you so beautifully clean that God accepts you as you approach the throne of grace. Psalm 50:14-15 suggests that in your day of trouble a sacrifice of thanksgiving is the proper prelude to your prayer for deliverance. In other words, praise makes your petition more effective. God has done so much for us already for which we have so often inadequately thanked Him, that adoring praise warms the heart of God and prepares the way for speedy answers.

If there ever was an expert in spiritual warfare, it was Martin Luther. He was very aware of the demonic forces fighting against him. Luther wrote: "When I cannot pray I always sing." Praise brings heaven's power upon you. God has delivered people from sinful habits through praise. Every time the temptation returned, they praised the Lord some more until the pressure lifted. Other people have been healed while praising the Lord. John Wesley, too, knew the secret: "Praise opens the door to more grace."

WESLEY DUEWEL, IN *TOUCH THE WORLD THROUGH PRAYER*

GOD ABOVE ALL

Teach me your way, O LORD, that I may walk
in your truth; unite my heart to fear your name.
(PSALM 86:11)

Another saying of Jesus, and a most disturbing one, was put in the form of a question, "How can ye believe, which receive honor one of another, and seek not the honor that cometh from God alone?" If I understand this correctly Christ taught here the alarming doctrine that the desire for honor among men made belief impossible. Is this sin at the root of religious unbelief? Could it be that those "intellectual difficulties" which men blame for their inability to believe are but smoke screens to conceal the real cause that lies behind them? Was it this greedy desire for honor from man that made men into Pharisees? Is this the secret back of religious self-righteousness and empty worship? I believe it may be. The whole course of the life is upset by failure to put God where He belongs. We exalt ourselves instead of God and the curse follows.

In our desire after God let us keep always in mind that God also hath desire, and His desire is toward the sons of men, and more particularly toward those sons of men who will make the once-for-all decision to exalt Him over all. Such are these precious to God above all treasures of earth or sea. In them God finds a theater where He can display His exceeding kindness toward us in Christ Jesus. With them God can walk unhindered, toward them He can act like the God He is.

In speaking thus I have one fear; it is that I may convince the mind before God can win the heart. For this God-above-all position is one not easy to take. The mind may approve it while not having the consent of the will to put it into effect. While the imagination races ahead to honor God, the will may lag behind and the man never guess how divided his heart is. The whole man must make the decision before the heart can know any real satisfaction. God wants us all, and He will not rest till He gets us all. No part of the man will do.

A. W. TOZER, IN *THE PURSUIT OF GOD*

LOVE AND VIRTUE

Little children, let us not love in word or talk but in deed and in truth.
(1 JOHN 3:18)

As God is the fountain and principle of all virtue, we possess all in the possession of Himself; and in proportion as we approach towards this possession, in like proportion do we rise into the most eminent virtues. For all virtue is but as a mask, an outside appearance changeable as our garments, if it doth not spring up, and issue from within; and then, indeed, it is genuine, essential, and permanent: "The beauty of the King's daughter proceeds from within" saith David (Psalm 45:13). These souls, above all others, practice virtue in the most eminent degree, though they advert not to virtue in particular; God, to whom they are united, carries them to the most extensive practice of it; He is exceedingly jealous over them, and prohibits them the taste of any pleasure but in Himself.

What a hungering for sufferings have those souls, who thus glow with Divine Love! How prone to precipitate into excessive austerities, were they permitted to pursue their own inclinations! They think of nought save how they may please their Beloved: as their self-love abates, they neglect and forget themselves; and as their love to God increases, so do self-detestation and disregard to the creature.

O was this easy method acquired, a method so suited to all, to the dull and ignorant as well as to the acute and learned, how easily would the whole Church of God be reformed! Love only is required: "Love;" saith Saint Augustine, "and then do what you please." For when we truly love, we cannot have so much as a will to anything that might offend the Object of our affections.

JEANNE GUYON, IN *A SHORT AND EASY METHOD OF PRAYER*

How God Interprets Prayers

*[Jesus] said to him, "Your prayers and your alms
have ascended as a memorial before God."*

(Acts 10:4)

When a request is refused, it is as truly answered as when it is granted.
Refusal may be the only answer possible to love and wisdom and truth. A
child may cry for a razor, and full-grown people may cry for things equally
unsuitable, unsafe, and unwise. Many have lived to thank God that He
withstood their agonizing entreaties at some particular time or for some
particular thing that seemed indispensable.

God never refuses without reason. He knows the past, in which there
may be reasons for present disqualification. Forgiven sin may disable.
Moses and David were both examples of this (Deuteronomy 32:49-52;
2 Samuel 12:14). There are vessels that break on the wheel, and though
another may be made, the original is impossible. Diseases may be healed,
but a lost limb cannot be restored. The Lord knows the future as well as the
past. The immediate may imperil the future. The eagerness for a mess of
pottage may involve the loss of an inheritance. Esau got the answer to his
entreaty at dinner time. Jacob got his at dawn. God spared Hezekiah fifteen
years, but he had better have gone when the Lord sent for him.

Delays are not denials, and it pays to wait on God's time. Moses got
into Canaan, and Elijah went to heaven by a more glorious way than that of
the juniper tree. No inspired prayer of faith is ever refused. "No" is never
God's last word. If the prayer seems unanswered, it is because it is lost in
the glory of the answer when it comes. God may refuse the route because
He knows a better one, and He took Moses into Canaan by a better way and
in better company. So in Glory shall we find our prayers have been interpreted according to the infinite wisdom and eternal love of God our Father
who bids us pray.

Samuel Chadwick, in *The Path of Prayer*

How to Ascertain the Will of God

You are my rock and my fortress; and for
your name's sake you lead me and guide me.

(Psalm 31:3)

1. I seek at the beginning to get my heart into such a state that it has no will of its own in regard to a given matter. Nine-tenths of the trouble with people generally is just here. Nine-tenths of the difficulties are overcome when our hearts are ready to do the Lord's will, whatever it may be. When one is truly in this state, it is usually but a little way to the knowledge of what His will is.

2. Having done this, I do not leave the result to feeling or simple impression. If so, I make myself liable to great delusions.

3. I seek the Will of the Spirit of God through, or in connection with, the Word of God. The Spirit and the Word must be combined. If I look to the Spirit alone without the Word, I lay myself open to great delusions also. If the Holy Ghost guides us at all, He will do it according to the Scriptures and never contrary to them.

4. Next I take into account providential circumstances. These often plainly indicate God's Will in connection with His Word and Spirit.

5. I ask God in prayer to reveal His Will to me aright.

6. Thus, through prayer to God, the study of the Word, and reflection, I come to a deliberate judgment according to the best of my ability and knowledge, and if my mind is thus at peace, and continues so after two or three more petitions, I proceed accordingly. In trivial matters, and in transactions involving most important issues, I have found this method always effective.

George Müller, in *Answers to Prayer*

176

MAKE REQUESTS OF GOD

If we know that he hears us in whatever we ask, we know
that we have the requests that we have asked of him.
(1 JOHN 5:15)

If you meant in your last letter that we can scrap the whole idea of petition-ary prayer — prayer which, as you put it, calls upon God to "engineer" particular events in the objective world — and confine ourselves to acts of penitence and adoration, I disagree with you. It may be true that Christianity would be, intellectually, a far easier religion if it told us to do this. And I can understand the people who think it would also be a more high-minded religion. But remember the psalm: "Lord, I am not high minded." Or better still, remember the New Testament. The most unblushingly petitionary prayers are there recommended to us both by precept and example. Our Lord in Gethsemane made a petitionary prayer (and did not get what He asked for). You'll remind me that He asked with a reservation — "neverthe-less, not my will but thine." This makes an enormous difference. But the difference which it precisely does not make is that of removing the prayer's petitionary character. When poor Bill, on a famous occasion, asked us to advance him £100, he said, "If you are sure you can spare it," and "I shall quite understand if you'd rather not." This made his request very different from the nagging or even threatening request which a different sort of man might have made. But it was still a request.

The servant is not greater, and must not be more high-minded, than the master. Whatever the theoretical difficulties are, we must continue to make requests of God. And on this point we can get no help from those who keep on reminding that this is the lowest and least essential kind of prayer. They may be right; but so what?

C. S. LEWIS, IN *LETTERS TO MALCOLM*

LIVING AS HIS CHILD

He predestined us for adoption as sons through
Jesus Christ, according to the purpose of his will.

(EPHESIANS 1:5)

The Lord would remind us that the prayer of a child owes its influence entirely to the relation in which he stands to the parent. The prayer can exert that influence only when the child is really living in that relationship, in the home, in the love, in the service of the Father. The power of the promise, "Ask, and it shall be given you," lies in the loving relationship between us as children and the Father in heaven; when we live and walk in that relationship, the prayer of faith and its answer will be the natural result. And so the lesson we have today in the school of prayer is this: Live as a child of God, then you will be able to pray as a child, and as a child you will most assuredly be heard.

And what is the true child-life? The answer can be found in any home. The child that by preference forsakes the father's house, that finds no pleasure in the presence and love and obedience of the father, and still thinks to ask and obtain what he will, will surely be disappointed. On the contrary, he to whom the intercourse and will and honor and love of the father are the joy of his life, will find that it is the father's joy to grant his requests. Scripture says, "As many as are *led* by the Spirit of God, they are the children of God:" the childlike privilege of asking all is inseparable from the childlike life under the leading of the Spirit. He that gives himself to be led by the Spirit in his life, will be led by Him in his prayers too. And he will find that Fatherlike giving is the Divine response to childlike living.

ANDREW MURRAY, IN *WITH CHRIST IN THE SCHOOL OF PRAYER*

Inexpressible Cries to God

Behold, I am of small account; what shall I answer you? I lay my hand on my mouth.

(Job 40:4)

A poor prayer is just so many words. A person who *truly prays* one prayer shall after that never be able to express with his mouth or pen the unutterable desires, feelings, and longing that went to God in that prayer.

The best prayers have often more groans than words. And those words that it has are but a lean and shallow representation of the heart, life, and spirit of that prayer. You do not find any words of prayer, that we read of, come out of the mouth of Moses, when he was going out of Egypt, and was followed by Pharaoh, and yet he made heaven ring again with his cry: "Then the Lord said to Moses, 'Why are you crying out to me? Tell the Israelites to move on'" (Exodus 14:15, NIV). Moses released inexpressible and unsearchable groans and cryings of his soul in and with the Spirit. God is the God of spirits, and his eyes look further than at the outside of any whatsoever: "But Moses and Aaron fell face down and cried out, 'O God, God of the spirits of all mankind, will you be angry with the entire assembly when only one man sins?'" (Numbers 16:22, NIV). I doubt that this is thought of by most of those who would be looked upon as praying people.

The nearer a person comes to fulfilling any work that God has commanded him to do according to his will, so much the more hard and difficult it is. And the reason is that man by himself is not able to do it; he must have the aid of the Holy Spirit. Now prayer is not only a duty, but one of the most eminent of duties; and therefore, so much the more difficult. Paul understood this, for he said, "I will pray with the Spirit." He knew well that it was not what others wrote or said that could make him a praying person. Nothing less than the Spirit could do it.

John Bunyan, in *Pilgrim's Prayer Book*

WILLING HIS WILL

Let us be grateful for receiving a kingdom that cannot be shaken, and thus let us offer to God acceptable worship, with reverence and awe.

(HEBREWS 12:28)

Down here on this fallen and broken planet, the planet we can't help but feel we have pretty well used up, it is hard to imagine God's kingdom coming, but we have been promised that it will, and for that coming we lift up our voice in prayer. We are telling our Father that that is what we want more than anything else. That is the real object of our prayer: *his* rule and reign and right ordering of all that is wrong.

As we put ourselves on his side, we hallow his name. As we lay our individual prayers before him, we do so recognizing that the answer has to fit into the coming of the kingdom and the holiness of the name, which means that the answer may be quite other than we suppose. The kingdom of God is a place where all is in perfect order, nothing is out of place, because it is the place where his will is always done. Therefore, when we ask for the coming of his kingdom, we are asking for the doing of his will.

This is the point at which earth and heaven meet, the point at which my will must come into harmony with God's. Anything I am asking that is not in harmony with the way things are done in heaven has got to go. If in the integrity of my heart I speak the words, *Thy will be done*, I must be willing, if the answer requires it, that *my* will be undone. It is a prayer of commitment and relinquishment. The cost to Jesus of bringing his Father's kingdom on earth was the Cross of Calvary. Facing that cost, he sweated in Gethsemane: "O my Father, if it be possible" (Matthew 26:39). Though his human flesh shrank at the prospect of death, he surrendered his own will to the will of the Father.

And thus he teaches us to pray for the coming of the kingdom in the only way the kingdom can possibly come: through the doing of the Father's will. There is no other way.

ELISABETH ELLIOT, IN *GOD'S GUIDANCE*

Turning On the Current

He who did not spare his own Son but gave him up for us all,
how will he not also with him graciously give us all things?
(Romans 8:32)

To pray is nothing more involved than to let Jesus come into our hearts, to give Him access with all His power to our needs. From this it is clear that success in prayer does not depend upon the assurance of the one who prays, nor upon his boldness, nor any such thing, but upon this one thing, that he opens his heart to Jesus.

And this is, as we have seen before, not a question of power but of will. Will I have Jesus come in to my need?

But this depends again on how helpless I am. Prayer is a mysterious instrumentality and can, in the final analysis, be employed to full effect and with perfect success only by those who are helpless.

Using an illustration from everyday life, we may compare prayer to an electric wiring system. The electric current is available, but it must be turned on. For that purpose we have what is known as a switch. All we need to do is to move the switch slightly, and the electric current flashes through the whole house. And we know, of course, that not much power is required to turn on a switch.

When man fell into sin, his soul was not only cut off from God, but the whole wiring system was destroyed. To restore it, Jesus had to suffer and die. The wiring is now in order again. We may all re-establish contact with, and make use of, the powers of the heavenly world. And prayer is the mysterious little instrumentality whereby the contact is made, enabling the powers of His salvation to reach our souls and our bodies, and, through us, to others, as far as our zeal and perseverance will permit.

Ole Hallesby, in *Prayer*

DISSOLVED INTO CHRIST

I am hard pressed between the two. My desire is
to depart and be with Christ, for that is far better.

(PHILIPPIANS 1:23)

Tuesday, Aug. 23. Studied in the forenoon, and enjoyed some freedom. In the afternoon, labored abroad: endeavored to pray; but found not much sweetness or intenseness of mind. Towards night, was very weary, and tired of this world of sorrow: the thoughts of death and immortality appeared very desirable, and even refreshed my soul. Those lines turned in my mind with pleasure,

> Come, death, shake hands,
> I'll kiss thy bands:
> 'Tis happiness for me to die.
> What! dost thou think that I will shrink?
> I'll go to immortality.

In evening prayer God was pleased to draw near my soul, though very sinful and unworthy: was enabled to wrestle with God, and to persevere in my requests for grace. I poured out my soul for all the world, friends, and enemies. My soul was concerned, not so much for souls as such, but rather for Christ's kingdom, that it might appear in the world, that God might be known to be God in the whole earth. And, oh, my soul abhorred the very thought of a *party* in religion! Let the truth of God appear, wherever it is; and God have the glory for ever. Amen. This was indeed a comfortable season. I thought I had some small taste of, and real relish for, the enjoyments and employments of the upper world. O that my soul was more attempered 'to it! I thought if God should say, "Cease making any provision for this life, for you shall in a few days go out of time into eternity," my soul would leap for joy. O that I may both "desire to be dissolved, to be with Christ," and likewise "wait patiently all the days of my appointed time till my change come!" But, alas! I am very unfit for the business and blessedness of heaven. O for *more holiness*!

JONATHAN EDWARDS, IN *THE LIFE AND DIARY OF DAVID BRAINERD*

DOUBT NOT

If you are not firm in faith, you will not be firm at all.
(ISAIAH 7:9)

A notable occasion we have as Jesus comes down from the Mount of Transfiguration. He finds His disciples defeated, humiliated and confused in the presence of their enemies. A father has brought his child possessed with a demon to have the demon cast out. They essayed to do it but failed. They had been commissioned by Jesus and sent to do that very work, but had signally failed. "And when he was come into the house, his disciples asked him privately, saying, Why could not we cast him out? And he said unto them, This kind can come forth by nothing but by prayer and fasting." Their faith had not been cultured by prayer. They failed in prayer before they failed in ability to do their work. They failed in faith because they had failed in prayer. That one thing which was necessary to do God's work was prayer. The work which God sends us to do cannot be done without prayer.

In Christ's teaching on prayer we have another pertinent statement. It was in connection with the cursing of the barren fig tree:

"Jesus answered and said unto them, Verily I say unto you, if ye have faith, and doubt not, ye shall not only do this which is done to the fig tree, but also if ye shall say unto this mountain, Be thou removed and be thou cast into the sea; it shall be done.

"And all things whatsoever ye shall ask in prayer, believing, ye shall receive."

In this passage we have faith and prayer, their possibilities and powers conjoined. A fig tree had been blasted to the roots by the word of the Lord Jesus. The power and quickness of the result surprised the disciples. Jesus says to them that it need be no surprise to them or such a difficult work to be done. "If ye have faith" its possibilities to affect will not be confined to the little fig tree, but the gigantic, rock-ribbed, rock-founded mountains can be uprooted and moved into the sea. Prayer is leverage of this great power of faith.

E. M. BOUNDS, IN *THE REALITY OF PRAYER*

The Secret of Life

The king said to me, "What are you requesting?" So I prayed to the
God of heaven. And I said to the king, "If it pleases the king,
and if your servant has found favor in your sight, that you send
me to Judah, to the city of my fathers' graves, that I may rebuild it."

(Nehemiah 2:4-5)

There is nothing about which we may not pray, but prayer will not avail if it is a mere whim or an idle wish. Nehemiah prayed over his work, but he made it his business to know all about the things of which he prayed. His work prospered because he worked at his work. It is no use to pray about work and then neglect it, or play the fool in it, for lack of courage, efficiency, and sense. He prayed and used his wits. He knew the Lord would send supplies, but he took care to have the king's letters. He knew the Lord would protect, but he added a sword to the equipment of the builder's trowel. Prayer gives vision in the secret place, intelligence in work, sense in judgment, courage in temptation, tenacity in adversity, and a joyous assurance in the will of God. A weaver who prayed over his work, as Nehemiah prayed over his, came to be known as the man who wove every yard of cloth for the Lord Jesus Christ. He never made a fortune, but his work prospered, and his character was of rare worth. Every task and every duty may be sanctified in the word of God and in prayer. The prayer life in which there are no miracles may be the greatest miracle of all.

The secret of life is in the secret place where God waits. Even to those to whom privacy is impossible there is a sanctuary of the soul into which they can withdraw. I want to bear my witness to the priceless value of the habit of secret prayer. There is nothing about which I do not pray. I go over all my life in the presence of God. All my problems are solved there. All questions of liberty as well as duty are settled there. I seek counsel of God, and submit all things to the judgment of God. The sanctuary of my soul is there.

Samuel Chadwick, in *The Path of Prayer*

Persevering in Prayer

[Pray] at all times in the Spirit, with all prayer and supplication. To that end keep alert with all perseverance, making supplication for all the saints.
(Ephesians 6:18)

Can we pray in prayer, or are we being beguiled by the devil? Have we been lured into a judicious winsomeness? Are we not quite so intense as we used to be? Have black and white become a neutral grey? Are we no longer so intense about sin as we used to be? Then we are out of place, we are exactly in the relationship of traitors, we can make known the position that can easily be taken by the devil unawares.

"Watch and pray," said Jesus in the centre of His own agony. If we don't, we shall slip into the lure of wrong roads without knowing it. The only way to keep right is to watch and pray. Prayer on any other basis than that on which it is placed in the New Testament is stupid, and the basis of prayer is not human earnestness, not human need, not the human will, it is Redemption, and its living centre is a personal Holy Ghost. A child can pray. Through His own agony in Redemption, God has made it as easy to pray as it sounds. There is nothing a rationally-minded being can ridicule more easily than prayer. "Praying always" — the unutterable simplicity of it! No panic, no flurry, always at leisure from ourselves on the inside.

It is all very well to have prayer meetings, but are we continually practicing in the armor of God, keeping our hearts stout in the courage of God's Spirit and taking our orders from Him? Or are we making an ingenious compromise? There is only one service that has no snares, and that is prayer. Preaching has snares to the natural heart; so has public service. Prayer has no snare because it is based on the Redemption of the Lord Jesus Christ made efficacious all the time by the Holy Spirit.

Oswald Chambers, in *If You Will Ask*

Is Not This the Blood?

How can we who died to sin still live in it?

(Romans 6:2)

With open face we behold as in a glass the glory of the Lord; and as we drink into the spirit and rejoice in the truth, "we are being changed into the same image, from glory to glory, as by the Spirit of the Lord." Therefore [Jesus] prays, "Sanctify them through thy truth." How can the eyes that are fixed upon God in Christ engage in sin? How can the ears that are listening to His voice be attentive to iniquity? How can the hands that clasp His feet "pull at sin as with a cart rope"? How can the feet anointed to follow Him, and whose bonds He has unloosened, wander willfully into the byways of sin and error? When we are led astray, it is because the eye is not on Christ, the ear is not listening to Christ, and the heart is not filled with Christ, and then, alas! alas! other things come in; but when we are engaged with the Truth as it is in Jesus, in the light and teaching of the Holy Ghost, sin and self lose their attractiveness; and when the world, the flesh, and the devil present to us their temptations, we shall feel as David did when the three worthies broke through the Philistines' hosts and brought him the water for which he had thirsted from the well of Bethlehem;

> [He] poured it out to the Lord, and said, "My God forbid it me, that I should do this thing: shall I drink the bloods of these men that have put their lives in jeopardy?" (1 Chronicles 11:18-19, KJV)

This will be the answer of conscience and of the heart to every lust. Is not this the blood of my Lord Jesus Christ, "who gave himself for my sins, that he might deliver" me "from this present evil world"?

Marcus Rainsford, in *Our Lord Prays for His Own*

THE POWER OF GOD'S LOVE

Anyone who does not love does not know God, because God is love.
(1 JOHN 4:8)

Prayer is given us as wings wherewith to mount, but also to shield our face when they have carried us before the great white throne. It is in prayer that the holiness comes home as love, and the love is established as holiness. At every step our thought is transformed to prayer, and our prayer opens new ranges of thought. His great revelation is His holiness, always outgoing in atoning love. The Christian revelation is not "God is love" so much as "love is God." That is, it is not God's love, but the infinite power of God's love, its finality, omnipotence, and absoluteness. It is not passionate and helpless love, but it has power to subdue everything that rises against it. And that is the holiness of love — the eternal thing in it. We receive the last reconciliation. Then the very wrath of God becomes a glory. The red in the sky is the new dawn. Our self-accusation becomes a new mode of praise. Our loaded hearts spring light again. Our heavy conscience turns to grave moral power. A new love is born for our kind. A new and tender patience steals upon us. We see new ways of helping, serving, and saving. We issue into a new world. We are one with the Christ not only on His cross, but in His resurrection. Think of the resurrection power and calm, of that solemn final peace, that infinite satisfaction in the eternal thing eternally achieved, which filled His soul when He had emerged from death, when man's worst had been done, and God's best had been won, for ever and for all. We have our times of entrance into that Christ. As we were one with Him in the likeness of His death, so we are in the likeness of His resurrection. We overcome our mistakes, negligences, sins; nay, we rise above the sin of the whole world, which will not let our souls be as good as they are. We overcome the world, and take courage, and are of new cheer.

P. T. FORSYTH, IN *THE SOUL OF PRAYER*

GOD'S TIME WILL COME

In the fear of the LORD one has strong confidence,
and his children will have a refuge.

(PROVERBS 14:26)

To the man or woman who is acquainted with God and who knows how to pray, there is nothing remarkable in the answers that come. They are sure of being heard, since they ask in accordance with what they know to be the mind and the will of God.

D. L. Moody gives this illustration of the power of prayer:

While in Edinburgh, a man was pointed out to me by a friend, who said:
"That man is chairman of the Edinburgh Infidel Club."
I went and sat beside him and said, "My friend, I am glad to see you in our meeting. Are you concerned about your welfare?"
"I do not believe in any hereafter."
"Well, just get down on your knees and let me pray for you."
"No, I do not believe in prayer."
I knelt beside him as he sat, and prayed. He made a great deal of sport of it. A year after I met him again, I took him by the hand and said: "Hasn't God answered my prayer yet?"
"There is no God. If you believe in one who answers prayers, try your hand on me."
"Well, a great many are now praying for you, and God's time will come, and I believe you will be saved yet."
Some time afterwards I got a letter from a leading barrister in Edinburgh telling me that my infidel friend had come to Christ, and that seventeen of his club men had followed his example. I did not know how God would answer prayer, but I knew He would answer. Let us come boldly to God.

When we live in fellowship with Him, we come with confidence into His presence, asking in the full confidence of receiving and meeting with the justification of our faith.

E. M. BOUNDS, IN *PURPOSE IN PRAYER*

PRAYER IS THE KEY

His delight is not in the strength of the horse,
nor his pleasure in the legs of a man.
(PSALM 147:10)

We live in an age of hustle and bustle, of man's efforts and man's determination, of man's confidence in himself and in his own power to achieve things, an age of human organization, and human machinery, and human push, and human scheming, and human achievement; in the things of God this means no real achievement at all. I think it would be perfectly safe to say that the church of Christ was never in all its history so fully and so skillfully and so thoroughly organized as it is today. Our machinery is wonderful, it is just perfect; but alas it is machinery without power; and when things do not go right, instead of going to the real source of our failure, our neglect to depend upon God and to look to God for power, we look around to see if there is not some new organization we can set up, some new wheel that we can add to our machinery. We have altogether too many wheels already. What we need is not so much some new organization, some new wheel, but "the Spirit of the living creature in the wheels" whom we already possess.

Prayer has as much power today, when men and women are themselves on praying ground and meeting the conditions of prevailing prayer, as it has ever had. God has not changed; and His ear is just as quick to hear the voice of real prayer, and His hand is just as long and strong to save, as it ever was. "Behold, the Lord's hand is not shortened, that it cannot save; neither his ear heavy, that it cannot hear." But "our iniquities" may "have separated between us and our God, and our sins" may "have hid his face from us, that he will not hear" (Isaiah 59:1-2, KJV). Prayer is the key that unlocks all the storehouses of God's infinite grace and power. All that God is, and all that God has, is at the disposal of prayer. But we must use the key.

R. A. TORREY, IN *THE POWER OF PRAYER*

What Prayer Is

You will call upon me and come and pray to me, and I will hear you.
You will seek me and find me, when you seek me with all your heart.

(Jeremiah 29:12-13)

Only a child of God can truly pray to God. Only a son can enter His presence. It is gloriously true that anyone can cry to Him for help — for pardon and mercy. But that is scarcely prayer. Prayer is much more than that. Prayer is going into "the secret place of the Most High," and abiding under the shadow of the Almighty (Psalm 91:1, KJV). Prayer is a making known to God our wants and desires, and holding out the hand of faith to take His gifts. Prayer is the result of the Holy Spirit dwelling within us. It is communion with God. Now, there can scarcely be communion between a king and a rebel. What communion hath light with darkness (2 Corinthians 6:14)? In ourselves we have no right to pray. We have access to God only through the Lord Jesus Christ (Ephesians 2:18; 3:12).

Prayer is much more than the cry of a drowning man — of a man sinking in the whirlpool of sin: "Lord, save me! I am lost! I am undone! Redeem me! Save me!" Anyone can do this, and that is a petition which is never unanswered, and one, if sincere, to which the answer is never delayed. But that is not prayer in the Bible sense. Even the lions, roaring after their prey, seek their meat from God; but that is not prayer.

We know that our Lord said, "Every one that asketh receiveth" (Matthew 7:8, KJV). He did say so, but to whom? He was speaking to His disciples (Matthew 5:1-2). Yes, prayer is communion with God: the "home-life" of the soul, as one describes it. And I much question whether there can be any communion with Him unless the Holy Spirit dwells in the heart, and we have "received" the Son, and so have the right to be called "children of God" (John 1:12, KJV).

Prayer is the privilege of a child. Children of God alone can claim from the heavenly Father the things which He hath prepared for them that love Him.

An Unknown Christian, in *The Kneeling Christian*

He Is Worthy of All

Faith by itself, if it does not have works, is dead.

(James 2:17)

There is a danger in our evangelical religion of looking too much at what it offers from one side, as a certain experience to be obtained in prayer and faith. There is another side which God's word puts very strongly, that of obedience as the only path to blessing. What we need is to realize that in our relationship to the Infinite Being whom we call God who has created and redeemed us, the first sentiment that ought to animate us is that of subjection: the surrender to His supremacy, His glory, His will, His pleasure, ought to be the first and uppermost thought of our life. The question is not how we are to obtain and enjoy His favor, for in this the main thing may still be self. But what this Being in the very nature of things rightfully claims, and is infinitely and unspeakably worthy of, is that His glory and pleasure should be my one object. Surrender to His perfect and blessed will, a life of service and obedience, is the beauty and the charm of heaven. Service and obedience, these were the thoughts that were uppermost in the mind of the Son, when He dwelt upon earth. Service and obedience, these must become with us the chief objects of desire and aim, more so than rest or light, or joy or strength: in them we shall find the path to all the higher blessedness that awaits us.

Obedience and faith are but two aspects of one act — surrender to God and His will. As faith strengthens for obedience, it is in turn strengthened by it: faith is made perfect by works. It is the man who is entirely consecrated to God and His will who will find the power come to claim everything that His God has promised to be for him.

ANDREW MURRAY, IN *WITH CHRIST IN THE SCHOOL OF PRAYER*

THE GAUGE OF GRACE

The Lord said to him, "Arise and go to the street called Straight, and inquire at the house of Judas for one called Saul of Tarsus, for behold, he is praying."

(ACTS 9:11, NKJV)

In the conversion of Saul of Tarsus there is a unique revelation of the mind of God concerning prayer. There are three persons in that incident of prayer. There are the man who prayed, the God who heard, and the man through whom the answer came. God is central. It is to Him prayer is made, through Him prayer is interpreted, and by Him prayer is answered.

God speaks of prayer in terms of wonder: "Behold, he is praying." The language is that of humanity, but it is the only speech man knows, and however inadequate it may be, it stands for corresponding reality in God. Can God wonder? Can there be in Him elements of surprise and amazement? Can it be that there are things that to God are wonderful? That is how God speaks, and to Him there is nothing more gloriously wonderful than prayer. *Behold!* In that word there is wonder, rapture, exultation. In the estimate of God prayer is more wonderful than all the wonders of the heavens, more glorious than all the mysteries of the earth, more mighty than all the forces of creation.

God interprets prayer as a sign of all that happened to Saul of Tarsus on the Damascus road. That is what it meant to God, and that is what it always means to Him. Prayer is the symbol and proof and gauge of grace. All that happens in the converting work of grace whereby we receive the adoption of sons is that, being sons, we begin to pray. Saul of Tarsus had been a praying man all his life, but it was not until then that he began to pray as God interprets prayer.

SAMUEL CHADWICK, IN *THE PATH OF PRAYER*

HOLY BOLDNESS

Since we have such a hope, we are very bold.

(2 CORINTHIANS 3:12)

God called Moses to lead Israel out of Egypt, not to defend them in Egypt; to attack and defeat the enemy nations, not to protect Israel from them. God sent Joshua to invade and conquer, not to negotiate detente. The Holy Spirit was given at Pentecost, not to keep the church blessed and comfortable, but to make the church invincible.

The weapons of your spiritual warfare, says Paul, are not defensive weapons, but weapons of attack. "The weapons we fight with are not the weapons of the world. On the contrary, they have divine power to demolish strongholds. We demolish arguments [from Satan] and every pretension [literally, 'lofty thing'] that sets itself up against the knowledge of God, and we take captive every thought to make it obedient to Christ" (2 Corinthians 10:4-5, NIV). We are not to build a bypass when Satan throws up a mountain of resistance against us; we are to challenge Satan and hurl his mountain into the sea (Matthew 17:20). We are not to "hold the fort" until Jesus comes and rescues us; we are to storm the gates of Hades (16:18).

Ask God to give you a militant spirit. Ask Him to point out to you the specific needs for which to pray. Ask Him to show you the blindness, the slavery, and the lostness of the unsaved. Ask God to help you feel His longing love for the sinner, His hatred for the sin which is destroying the sinner, and His passion for the church, the kingdom, and the waiting harvest.

Ask God to give you a new joy and expectancy in prayer, a holy boldness to see Christ triumph and Satan defeated. Ask God to give you increased faith to see God's promise fulfilled and Satan put to shame. Ask God to light a holy fire in your soul by the power of the Holy Spirit, to transform your praying from weakness to prevailing power and an urgent insistence to see God's will be done on earth as it is in heaven.

WESLEY DUEWEL, IN *TOUCH THE WORLD THROUGH PRAYER*

Help Must Be at Hand

By the help of your God, return, hold fast to love
and justice, and wait continually for your God.

(Hosea 12:6)

There are few secrets in China, and soon the patients knew all about the financial basis upon which the hospital was now run, and they were watching eagerly for the outcome. This was something more to think and talk about. As the money left by Dr. Parker was used up and Hudson Taylor's own supplies ran low, many conjectured as to what would happen next. Needless to say, Hudson Taylor gave himself to prayer at this time. It was, perhaps, a more open, and in that sense more crucial, test than any that had come to him previously, and he realized that the faith of many was at stake, as well as the continuance of the hospital work. But day after day went by without bringing the expected answer. Finally one morning Kuei-hua, the cook, appeared with serious news. The very last bag of rice had been opened, and it was disappearing rapidly. "Then," replied Hudson Taylor, "the Lord's time for helping us must be close at hand." And so it was. Even before they emptied that bag of rice, a letter reached the young missionary that was among the most remarkable he had ever received. It was from Mr. William Berger, and it contained a check for 50 pounds, like others that had come before. Only, in this case, the letter went on to say that a heavy burden had come upon the writer, the burden of wealth to use for God. Fifty pounds! There it lay on the table, and his far-off friend, knowing nothing about that last bag of rice or the many needs of the hospital, actually asked if he might send them more. No wonder Hudson Taylor was overwhelmed with thankfulness and awe. Suppose he had held back from taking charge of the hospital on account of lack of means, or, rather, lack of faith? Lack of faith — with such promises and such a God? The praise meeting held in the hospital chapel resounded with songs and shouts of joy.

Dr. and Mrs. Howard Taylor, in *Hudson Taylor's Spiritual Secret*

THE NAME ABOVE ALL

His name shall be called Wonderful Counselor,
Mighty God, Everlasting Father, Prince of Peace.
(ISAIAH 9:6)

In Africa during the earlier part of this century, men called "white hunters" built up for themselves a good reputation as guides. They knew where the animals were and they charged high prices to lead foreign hunters to where they could shoot them. It was not only the big game the foreigners paid for but the big name of the guide as well. A high reputation carries a high responsibility.

Old Testament writers made much of the name of God. Israel was a nation specifically set apart as a place for God to put his name. Appeals were made on the basis of the name. "For thy name's sake lead me, and guide me," the psalmist prayed. Not because of who I am, not in recognition of my reputation, but because of who you are. "And his name will be called 'Wonderful Counselor.'" "The Lord is my banner." "Lord God of Hosts." No questions of merit can arise with regard to that name. It is above every name. Therefore I can come today on the ground of that name's merit.

The prayer that Jesus taught his disciples begins with the petition, "Our Father who art in heaven, hallowed be thy name." Whatever our requests may be that bring us to his feet, they should begin with a careful consideration of the meaning of this form of address. If we say the words slowly and thoughtfully, they cannot help but color the rest of the prayer. If it is guidance we are asking, we may be very wrong in our hopes as to the direction it will take. We may be ill-prepared in heart for the road God will choose for us. But, as George MacDonald wrote, "The thought of him to whom that prayer goes will purify and correct the desire."

If we do not have God's unequivocal promise, the words "Guide me, for the sake of your name" would sound outrageously presumptuous. But the truth is that God said he would do just this. There is nothing presumptuous or precarious about it. The validity of the divine word is at stake, and that is a very sure foundation.

ELISABETH ELLIOT, IN *GOD'S GUIDANCE*

CAST YOURSELF ON HIS MERCY

I acknowledged my sin to you, and I did not cover my iniquity.
(PSALM 32:5)

When, in the course of the day's engagements, our conscience witnesses against us that we have sinned, we should at once confess our guilt, claim by faith the cleansing of the blood of Christ, and so wash our hands in innocence. And afterwards, as soon as we have a convenient opportunity, we ought to review with deliberation the wrong that we have done. As we consider it *with God* we shall be impressed by its sinfulness, as we were not at the time of its committal. And if the sin is one which we have committed before, one to which perhaps our nature lies open, we must cast ourselves in utter faith upon the strong mercy of God, pleading with Him in the name of Christ that we may never again so grieve Him. As our hearts grow more tender in the presence of God, the remembrance of former sins which have already been acknowledged and forgiven will from time to time imprint a fresh stain upon our conscience. In such a case nature itself seems to teach us that we ought anew to implore the pardoning grace of God. For we bend, not before the judgment seat of the Divine Lawgiver, but before our Father, to whom we have been reconciled through Christ. A more adequate conception of the offense which we have committed ought surely to be followed by a deeper penitence for the wrong done. Under the guidance of the Holy Spirit we shall often be led to pray with the Psalmist, "Remember not the sins of my youth" (Psalm 25:7, KJV), even though these have long since been dealt with and done away. Conviction of sin will naturally prompt to confession. When such promptings are disregarded, the Spirit who has wrought in us that conviction is grieved.

DAVID MCINTYRE, IN *THE HIDDEN LIFE OF PRAYER*

Don't Be Ashamed

> *Search me, O God, and know my heart! Try me and*
> *know my thoughts! And see if there be any grievous*
> *way in me, and lead me in the way everlasting!*
> (Psalm 139:23-24)

We remember the response of Adam and his wife after their willful disobedience of God's one prohibition. When they "heard the sound of the Lord God as he was walking in the garden in the cool of the day . . . they hid from the Lord God among the trees of the garden" (Genesis 3:8, NIV). Shame encourages us to hide from the presence of God; shame squirrels behind a masking foliage of pleasantries while refusing to be honest; shame fosters flight and escapism; shame engenders prayerlessness.

What is God's response? God sought Adam and Eve and dealt with their sin. We cannot successfully hide from God anyway, "for a man's ways are in full view of the Lord, and he examines all his paths" (Proverbs 5:21, NIV). "Nothing in all creation is hidden from God's sight. Everything is uncovered and laid bare before the eyes of him to whom we must give account" (Hebrews 4:13, NIV). But if it is futile to run from God, our sense of shame can scarcely be an adequate ground to excuse our prayerlessness. Rather, it ought to be a goad that drives us back to the only one who can forgive us and grant us utter absolution, back to the freedom of conscience and the boldness in prayer that follow in the wake of the joyful knowledge that we have been accepted by a holy God because of his grace.

D. A. Carson, in *A Call to Spiritual Reformation*

Seek Jesus First

Which of you by being anxious can add a single hour to his span of life?
(Matthew 6:27)

If the Creator thus sustains the birds and lilies, should he not much more as a Father nourish his own children, who daily pray to him? Should he not be able to grant them the necessities of life, when all earthly goods belong to him, and when he can distribute them according to his pleasure?

Anxiety is characteristic of the Gentiles, for they rely on their own strength and work instead of relying on God. They do not know that the Father knows that we have need of all these things, and so they try to do for themselves what they do not expect from God. But the disciples know that the rule is "Seek ye first the kingdom of God and his righteousness and all these things shall be added unto you." Anxiety for food and clothing is clearly not the same thing as anxiety for the kingdom of God, however much we should like to persuade ourselves that when we are working for our families and concerning ourselves with bread and houses we are thereby building the kingdom, as though the kingdom could be realized only through our worldly cares. The kingdom of God and his righteousness are sharply distinguished from the gifts of the world which come our way. That kingdom is not other than the righteousness of Matthew 5 and 6, the righteousness of the cross and of following Christ beneath that cross. Fellowship with Jesus and obedience to his commandment come first, and all else follows. Worldly cares are not part of our discipleship, but distinct and subordinate concerns. Before we start taking thought for our life, our food and clothing, our work and families, we must seek the righteousness of Christ. We have here either a crushing burden, which holds out no hope for the poor and wretched, or else it is the quintessence of the gospel, which brings the promise of freedom and perfect joy.

Dietrich Bonhoeffer, in *The Cost of Discipleship*

TOO HARD FOR GOD?

I can do all things through him who strengthens me.

(PHILIPPIANS 4:13)

A man once went to George Muller and said he wanted him to pray for a certain thing. The man stated that he had asked God a great many times to grant him his request, but He had not seen fit to do it. Mr. Muller took out his notebook, and showed the man the name of a person for whom, he said, he had prayed for twenty-four years. The prayer, Mr. Muller added, was not answered yet; but the Lord had given him assurance that that person was going to be converted, and his faith rested there.

We sometimes find that our prayers are answered right away while we are praying; at other times the answer is delayed. But especially when men pray for mercy, how quickly the answer comes! Look at Paul, when he cried, "O Lord, what wilt Thou have me to do?" The answer came at once. Then the publican who went up to the temple to pray — he got an immediate answer. The thief on the cross prayed, "Lord, remember me when Thou comest into Thy kingdom!" and the answer came immediately — then and there. There are many cases of a similar kind in the Bible, but there are also others who prayed long and often. The Lord delights in hearing His children make their requests known unto Him — telling their troubles all out to Him; and then we should wait for His time. We do not know when that is. I think we shall find a great many of our prayers that we thought unanswered answered when we get to heaven. If it is the true prayer of faith, God will not disappoint us. Let us not doubt God. Jeremiah prayed, and said: "Ah Lord GOD! behold, thou hast made the heaven and the earth by thy great power and stretched out arm, and there is nothing too hard for thee" (Jeremiah 32:17, KJV). Nothing is too hard for God; that is a good thing to take for a motto.

D. L. MOODY, IN *PREVAILING PRAYER*

A SOUL STAYED UPON GOD

Commit your way to the LORD; trust in him, and he will act.

(PSALM 37:5)

Sometimes all has been dark, exceedingly dark, with reference to my service among the saints, judging from natural appearances; yea, when I should have been overwhelmed indeed in grief and despair, had I looked at things after the outward appearance; at such times I have sought to encourage myself in God, by laying hold in faith on His mighty power, His unchangeable love, and His infinite wisdom, and I have said to myself: God is able and willing to deliver me, if it be good for me; for it is written: "He that spared not His own Son, but delivered Him up for us all, how shall He not with Him also freely give us all things?" (Romans 8:32, KJV). This, this it was which, being believed by me through grace, kept my soul in peace. Further, when in connection with the Orphan-Houses, Day Schools, etc., trials have come upon me which were far heavier than the want of means my soul was stayed upon God; I believed His word of promise which was applicable to such cases; I poured out my soul before God, and arose from my knees in peace, because the trouble that was in the soul was in believing prayer cast upon God, and thus I was kept in peace, though I saw it to be the will of God to remain far away from the work. Further, when I needed houses, fellow-labourers, masters and mistresses for the Orphans or for the Day Schools, I have been enabled to look for all to the Lord and trust in Him for help. Dear reader, I may seem to boast; but, by the grace of God, I do not boast in thus speaking. From my inmost soul I do ascribe it to God alone that He has enabled me to trust in Him, and that hitherto He has not suffered my confidence in Him to fail.

GEORGE MÜLLER, IN *ANSWERS TO PRAYER*

The Secret of Christian Quietness

Say to those who have an anxious heart, "Be strong; fear not!"
(Isaiah 35:4)

Be yourself exactly before God, and present your problems, the things you know you have come to your wits' end about. The New Testament view of a Christian is that he is one in whom the Son of God has been revealed, and prayer deals with the nourishment of that life. One way it is nourished is by refusing to worry over anything, for worry means there is something over which we cannot have our own way, and is in reality personal irritation with God. Jesus Christ says, "Don't worry about your life."

Never let anything push you to your wits' end, because you will get worried, and worry makes you self-interested and disturbs the nourishment of the life of God. Give thanks to God that *He* is there, no matter what is happening. Many a man has found God in the belly of hell in the trenches during the days of war, i.e., they came to their wits' end and discovered God. The secret of Christian quietness is not indifference, but the knowledge that God is my Father, He loves me, I shall never think of anything He will forget, and worry becomes an impossibility.

It is not so true that "prayer changes things" as that prayer changes *me* and then I change things; consequently we must not ask God to do what He has created us to do. For instance, Jesus Christ is not a social reformer; He came to alter us first, and if there is any social reform to be done on earth, we must do it. God has so constituted things that prayer on the basis of Redemption alters the way a man looks at things. Prayer is not a question of altering things externally, but of working wonders in a man's disposition. When you pray, *things* remain the same, but *you* begin to be different.

OSWALD CHAMBERS, IN *IF YOU WILL ASK*

Coming Before the Good King

> *He arose and came to his father. But while he was still*
> *a long way off, his father saw him and felt compassion,*
> *and ran and embraced him and kissed him.*
>
> (Luke 15:20)

I consider myself as the most wretched of men, full of sores and corruption, and who has committed all sorts of crimes against his King; touched with a sensible regret I confess to Him all my wickedness, I ask His forgiveness, I abandon myself in His hands, that He may do what He pleases with me. This King, full of mercy and goodness, very far from chastising me, embraces me with love, makes me eat at His table, serves me with His own hands, gives me the key of His treasures; He converses and delights Himself with me incessantly, in a thousand and a thousand ways, and treats me in all respects as His favorite. It is thus I consider myself from time to time in His holy presence.

My most usual method is this simple attention, and such a general passionate regard to God; to whom I find myself often attached with greater sweetness and delight than that of an infant at the mother's breast: so that if I dare use the expression, I should choose to call this state the bosom of God, for the inexpressible sweetness which I taste and experience there. If sometimes my thoughts wander from it by necessity or infirmity, I am presently recalled by inward motions, so charming and delicious that I am ashamed to mention them.

I desire your reverence to reflect rather upon my great wretchedness, of which you are fully informed, than upon the great favors which God does me, all unworthy and ungrateful as I am.

As for my set hours of prayer, they are only a continuation of the same exercise. Sometimes I consider myself there, as a stone before a carver, whereof he is to make a statue: presenting myself thus before God, I desire Him to make His perfect image in my soul, and render me entirely like Himself.

Brother Lawrence, in *The Practice of the Presence of God*

GOD'S LOAN TO US

> *Who sees anything different in you? What do you have*
> *that you did not receive? If then you received it,*
> *why do you boast as if you did not receive it?*
> (1 CORINTHIANS 4:7)

We are often hindered from giving up our treasures to the Lord out of fear for their safety; this is especially true when those treasures are loved relatives and friends. But we need have no such fears. Our Lord came not to destroy but to save. Everything is safe which we commit to Him, and nothing is really safe which is not so committed.

Our gifts and talents should also be turned over to Him. They should be recognized for what they are, God's loan to us, and should never be considered in any sense our own. We have no more right to claim credit for special abilities than for blue eyes or strong muscles.

The Christian who is alive enough to know himself even slightly will recognize the symptoms of this possession malady, and will grieve to find them in his own heart. If the longing after God is strong enough within him he will want to do something about the matter. Now, what should he do?

First of all he should put away all defense and make no attempt to excuse himself either in his own eyes or before the Lord. Whoever defends himself will have himself for his defense, and he will have no other; but let him come defenseless before the Lord and he will have for his defender no less than God Himself.

Then he should remember that this is holy business. No careless or casual dealings will suffice. Let him come to God in full determination to be heard. Let him insist that God accept his all, that He take things out of his heart and Himself reign there in power. It may be he will need to become specific, to name things and people by their names one by one. If he will become drastic enough he can shorten the time of his travail from years to minutes and enter the good land long before his slower brethren who coddle their feelings and insist upon caution in their dealings with God.

A. W. TOZER, IN *THE PURSUIT OF GOD*

Cooperation with God

Come now, let us reason together, says the Lord.
(Isaiah 1:18)

Faith is faith in another. In prayer we do not so much work as interwork. We are fellow workers with God in a reciprocity. And as God is the freest Being in existence, such co-operant prayer is the freest things that man can do. If we were free in sinning, how much more free in the praying which undoes sin! If we were free to break God's will, how much more free to turn it or to accept it! Petitionary prayer is man's cooperation in kind with God amidst a world He freely made for freedom. The world was made by a freedom which not only left room for the kindred freedom of prayer, but which so ordered all things in its own interest that in their deepest depths they conspire to produce prayer. To pray in faith is to answer God's freedom in its own great note. It means we are taken up into the fundamental movement of the world. It is to realize that for which the whole world, the world as a whole, was made. It is an earnest of the world's consummation. We are doing what the whole world was created to do. We overleap in the spirit all between now and then, as in the return to Jesus we overleap the two thousand years that intervene. The object the Father's loving purpose had in appointing the whole providential order was intercourse with man's soul. That order of the world is, therefore, no rigid fixture, nor is it even a fated evolution. It is elastic, adjustable, flexible, with margins for freedom, for free modification in God and man; always keeping in view that final goal of communion, and growing into it by a spiritual interplay in which the whole of Nature is involved. The goal of the whole cosmic order is the "manifestation of the sons of God," the realization of complete sonship, its powers and its confidences.

P. T. Forsyth, in *The Soul of Prayer*

The Great Need to Make Disciples

Go therefore and make disciples of all nations, baptizing them in the name of the Father and of the Son and of the Holy Spirit.
(Matthew 28:19)

It is of supreme importance that all Christians understand that this commission to convert the world is given to them by Christ individually.

Everyone has been given the great responsibility to win as many souls as possible to Christ. This is the great privilege and the great duty of all the disciples of Christ. There are many ways we can be a part of this work. But every one of us ought to possess this power so that, whether we preach or pray, or write, or print, or trade, or travel, take care of children, or administer the government of the state, or whatever we do, our whole life and influence should be permeated with this power. Christ says, "If any man believe in Me, out of his inmost being shall flow rivers of living water" — that is, a Christian influence having in it the element of power to impress the truth of Christ upon the hearts of men, shall proceed from Him. The great need of the Church at present is, first, the clear conviction that this commission to convert the world is given to each of Christ's disciples as his lifework. I fear I must say that most professing Christians do not seem to have been compelled to action by this truth. The work of saving souls they leave to ministers.

The second great need is a clear conviction of the necessity of this gift of power upon every individual soul. Many professing Christians assume it belongs especially and only to those who are called to preach the gospel as a lifework. They fail to realize that all are called to preach the gospel, that the whole life of every Christian is to be a proclamation of the glad tidings.

Charles Finney, in *Power from on High*

JORN'S LOT

> *The LORD is my chosen portion and my cup; you hold*
> *my lot. The lines have fallen for me in pleasant places;*
> *indeed, I have a beautiful inheritance.*
>
> (PSALM 16:5-6)

One of the tenants on my father's farm was one of these faithful intercessors. His name was Jorn. Our Lord had imposed severe limitations upon him from his birth. His eyes were weak, and as a result it was always difficult for him to earn a living. Trials and tribulations became Jorn's lot, and many a day was dark and dreary.

But he humbled himself beneath the mighty hand of God, and little by little, in the school of difficult experiences, he learned the holy art of prayer. He would pray for his home community day and night. And, in due time, God exalted him. He became the spiritual counselor of the whole parish. People came to his little hut from the whole vicinity to get advice and help. And if Jorn could not help them in any other way, he could give them some of the unfeigned love of his own tender heart. Besides, he prayed for them; and as the years passed, many a soul left his humble dwelling with a lighter tread and a happier heart.

In the later years of his life he was very poorly. Two elderly Christian women, who were with him and cared for him, told me that he would be awake a great deal at night, and that, while thus awake, they could hear him pray for all the people of the parish. And he did not make as light of it as we are apt to do. As a rule we are always in a hurry, so we take them all in one group to the Lord and ask Him in one prayer to bless them all.

But old Jorn didn't do it that way. He mentioned each one of them by name, as in his thoughts he went from house to house. Even children whom he had not seen, but who he knew had been born, he felt that he had to carry to the throne of grace upon the arms of prayer.

OLE HALLESBY, IN *PRAYER*

THE POWER OF PRIVATE PRAYER

Rising very early in the morning, while it was still dark, he departed and went out to a desolate place, and there he prayed.

(MARK 1:35)

Hypocrites never pray in secret. Prayers that are a pretense require an audience. They are intended to be heard of men, and they have their reward in skill of phrasing, a show of earnestness, and a reputation for piety. These things do not count with God. They cannot live in His presence. Prayer is between the soul and God alone.

The soul needs its silent spaces. It is in them we learn to pray. There, alone, shut in with God, our Lord bids us pray to our Father who is in secret, and seeth in secret. There is no test like solitude. Fear takes possession of most minds in the stillness of the solitary place. The heart shrinks from being alone with God who seeth in secret! Who shall abide in His presence? Who can dwell with God, who is shadowless light? Hearts must be pure and hands clean that dare shut the door and be alone with God. It would revolutionize the lives of most men if they were shut in with God in some secret place for half an hour a day.

For such praying all the faculties of the soul need to be awake and alert. When our Lord took Peter and James and John with Him to the secret place of prayer, they were heavy with sleep. It was the same in the mount of glory and the garden of agony, and it was not until they were fully awake that they saw the glory or realized the anguish. There are some silent places of rare wisdom where men may not talk, but they find it possible to sleep. Mooning is not meditation, and drowsy repose is not praying. The secret place of prayer calls for every faculty of mind and heart. In private prayer the soul stands naked and alone in the presence of God. Thought is personal, prayer is original, motive is challenged. Corporate prayer gives a spirit of fellowship; private prayer disciplines personality. Who can measure the influence of an hour a day spent alone with God?

SAMUEL CHADWICK, IN *THE PATH OF PRAYER*

PRESS ON TO KNOW GOD

Draw near to God, and he will draw near to you.
(JAMES 4:8)

To be truly converted is to avert wholly from the creature, and turn wholly unto God.

For the attainment of salvation it is absolutely necessary that we should forsake outward sin and turn unto righteousness: but this alone is not perfect conversion, which consists in a total change of the whole man from an outward to an inward life.

When the soul is once turned to God a wonderful facility is found in continuing steadfast in conversion; and the longer it remains thus converted, the nearer it approaches, and the more firmly it adheres to God; and the nearer it draws to Him, of necessity it is the farther removed from the creature, which is so contrary to Him: so that it is so effectually established and rooted in its conversion that it becomes habitual, and, as it were, natural.

Now we must not suppose that this is effected by a violent exertion of its own powers; for it is not capable of, nor should it attempt any other co-operation with Divine Grace, than that of endeavouring to withdraw itself from external objects and to turn inwards: after which it has nothing farther to do than to continue steadfast in adherence to God.

God has an attractive virtue which draws the soul more and more powerfully to Himself, the nearer it approaches towards Him, and, in attracting, He purifies and refines it. The soul co-operates with the attractions of God, by a free and affectionate correspondence. This kind of introversion is both easy and efficacious, advancing the soul naturally and without constraint, because God Himself is its center.

JEANNE GUYON, IN *A SHORT AND EASY METHOD OF PRAYER*

Genuine Prayer in the Spirit

Have mercy on me, O God, according to your steadfast love;
according to your abundant mercy blot out my transgressions.
(Psalm 51:1)

Man by himself is so full of all manner of wickedness, that he cannot make a word or a thought or prayer clean and acceptable to God; he must have the guidance of the Holy Spirit. For this reason, the Pharisees, with all their fine prayers, were rejected. The Pharisees were excellently able to express themselves in words, and also for length of time spent in prayer they were very notable. But they had not the Spirit to help them, so they did what they did with their infirmities and weaknesses only. They fell far short of a sincere, sensible, affectionate pouring out of their souls to God, through the strength of the Holy Spirit. The prayer that ascends to heaven is the prayer that is sent there by the Holy Spirit, and it is that prayer which is effective.

Nothing but the Spirit can show a man clearly his misery by nature and put him into a posture of prayer. Talk is but talk and so our prayers are only mouth-worship if there is not a sense of misery in sin. O the cursed hypocrisy that is in most hearts and that accompanies many thousands of praying men! But the Spirit will show the soul its misery, where it is in its spiritual growth, and what is likely to become of it apart from Christ, and also the intolerableness of its condition apart from faith in the Savior. For it is the Spirit who effectively convinces of sin and misery without the Lord Jesus, and so puts the soul into a sweet, serious, sensible, affectionate way of praying to God according to his Word.

Even if men did see their sins, without the help of the Holy Spirit they *would* not pray. Instead, they would run away from God and utterly despair of mercy. Such were the cases of Adam and Eve, Cain, and Judas. When a man is indeed in despair over his sin and God's curse, then it is a difficult thing to persuade him to pray. Apart from the influence of the Holy Spirit a sinner will say, "It's no use" (Jeremiah 18:12, NIV).

John Bunyan, in *Pilgrim's Prayer Book*

Hearing the Voice

Oh, that my people would listen to me, that Israel would walk in my ways!
(Psalm 81:13)

Just as far as we listen to the voice and language that God speaks, and in the words of God receive His thoughts, His mind, His life, into our heart, we shall learn to speak in the voice and the language that God hears. It is the ear of the learner, wakened morning by morning, that prepares for the tongue of the learned, to speak to God as well as men, as should be (Isaiah 1:4).

Hearing the voice of God is something more than the thoughtful study of the Word. There may be a study and knowledge of the Word, in which there is but little real fellowship with the living God. But there is also a reading of the Word, in the very presence of the Father, and under the leading of the Spirit, in which the Word comes to us in living power from God Himself; it is to us the very voice of the Father, a real personal fellowship with Himself. It is the living voice of God that enters the heart, that brings blessing and strength, and awakens the response of a living faith that reaches the heart of God again.

It is on this hearing the voice that the power both to obey and believe depends. The chief thing is, not to know *what* God has said we must do, but that *God Himself* says it to us. It is not the law, and not the book, not the knowledge of what is right, that works obedience, but the personal influence of God and His living fellowship. And even so it is not the knowledge of *what* God has promised, but the presence of *God Himself* as the Promiser, that awakens faith and trust in prayer. It is only in the full presence of God that disobedience and unbelief become impossible.

Andrew Murray, in *With Christ in the School of Prayer*

You Are Not Condemned

*Immediately the father of the child cried out
and said, "I believe; help my unbelief!"*

(Mark 9:24)

All the known or unknown rebellions of my life are being taken care of through the power of Jesus Christ's resurrected life. I know, too, that He expects me to cooperate with Him in bringing my will under His control, so that all these rebellions can be stripped of their dominating power. When, face to face, I am alone with Him in prayer, and His love is pouring over me, somehow it is possible to hand over to Him the specific thing that I wanted to manage myself.

And you, my tender-hearted, overly conscientious friend, can rest in Him, too, so that your prayers will be answered, and so that you do not need to continue condemning yourself.

Who is he that condemns? Do you know the answer to that question? Do you condemn yourself? Oh, yes, we do, in a way that helps us turn positively to Christ. But the morbid, negative daily condemnation which is sapping the life out of you, and keeping you from receiving all He wants to give you, is wrong. Because He has already died for you. The Christ who died for you and rose again is the only One who can condemn you. And He does not (Romans 8:31-39). He loves you. He loves you more than you are loved by anyone else in this world or in the next. God loves you. The Son of Man is come not to condemn but to save (John 3:17).

When you do find something that condemns you, bring it at once to His feet, and it will be transformed. Because all the fruits of the Spirit are sins transformed. Resentment is changed to love. Sadness is changed to joy. Unbelief is changed to faith. Rebellion is changed to acceptance. These are simply the gifts which accompany the Giver. Where He is, and where He lives, are all the good things He wants to give to us. We don't pick faith out of the air, or off a limb.

Jesus Christ is our faith.

Rosalind Rinker, in *Prayer: Conversing with God*

GIVE YOUR LIFE

> *Many were gathered together, so that there was no more room,
> not even at the door. And [Jesus] was preaching the word to them.*
>
> (MARK 2:2)

Hyde felt that his place was in the Prayer Room, but he had to enter the platform at times, and his messages were delivered with tremendous power, as we would naturally expect when he came straight from the Prayer Room to deliver his message. I shall never forget the effect of one of his Bible readings on the congregation and on the whole convention. I realized very soon that he was delivering a solemn message, for there was a solemnity in the congregation that was almost oppressive. He spoke quietly, but all could hear him, and I felt that his *life* was in the Word. He once told me that one had to give *himself* if he wanted to serve God and help men, that it was not enough to give our time and our talents, that our life must be given. This was true, he said, both in praying and in preaching. Alas! how few of us give our life; when we think that our life is touched, we feel it is time to draw back. How often we have heard it said, "You will kill yourself if you work as you do, take it easy." But Hyde used to say, "Give your life for God and men," let that vital energy, that living power within, be poured out for me. Who is right? Hyde or the modern man? Hyde gave himself as he preached — he poured out his life as he prayed and men realized the power. I heard that immediately after the service, the Committee was called together to consider God's challenge to them, and for prayer that the message might influence men. At breakfast, men were in groups asking what should be done, and I know that many went away alone to have their lives re-adjusted by the Holy Spirit.

CAPTAIN E. G. CARRÉ, IN *A PRESENT-DAY CHALLENGE TO PRAYER*

THEY HAVE BEEN WITH JESUS

> *God, who said, "Let light shine out of darkness," has*
> *shone in our hearts to give the light of the knowledge*
> *of the glory of God in the face of Jesus Christ.*
> (2 CORINTHIANS 4:6)

It is when we pray, that the Holy Spirit takes of the things of Christ and reveals them unto us (John 16:15). It was when Moses prayed, "Show me, I pray thee, thy glory," that he not only saw somewhat of it, but shared something of that glory, and his own face shone with the light of it (Exodus 33:18; 34:29, KJV). And when we, too, gaze upon the "glory of God in the face of Jesus Christ" (2 Corinthians 4:6), we shall see not only a glimpse of that glory, but we shall gain something of it ourselves.

Now, that is prayer, and the highest result of prayer. Nor is there any other way of securing that glory, that God may be glorified in us (Isaiah 60:21).

Let us often meditate upon Christ's glory — gaze upon it and so reflect it and receive it. This is what happened to our Lord's first disciples. They said in awed tones, "We beheld his glory!" Yes, but what followed? A few plain, unlettered, obscure fishermen companied with Christ a little while, seeing His glory; and lo! they themselves caught something of that glory. And then others marveled and "took knowledge of them that they had been with Jesus" (Acts 4:13, KJV). And when we can declare, with St. John, "Yea, and our fellowship is with the Father and with His Son Jesus Christ" (1 John 1:3, KJV), people will say the same of us: "They have been with Jesus!"

As we lift up our soul in prayer to the living God, we gain the beauty of holiness as surely as a flower becomes beautiful by living in the sunlight. Was not our Lord Himself transfigured when He prayed? And the "very fashion" of our countenance will change, and we shall have our Mount of Transfiguration when prayer has its rightful place in our lives. And men will see in our faces "the outward and visible sign of an inward and spiritual grace." Our value to God and to man is in exact proportion to the extent in which we reveal the glory of God to others.

AN UNKNOWN CHRISTIAN, IN *THE KNEELING CHRISTIAN*

SPEAKING TO CHRIST THROUGH THE SPIRIT

May the God of hope fill you with all joy and peace in believing,
so that by the power of the Holy Spirit you may abound in hope.

(ROMANS 15:13)

The Spirit of Christ reveals to us *our own wants*, that we may reveal them unto him: "We know not what we should pray for as we ought" (Romans 8:26); no teachings under those of the Spirit of God are able to make our souls acquainted with their own wants — its burdens, its temptations. For a soul to know its wants, its infirmities, is a heavenly discovery. He that hath this assistance, his prayer is more than half made before he begins to pray. His conscience is affected with what he hath to do; his mind and spirit contend within him, there especially where he finds himself most straitened. He brings his burden on his shoulders, and unloads himself on the Lord Christ. He finds (not by a perplexing conviction, but a holy sense and weariness of sin) where he is dead, where dull and cold, wherein unbelieving, wherein tempted above all his strength, where the light of God's countenance is wanting. And all these the soul hath a sense of by the Spirit, an inexpressible sense and experience. Without this, prayer is not prayer; men's voices may be heard, but they speak not in their hearts. Sense of want is the spring of desire; natural of natural; spiritual of spiritual. Without this sense given by the Holy Ghost, there is neither desire nor prayer.

But he that hath this assistance can provide no clothing that is large and broad enough to set forth the desires of his heart; and therefore, in the close of his best and most fervent supplications, such a person finds a double dissatisfaction in them: 1) That they are not *a righteousness* to be rested on; that if God should mark what is in them amiss, they could not abide the trial. 2) That his heart in them is not *poured out*, nor delivered in any proportion to the holy desires and labourings that were conceived therein; though he may in Christ have great refreshment by them. The more the saints speak, the more they find they have left unspoken.

JOHN OWEN, IN *OF COMMUNION WITH GOD THE FATHER, SON AND HOLY GHOST*

Don't Be Content with Mediocrity

Awake, O sleeper, and arise from the dead, and Christ will shine on you.
(Ephesians 5:14)

Some Christians want enough of Christ to be identified with him but not enough to be seriously inconvenienced; they genuinely cling to basic Christian orthodoxy but do not want to engage in serious Bible study; they value moral probity, especially of the public sort, but do not engage in war against inner corruptions; they fret over the quality of the preacher's sermon but do not worry much over the quality of their own prayer life. Such Christians are content with mediocrity.

What is God's response? Many passages could be brought to bear on the condition. One of the most intriguing is the letter written by James, the half-brother of our Lord. Writing to Christians, he nevertheless finds it necessary to say, "You quarrel and fight. You do not have, because you do not ask God" (James 4:2, NIV). Here are Christians, bickering and squabbling, profoundly frustrated because of their prayerlessness. When they do pray, they are no better off: "When you ask, you do not receive, because you ask with wrong motives, that you may spend what you get on your pleasures" (James 4:3, NIV).

From God's perspective, such Christians are "adulterous people" (verse 4, NIV), because while nominally maintaining an intimate relationship with God, they are trying to foster an intimate relationship with the world. "You adulterous people, don't you know that friendship with the world is hatred toward God [in exactly the same way that physically adulterous relationship is hatred toward the spouse]? Anyone who chooses to be a friend of the world becomes an enemy of God" (verse 4, NIV).

God's response is utterly uncompromising: "Submit yourselves, then, to God. Resist the devil, and he will flee from you. Come near to God and he will come near to you. Wash your hands, you sinners, and purify your hearts, you double-minded. Grieve, mourn and wail. Change your laughter to mourning and your joy to gloom. Humble yourselves before the Lord, and he will lift you up" (verses 7-10, NIV).

The sad truth is that at various times all of us need to apply these words to our lives.

D. A. Carson, in *A Call to Spiritual Reformation*

THE FAITH TO ASK GOD'S WILL

> *Those who trust in the LORD are like Mount Zion,*
> *which cannot be moved, but abides forever.*
>
> (PSALM 125:1)

Advice is a commodity we suddenly need and set out to get. We might spend a few dollars for a magazine, or a few dollars to have our tea leaves read, with the attitude, "Oh, well, it might work. What can I lose?" If we like what we hear, we can follow the advice. If not, we reject it. We might get the advice of friends without having to pay for it, and when we are in serious difficulty we may be willing to pay a great deal for professional advice. The higher the fee, the more concerned we will be to ascertain the qualifications of the source we are consulting. Is it trustworthy? But ours is still the choice — we can take it or leave it, according to our inclinations.

The Christian does not come to God for advice. He comes asking for God's will and, in the truest sense, there is no option here. Once it is known, it must be done. "Whoever knows what is right to do and fails to do it, for him it is sin."

God's fee may be a higher one than we are prepared to pay — it may cost everything. Anybody who honestly intends to follow will certainly be asked to deny himself. A wealthy young man once came to Jesus full of good intentions, but they were short-lived. He went away sorrowful because Jesus had asked him to sell everything he owned. That was too much.

To ask for the guidance of God is to make a choice, and this takes faith. It must be faith of a far higher kind than the breezy "If I like what I see I'll take it." It is the faith that has strength to wait for the rewards God holds, strength to believe they are worth waiting for, worth the price asked. Our prayers for God's guidance really begin here: *I trust him.*

ELISABETH ELLIOT, IN *GOD'S GUIDANCE*

TOTAL HONESTY

*Evening and morning and at noon I utter my
complaint and moan, and he hears my voice.*
(PSALM 55:17)

Honest dealing becomes us when we kneel in His pure presence.

In our address to God we like to speak of Him as we think we ought to speak, and there are times when our words far outrun our feelings. But it is best that we should be perfectly frank before Him. He will allow us to say anything we will, so long as we say it to Himself. "I will say unto God, my rock," exclaims the psalmist, "Why hast Thou forgotten me?" (Psalm 42:9, KJV). If he had said, "Lord, Thou canst not forget: Thou hast graven my name on the palms of Thy hands," he would have spoken more worthily, but less truly. On one occasion Jeremiah failed to interpret God aright. He cried, as if in anger, "O Lord, Thou hast deceived me, and I was deceived: Thou art stronger than I, and hast prevailed" (Jeremiah 20:7, KJV). These are terrible words to utter before Him who is changeless truth. But the prophet spoke as he felt, and the Lord not only pardoned him, He met and blessed him there.

It is possible that some who read these words may have a complaint against God. A controversy of long standing has come between your soul and His grace. If you were to utter the word that is trembling on your lips, you would say to Him, "Why hast Thou dealt thus with me?" Then dare to say, with reverence and with boldness, all that is in your heart. "Produce your cause, saith the Lord; bring forth your strong reasons, saith the King of Jacob" (Isaiah 41:21, KJV). Carry your grievance into the light of His countenance; charge your complaint home. Then listen to His answer. For surely, in gentleness and truth, He will clear Himself of the charge of unkindness that you bring against Him. And in His light you shall see light.

DAVID MCINTYRE, IN *THE HIDDEN LIFE OF PRAYER*

God's Presence on the Wearisome Journey

Sow for yourselves righteousness; reap steadfast love;
break up your fallow ground, for it is the time to seek the Lord,
that he may come and rain righteousness upon you.

(Hosea 10:12)

Tuesday, April 17. Rode to Millington again; and felt perplexed when I set out; was feeble in body, and weak in faith. I was going to preach a lecture; and feared I should never have assistance enough to get through. But contriving to ride alone, at a distance from the company that was going, I spent the time in lifting up my heart to God: had not gone far before my soul was abundantly strengthened with those words, "If God be for us, who can be against us?" I went on, confiding in God; and fearing nothing so much as self-confidence. In this frame I went to the house of God, and enjoyed some assistance. Afterwards felt the spirit of love and meekness in conversation with some friends. Then rode home to my brother's; and in the evening, singing hymns with friends, my soul seemed to melt; and in prayer afterwards, enjoyed the exercise of *faith*, and was enabled to be *fervent in spirit*: found more of God's presence, than I have done any time in my late wearisome journey. Eternity appeared very near; my nature was very weak, and seemed ready to be dissolved; the sun declining, and the shadows of the evening drawing on apace. O I longed to fill up the remaining moments all for God! Though my body was so feeble, and wearied with preaching, and much private conversation, yet I wanted to sit up all night to do something for God. To God, the giver of these refreshments, be glory for ever and ever. Amen.

Jonathan Edwards, in *The Life and Diary of David Brainerd*

THE GLORY OF REDEMPTION

In love he predestined us for adoption as sons through
Jesus Christ, according to the purpose of his will, to the praise
of his glorious grace, with which he has blessed us in the Beloved.

(EPHESIANS 1:4-6)

The glory of the Lord is manifested in the kingdom of His providence; He upholds all things that He hath made with the word of His power, "By the greatness of his might, for that he is strong in power; not one faileth" (Isaiah 40:26, KJV).

But much more in upholding, sustaining, keeping, blessing, and supplying the need of His people, is He glorified. It is in His dealings with the sons of men that the Lord Jesus Christ is most manifest, and, therefore, most glorifies Himself, as it is in giving the Lord Jesus Christ to the sons of men, Jehovah has most glorified Himself. We are the empty vessels, into which the Lord Jesus Christ pours the fullness of His grace, and into which, by-and-by, He will pour forth the fullness of His glory. It is in redeeming sinners Jesus is most glorified; it cost Him but a word to create the worlds, but to redeem a sinner's soul cost Him all that He had, including His tremendous stoop from heaven's glory to earth's wilderness, the cross, and the curse. It is in regenerating sinners that the Lord Jesus manifests His glory. Who but Himself could take a dead soul, and regenerate it with His own eternal life? This is truly a wonderful display of the glory of His grace; matter does not resist His power, the sinner does; sun, moon, stars, earth, and skies gave Him no opposition when He created them — but the world, the flesh, and the devil do their utmost to resist Him in His new creation; and if His glory is manifested in the natural creation, which never did or could resist His power, how much more in His new creation. It is in the conversion of sinners Christ is glorified, turning them "from darkness to light, and from the power of Satan unto God" (Acts 26:18, KJV).

MARCUS RAINSFORD, IN *OUR LORD PRAYS FOR HIS OWN*

ENTERING THE PRESENCE

*We all, with unveiled face, beholding the glory of the Lord, are being
transformed into the same image from one degree of glory to another.*

(2 CORINTHIANS 3:18)

The interior journey of the soul from the wilds of sin into the enjoyed
Presence of God is beautifully illustrated in the Old Testament tabernacle.
The returning sinner first entered the outer court where he offered a blood
sacrifice on the brazen altar and washed himself in the laver that stood
near it. Then through a veil he passed into the holy place where no natural
light could come, but the golden candlestick which spoke of Jesus the Light
of the World threw its soft glow over all. There also was the shewbread to
tell of Jesus, the Bread of Life, and the altar of incense, a figure of unceasing
prayer.

Though the worshipper had enjoyed so much, still he had not yet
entered the Presence of God. Another veil separated from the Holy of
Holies where above the mercy seat dwelt the very God Himself in awful
and glorious manifestation. While the tabernacle stood, only the high
priest could enter there, and that but once a year, with blood which he
offered for his sins and the sins of the people. It was this last veil which was
rent when our Lord gave up the ghost on Calvary, and the sacred writer
explains that this rending of the veil opened the way for every worshipper
in the world to come by the new and living way straight into the divine
Presence.

Everything in the New Testament accords with this Old Testament
picture. Ransomed men need no longer pause in fear to enter the Holy of
Holies. God wills that we should push on into his presence and live our
whole life there. This is to be known to us in conscious experience. It is
more than a doctrine to be held, it is a life to be enjoyed every moment of
every day.

A. W. TOZER, IN *THE PURSUIT OF GOD*

INVEST TIME IN PRAYER

The reward for humility and fear of the Lord is riches and honor and life.
(PROVERBS 22:4)

The rewards of prayer are indescribably greater than any dividends paid by an earthly investment. The Bible teaches that a sinner who denies God is of all men a fool. I sometimes wonder if some Christians also should not be classified as fools. A Christian whose prayers are almost always self-centered "give me" prayers, who can spend an hour a day reading the newspaper and not even five minutes reading God's Word, who averages more than two hours a day watching television and cannot give one hour to prayer — surely he or she is, of all people, most foolish!

That person knows the power of God, the glory of heaven, the length of eternity, the certainty of God's rewards for all we do for Him, yet places most of the emphasis of life on that which will have no value in eternity. That person wastes earthly time and loses eternal rewards. Much of the life investment of such a Christian will be burned up in a flash at the fiery judgment seat of Christ before which we all shall stand (Romans 14:10-12; 2 Corinthians 5:9-10). This Christian, though saved, is building on Christ with the materials of wood, hay, and straw (1 Corinthians 3:11-15). Paul says that individual will "suffer loss."

Prayer is your opportunity to transmute minutes and hours into eternal reward, earthly time into eternal blessings. Prayer is one of the most godly activities anyone on earth can engage in, perhaps the most godly of all. It is the constant activity of God the Son and God the Spirit. Surely time invested in partnership with Jesus and the Holy Spirit is the wisest use of time you can ever make.

WESLEY DUEWEL, IN *TOUCH THE WORLD THROUGH PRAYER*

WHERE ARE THE NINE?

Oh give thanks to the Lord, for he is good;
for his steadfast love endures forever!

(PSALM 118:1)

It is easy for us to think that God is so great and so highly exalted that it does not make any difference to Him whether we give thanks or not. It is, therefore, necessary for us to catch a vision of the heart of God. His is the most tender and most sensitive heart of all. Nothing is so small or inconsequential that it does not register an impression with Him, whether it be good or bad. Jesus says that He will not forget even a cup of cold water if it is given in grateful love of Him.

How much Jesus appreciates gratitude can be seen very clearly from the account of the ten lepers whom He restored to health (Luke 17:11-19). He had healed them by sending them to the priests to receive the certificate required by law to show that they had been cleansed of their leprosy. While they were on their way to the priests, they were suddenly cleansed, every one of them. Nine of them continued on their way to receive their certificates. And in so doing they were in reality complying with Jesus' words, "Go and show yourselves unto the priests."

One of them, however, turned about, went back to Jesus joyfully speaking His praises, fell down on his face before the Lord and returned thanks to Him.

Notice the impression it made upon Jesus. Listen to the tone in His query, "Were not the ten cleansed? But where are the nine? Were there none found that returned to give glory to God, save this stranger?"

Here we are also told by Jesus Himself that to give thanks means to give glory to God. This explains why it is so blessed to give thanks. Even though our efforts to thank God in prayer are weak, nevertheless we find that when we succeed in truly thanking God, we feel good at heart. The reason is that we have been created to give glory to God, now and forevermore.

OLE HALLESBY, IN *PRAYER*

THE DEBT YOU CANNOT PAY

You, who were dead in your trespasses and the uncircumcision of your flesh, God made alive together with him, having forgiven us all our trespasses, by canceling the record of debt that stood against us with its legal demands. This he set aside, nailing it to the cross.

(COLOSSIANS 2:13-14)

What is the nature of our debt to God? He has commanded us to be holy, even as He is holy; to be perfect, even as He is perfect. With one sin, one transgression, we fall hopelessly short of that standard, placing ourselves in a position of indebtedness we can never escape. You've heard the adage that everyone's entitled to one mistake. That's part of the entitlement mentality of the United States, where we think we have rights to all kinds of things. In truth, the only thing we're entitled to is everlasting punishment in hell. God never said we are entitled to one mistake, and if we were, how long ago did each of us use up our one mistake? We have sinned against God and His perfect holiness multiple times since we got out of our beds this morning. How great is our debt after a lifetime of sin?

The apostle Paul, speaking about unbelievers, said, "In accordance with your hardness and your impenitent heart, you are treasuring up for yourself wrath in the day of wrath and revelation of the righteous judgment of God" (Romans 2:5, NKJV). Paul was saying that every day a person lingers in this life without falling on his knees and asking God to forgive his debts, he is increasing that "treasury of wrath." The problem is that the mercy and patience of God convince impenitent people that since they've escaped the judgment of God so far, they will escape it forever. These are the kinds of people who say to me again and again, "It's nice that you're a Christian, but I don't feel the need for Jesus." When I hear that, I want to weep. I want to say: "Don't you understand that what you need more desperately than anything in the world is Jesus? Don't you feel the weight of that debt that you can't possibly pay?" I want to help them see that when that debt is called, it will be the most severe crisis they have ever faced, for they won't be able to pay.

Jesus loved people enough to warn them and to teach them to beg God for forgiveness.

R. C. SPROUL, IN *THE PRAYER OF THE LORD*

On His Knees at Last

Continue steadfastly in prayer, being watchful in it with thanksgiving.

(COLOSSIANS 4:2)

I heard of a wife in England who had an unconverted husband. She resolved that she would pray every day for twelve months for his conversion. Every day at twelve o'clock she went to her room alone and cried to God. Her husband would not allow her to speak to him on the subject; but she could speak to God on his behalf. It may be that you have a friend who does not wish to be spoken with about his salvation; you can do as this woman did — go and pray to God about it. The twelve months passed away, and there was no sign of his yielding. She resolved to pray for six months longer; so every day she went alone and prayed for the conversion of her husband. The six months passed, and still there was no sign, no answer. The question arose in her mind, could she give him up? "No," she said; "I will pray for him as long as God gives me breath." That very day, when he came home to dinner, instead of going into the dining room he went upstairs. She waited, and waited, and waited; but he did not come down to dinner. Finally she went to his room, and found him on his knees crying to God to have mercy upon him. God convicted him of sin; he not only became a Christian, but the Word of God had free course, and was glorified in him. God used him mightily. That was God answering the prayers of this Christian wife; she knocked, and knocked, till the answer came.

D. L. MOODY, IN *PREVAILING PRAYER*

TAKE YOUR TROUBLES TO GOD

In the world you will have tribulation. But take heart;
I have overcome the world.

(JOHN 16:33)

When we survey all the sources from which trouble comes, it all resolves itself into two invaluable truths: First, that our troubles at last are of the Lord. They come with His consent. He is in all of them, and is interested in us when they press and bruise us. And secondly, that our troubles, no matter what the cause, whether of ourselves, or men or devils, or even God Himself, we are warranted in taking them to God in prayer, in praying over them, and in seeking to get the greatest spiritual benefits out of them.

Prayer in the time of trouble tends to bring the spirit into perfect subjection to the will of God, to cause the will to be conformed to God's will, and saves from all murmurings over our lot, and delivers from everything like a rebellious heart or a spirit critical of the Lord. Prayer sanctifies trouble to our highest good. Prayer so prepares the heart that it softens under the disciplining hand of God. Prayer places us where God can bring to us the greatest good, spiritual and eternal. Prayer allows God to freely work with us and in us in the day of trouble. Prayer removes everything in the way of trouble, bringing to us the sweetest, the highest and greatest good. Prayer permits God's servant, trouble, to accomplish its mission in us, with us and for us.

The end of trouble is always good in the mind of God. If trouble fails in its mission, it is either because of prayerlessness or unbelief, or both. Being in harmony with God in the dispensations of His providence, always makes trouble a blessing. The good or evil of trouble is always determined by the spirit in which it is received.

E. M. BOUNDS, IN *THE ESSENTIALS OF PRAYER*

Unforgiveness Leads to Prayerlessness

Love your enemies, do good to those who hate you,
bless those who curse you, pray for those who abuse you.

(Luke 6:27-28)

We cannot live long in this world without coming across injustice, chronic lack of fairness. Many of us accept such sin with reasonable equanimity, reasoning that it is, after all, a fallen world. But when the injustice and unfairness is directed against us, our reaction may be much less philosophical. Then we may nurture a spirit of revenge, or a least of bitterness, malice, and gossip. Such sins in turn assure that our prayers are never more than formulaic; eventually such sin may lead to chronic prayerlessness. "How can I be expected to pray when I have suffered so much?"

What is God's response? At the end of Matthew's version of the Lord's Prayer, Jesus adds, "For if you forgive men when they sin against you, your heavenly Father will also forgive you. But if you do not forgive men their sins, your Father will not forgive your sins" (Matthew 6:14-15, NIV). The idea is not that by our act of forgiving others we somehow earn the Father's forgiveness, but that by our forgiving others we demonstrate we really want the Father's forgiveness. By such an approach to God we signal that our repentance is genuine and our contrition real. Christians must never approach God as if they enjoy an inside track with the Almighty that allows them to experience his blessings but not his discipline. Precisely because we know ourselves to be sinners in need of forgiveness, recognize that to ask for forgiveness while we withhold it from others is nothing more than cheap religious cant.

In fact, we can look at this matter of bitterness not only from the vantage of those who need forgiveness but from the vantage of those who have received it. The Bible tells us, "Get rid of all bitterness, rage, and anger, brawling and slander, along with every form of malice. Be kind and compassionate to one another, forgiving each other, just as in Christ God forgave you" (Ephesians 4:31-32, NIV). In the light of matchless forgiveness we have received because Christ bore our guilt, what conceivable right do we have to withhold forgiveness?

D. A. Carson, in *A Call to Spiritual Reformation*

So do not fear, for I am with you;
do not be dismayed, for I am your God.

Thank You

for requesting this resource

It's our hope that our resources bless you and draw you closer to God each day. We are so thankful for your prayers and support of our ministry.

Your friends at
Our Daily Bread Ministries

U5080

PRAY STRETCHED-OUT-ED-LY

Peter was kept in prison, but earnest
prayer for him was made to God by the church.
(ACTS 12:5)

God cannot always grant our petitions immediately. Sometimes we are not fitted to receive the gift. Sometimes He says "No" in order to give us something far better. Think, too, of the days when St. Peter was in prison. If your boy was unjustly imprisoned, expecting death at any moment, would you — could you — be content to pray just once, a "business-like" prayer: "O God, deliver my boy from the hands of these men"? Would you not be very much in prayer and very much in earnest?

This is how the Church prayed for St. Peter. "Long and fervent prayer was offered to God by the Church on his behalf" (Acts 12:5, WNT). Bible students will have noticed that the *American Standard Version* rendering, "without ceasing," reads "earnestly" in the *Revised Standard Version*. Dr. Torrey points out that neither translation gives the full force of the Greek. The word means literally "stretched-out-ed-ly." It represents the soul on the stretch of earnest and intense desire. Intense prayer was made for St. Peter. The very same word is used of our Lord in Gethsemane: "And being in an agony he prayed more earnestly, and his sweat became as it were great drops of blood falling down upon the ground" (Luke 22:44, KJV).

Ah! there was earnestness, even agony in prayer. Now, what about our prayers? Are we called upon to agonize in prayer? Many of God's dear saints say "No!" They think such agonizing in us would reveal great want of faith. Yet most of the experiences which befell our Lord are to be ours. We have been crucified with Christ, and we are risen with Him. Shall there be, with us, no travailing for souls?

Come back to human experience. Can we refrain from agonizing in prayer over dearly beloved children who are living in sin? I question if any believer can have the burden of souls upon him — a passion for souls — and not agonize in prayer.

AN UNKNOWN CHRISTIAN, IN *THE KNEELING CHRISTIAN*

CLEANSED AND TRANSFORMED COMPLETELY

Behold, you delight in truth in the inward being,
and you teach me wisdom in the secret heart.

(PSALM 51:6)

The great mystic work of the Holy Ghost is in those dim regions of personality where we cannot go. If you want to know what those regions are like, read Psalm 139. The Psalmist implies, "Thou art the God of the early mornings, the God of the late-at-nights, the God of the mountain peaks, the God of the sea; but, my God, my soul has further horizons than the early mornings, deeper darkness than the nights of earth, higher peaks than any mountain, greater depths than any sea can know. My God, Thou art the God of these, be my God! I cannot reach to the heights or depths, there are motives I cannot touch, dreams I cannot fathom, God search me, winnow out my way."

When God gives His calm, do we realise the magnitude of sanctification through His omnipotent might? Do we believe that God can garrison our imaginations, can sanctify us far beyond where we can go? Have we realised that if we walk in the light, as God is in the light, the blood of Jesus Christ cleanses us from all sin? If that means cleansing from sin in conscious experience only, God Almighty have mercy on us! The man who has become obtuse through sin is unconscious of sin. Being cleansed by the blood of Jesus means cleansing to the very heights and depths of our spirit if we walk in the light as God is in the light. None of us soak sufficiently in the terrific God-like revelation of sanctification, and many a child of God would never have been led astray by the counterfeits of Satan if they had allowed their minds to be bent on that great conception of Paul's, "your whole spirit"—from the vague beginnings of personality known only to God, to the topmost reach, preserved entire, garrisoned by the God of peace.

OSWALD CHAMBERS, IN *IF YOU WILL ASK*

PRAYER AT WORK IN OTHERS

I have prayed for you that your faith may not fail.
And when you have turned again, strengthen your brothers.
(LUKE 22:32)

Did you ever think how our Lord Jesus Himself accomplished things by praying that even He could not accomplish in any other way? Take for example the case of Simon Peter. He was full of self-confidence and therefore was in imminent danger. Our Lord endeavored by His teachings and by His warnings to deliver Peter from his self-confidence. He told Peter definitely of his coming temptation and of his fall, but Peter, filled with self-confidence, replied: "If all shall be offended in thee, I will never be offended" (Matthew 26:33, KJV). And again, "I will lay down my life for thee" (John 13:37, KJV). Teaching failed, warning failed, and then our Lord took to prayer. He said, "Simon, Simon, behold, Satan asked to have you, that he might sift you as wheat; but I made supplication for thee, that thy faith fail not; and do thou when once thou has turned again, establish thy brethren" (Luke 22:31-32, KJV). Satan got what he asked. But all the time Satan sifted, our Lord Jesus prayed, and Simon was perfectly safe even though he was in Satan's sieve; and all Satan succeeded in doing with him was to sift some of the chaff out of him, and Simon came out of Satan's sieve purer wheat than he ever was before.

It was our Lord's prayer for him that transformed the Simon who denied his Lord three times, and denied Him with oaths and curses, in the courtyard of Annas and Caiaphas, into Peter, *the man of rock*, who faced the very court that sentenced Jesus to death.

Prayer will reach down, down, down into the deepest depths of sin and ruin and take hold of men and women who seem lost beyond all possibility or hope of redemption and lift them up, up, up until they are fit for a place beside the Son of God.

R. A. TORREY, IN *THE POWER OF PRAYER*

Faith Must Be Tried

The testing of your faith produces steadfastness. And let steadfastness have its full effect, that you may be perfect and complete, lacking in nothing.

(James 1:3-4)

If we, indeed, desire our faith to be strengthened, we should not shrink from opportunities where our faith may be tried, and, therefore, through the trial, be strengthened. In our natural state we dislike dealing with God alone. Through our natural alienation from God we shrink from Him, and from eternal realities. This cleaves to us more or less, even after our regeneration. Hence it is, that more or less, even as believers, we have the same shrinking from standing with God alone — from depending upon Him alone — from looking to Him alone — and yet this is the very position in which we ought to be, if we wish our faith to be strengthened. The more I am in a position to be tried in faith with reference to my body, my family, my service for the Lord, my business, etc., the more shall I have opportunity of seeing God's help and deliverance; and every fresh instance, in which He helps and delivers me, will tend towards the increase of my faith. On this account, therefore, the believer should not shrink from situations, positions, circumstances, in which his faith may be tried; but should cheerfully embrace them as opportunities where he may see the hand of God stretched out on his behalf, to help and deliver him, and whereby he may thus have his faith strengthened. We should let God work for us, when the hour of the trial of our faith comes, and do not work a deliverance of our own. Wherever God has given faith, it is given, among other reasons, for the very purpose of being tried. Yea, however weak our faith may be, God will try it; only with this restriction, that as in every way, He leads on gently, gradually, patiently, so also with reference to the trial of our faith.

George Müller, in *Answers to Prayer*

PRAY ACCORDING TO SCRIPTURE

O God of Israel, let your word be confirmed,
which you have spoken to your servant David my father.
(1 KINGS 8:26)

It is prayer when it is within the compass of God's Word and it is blasphemy, or at best vain babbling, when the petition is contrary to the Book. David, therefore, while in prayer, kept his eye on the Word of God: "I am laid low in the dust; renew my life according to your word" (Psalm 119:25, NIV). And indeed the Holy Spirit does not immediately enliven the heart of the praying Christian without the Word, but only by, with, and through the Word. The Holy Spirit brings the Word to the heart, and opens the Word to us so that we are provoked to go to the Lord in prayer and tell him how it is with us. We also are led to argue and plead according to the Word.

This was the experience of Daniel, that mighty prophet of God. Daniel, understanding that the captivity of the children of Israel was near to an end, made his prayer to God (Daniel 9:1-3). So I say as the Spirit is the helper and the governor of the soul, when you pray according to the will of God, you should be guided by and pray according to the Word of God and his promises.

Hence our Lord Jesus Christ did come to a stop in his prayer for deliverance, although his life lay at stake for it. He said that he could pray to his Father, and that the Father could give him twelve legions of angels; but how then would the Scriptures be fulfilled (see Matthew 26:53-54)? Were there but a word for it in the Scriptures, then Jesus would have soon been out of the hands of his enemies and would have soon been helped by the angels. But the Scriptures would not warrant this type of praying because they had indicated that he was to die for our sins. True prayer, then, must be according to the Word of God and his promises.

JOHN BUNYAN, IN *PILGRIM'S PRAYER BOOK*

TRUE FELLOWSHIP THROUGH PRAYER

Complete my joy by being of the same mind,
having the same love, being in full accord and of one mind.

(PHILIPPIANS 2:2)

The worst sin is prayerlessness. Overt sin, or crime, or the glaring inconsistencies which often surprise us in Christian people are the effect of this, or its punishment. We are left by God for lack of seeking Him. The history of the saints shows often that their lapses were the fruit and nemesis of slackness or neglect in prayer. Their life, at seasons, also tended to become inhuman by their spiritual solitude. They left men, and were left by men, because they did not in their contemplation find God; they found but the thought or the atmosphere of God. Only living prayer keeps loneliness humane. It is the great producer of sympathy. Trusting the God of Christ, and transacting with Him, we come into tune with men. Our egoism retires before the coming of God, and into the clearance there comes with our Father our brother. We realize man as he is in God and for God, his Lover. When God fills our heart He makes more room for man than the humanist heart can find. Prayer is an act, indeed *the* act, of fellowship. We cannot truly pray even for ourselves without passing beyond ourselves and our individual experience. If we should begin with these the nature of prayer carries us beyond them, both to God and to man. Even private prayer is common prayer — the more so, possibly, as it retires from being public prayer.

Not to want to pray, then, is the sin behind sin. And it ends in not being able to pray. That is its punishment — spiritual dumbness, or at least aphasia, and starvation. We do not take our spiritual food, and so we falter, dwindle, and die. "In the sweat of your brow ye shall eat your bread." That has been said to be true both of physical and spiritual labour. It is true both of the life of bread and of the bread of life.

P. T. FORSYTH, IN *THE SOUL OF PRAYER*

LOOKING TO GOD IN FAITH

Those who look to him are radiant, and their faces shall never be ashamed.

(PSALM 34:5)

The recognition of who God is is a lifetime process. Nor does it end with our earthly life. "This is eternal life, that they know thee the only true God, and Jesus Christ whom thou hast sent." The process of knowing him modifies the quality of our lives. It is a continual fulfillment and a continual attraction. "Let us know," the prophet Hosea wrote; "let us press on to know the Lord; his going forth is sure as the dawn; he will come to us as the showers, as the spring rains that water the earth."

The quality of our lives is transformed not only by our initial response to Christ but also by the daily answer of faith to whatever a day holds. If we have, perhaps through some small incident, come to a new knowledge of our sin, we then recognize him as Savior. In our sorrow we learn that he is the Comforter. In perplexity he shows himself as our Counselor. Our weakness gives us occasion to call on him as the Mighty God, Strength, Fortress, Deliverer, and Refuge.

The prophet Habakkuk saw the God of Israel not as a tender Shepherd but as a raging Giant: "Thou didst bestride the earth in fury, thou didst trample the nations in anger. Thou wentest forth for the salvation of thy people, for the salvation of thy anointed. Thou didst crush the head of the wicked, laying him bare from thigh to neck. . . . Thou didst trample the sea with thy horses." This representation of power is followed by Habakkuk's testimony of faith: "God, the Lord, is my strength; he makes my feet like hind's feet, he makes me tread upon my high places." That fearful deity, that Giant who roars forth for the deliverance of his people, is the God who makes us able to walk where it seems there can be no walking.

ELISABETH ELLIOT, IN *GOD'S GUIDANCE*

PURE GOLD

You have been grieved by various trials, so that the tested genuineness of your faith — more precious than gold that perishes though it is tested by fire — may be found to result in praise and glory and honor at the revelation of Jesus Christ.

(1 PETER 1:6-7)

God purifies the soul by His Wisdom, as refiners do metals in the furnace. Gold cannot be purified but by fire, which gradually separates from and consumes all that is earthy and heterogeneous: it must be melted and dissolved, and all impure mixtures taken away by casting it again and again into the furnace; thus it is refined from all internal corruption, and even exalted to a state incapable of further purification.

The goldsmith now no longer discovers any adulterate mixture; its purity is perfect, its simplicity complete. The fire no longer touches it; and were it to remain an age in the furnace its purity would not be increased nor its substance diminished.

Further, the goldsmith never mingles together the pure and the impure gold, lest the dross of the one should corrupt the other; before they can be united they must first be equally refined; he therefore plunges the impure metal into the furnace till all its dross is purged away and it becomes fully prepared for incorporation and union with the pure gold.

This is what St. Paul means, when he declares, that "the fire shall try every man's work of what sort it is" (1 Corinthians 3:13). He adds, "If any man's work be burnt, he shall suffer loss; yet he himself shall be saved, yet so as by fire" (verse 15). He here intimates that there is a species of works so degraded by impure mixtures that though the mercy of God accepts them, yet they must pass through the fire to be purged from the contamination of Self.

JEANNE GUYON, IN *A SHORT AND EASY METHOD OF PRAYER*

Keep Asking

Beloved, if our heart does not condemn us, we have confidence
before God; and whatever we ask we receive from him, because
we keep his commandments and do what pleases him.

(1 John 3:21-22)

To have our prayers answered, we must keep on asking, keep on seeking, keep on knocking, for this is the continuing action of the Greek verb in Matthew 7:7-8 and also of Luke 11:5-13, the story of the man who wanted bread at midnight, and kept asking until he got it. Don't give up. Don't be discouraged, keep asking. Why? The only reason I know is that prayer changes me because I am in His presence, and then I either begin to change my requests, or I become able to cope with my circumstances which may or may not change.

So there are no unanswered prayers in one sense, because if we ask for what we want in His Name, and we are living in Him, and we keep on asking, the answer will come. It may be yes or it may be no, but God sends it, and it will be the best.

We do understand, however, that some answers to our prayers are delayed, and this is because God answers them in His way instead of in ours.

But hindered or obstructed prayer is a very real thing and is not the same as unanswered prayer. When we are not living in Christ or letting Him live in us, there is always a reason. John, in his first epistle (1 John 3:21-22) tells us that our guilty hearts will keep us from coming boldly to God. And our guilty hearts will keep us from asking and receiving what God wants to give us.

This explains how unforgiveness or resentment toward another can hinder our prayers. Unforgiveness on our part automatically creates guilt in us. If I cannot love my brother whom I can see, how can I love God whom I cannot see (1 John 4:20)? Love of God and love of our fellow man go together. *I will love God only as much as I love the person I dislike the most.*

Rosalind Rinker, in *Prayer: Conversing with God*

Coming to the Cure

You say, I am rich, I have prospered, and I need nothing,
not realizing that you are wretched, pitiable, poor, blind, and naked.
(Revelation 3:17)

At the moment of my conversion, or when I first exercised faith, I saw my ruinous error. I found that faith consisted not in an intellectual conviction that the things affirmed in the Bible about Christ are true, *but in the heart's trust in the person of Christ.* I learned that God's testimony concerning Christ was designed to lead me to trust Christ, to confide in His person as my Savior, and that to stop short in merely believing about Christ was a fatal mistake that inevitably left me in my sins. It was as if I were sick almost unto death and someone should recommend to me a physician who was surely able and willing to save my life, and I should listen to the testimony concerning him until fully convinced that he was both able and willing to save my life, and then should be told to believe in him and my life was secure. Now, if I understood this to mean nothing more than to accept the testimony with the firmest conviction, I should reply: "I do believe in him with an undoubting faith. I believe every word you have told me regarding him." But if I stopped here I should, of course, lose my life. In addition to this firm intellectual conviction of his willingness and ability it would be essential to apply to him, to come to him, to trust his person, to accept his treatment. When I had intellectually accepted the testimony concerning him with an unwavering belief, the next and the indispensable thing would be a voluntary act of trust or confidence in his person, a committal of my life to him and his sovereign treatment in the cure of my disease.

Charles Finney, in *Power from on High*

Intercession with God

He is able to save to the uttermost those who draw near to God through him, since he always lives to make intercession for them.

(Hebrews 7:25)

God has chosen to accomplish many of His sovereign purposes with our help. Paul repeatedly reminds us that God has appointed us to a sacred partnership for the purpose of gospel advance. Paul emphasizes our sacred responsibility to work with God. Every form of obedience to God is urgent, but there are many situations in which we are limited. We may not be at the place of need. We may lack special skills or training. But we can always work with God through prayer.

Through prayer we can cooperate with Him in any place, at any time, and for any kind of need. We are created to pray. We were saved by God's grace to enter into a ministry of prayer. We have the liberty, the right, and the position of official children of God, called to work with God, chosen for this specific purpose.

Furthermore, God said in Exodus 19:5-6, "Although the whole earth is mine, you will be for me a kingdom of priests." Isaiah prophesied, "You will be called priests of the Lord" (Isaiah 61:6, NIV). Why did Jesus make us "priests" to serve God (Revelation 1:6)? Why are all Christians called "a holy priesthood" (1 Peter 2:5, NIV), "a royal priesthood" (verse 9)?

Obviously, part of God's purpose in designating us priests is that we are to worship and praise Him. But it includes far more than that. We are to be a "*royal* priesthood." Christ today rules the world through prayer. We are to share this rule by intercession for others even as Christ constantly intercedes for them (Hebrews 7:25). We have been given official access to heaven's throne room so that we may join our intercession with that of Christ!

If Christ intercedes, why is our intercession necessary? What could our puny prayers possibly add to His powerful intercession? God has been pleased to build into His eternal plan that we His children join with Christ in His intercessory role and rule today.

Wesley Duewel, in *Touch the World Through Prayer*

BE THOU MY VISION

> *Let us run with endurance the race that is set before us,*
> *looking to Jesus, the founder and perfecter of our faith.*
> (HEBREWS 12:1-2)

While we are looking at God we do not see ourselves — blessed riddance. The man who has struggled to purify himself and has had nothing but repeated failures will experience real relief when he stops tinkering with his soul and looks away to the perfect One. While he looks at Christ the very things he has so long been trying to do will be getting done within him. It will be God working in him to will and to do.

Faith is not in itself a meritorious act; the merit is in the One toward Whom it is directed. Faith is a redirecting of our sight, a getting out of the focus of our own vision and getting God into focus. Sin has twisted our vision inward and made it self-regarding. Unbelief has put self where God should be, and is perilously close to the sin of Lucifer who said, "I will set my throne above the throne of God." Faith looks out instead of in and the whole life falls into line.

All this may seem too simple. But we have no apology to make. To those who would seek to climb into heaven after help or descend into hell God says, "The word is nigh thee, even in the word of faith." The word induces us to lift up our eyes unto the Lord and the blessed work of faith begins.

When we lift our inward eyes to gaze upon God we are sure to meet friendly eyes gazing back at us, for it is written that the eyes of the Lord run to and fro throughout all the earth. The sweet language of experience is "Thou God seest me." When the eyes of the soul looking out meet the eyes of God looking in, heaven has begun right here on this earth.

A. W. TOZER, IN *THE PURSUIT OF GOD*

PRAY UNDISTRACTEDLY

Set your minds on things that are above, not on things that are on earth.
(COLOSSIANS 3:2)

As you kneel to speak with your Lord, it seems as though everything you have to do appears vividly before your mind's eye. You see especially how much there is to do, and how urgent it is that it be done, at least some of it. As these thoughts occur, you become more and more restless. You try to keep your thoughts collected and to speak with God, but you succeed only for a moment now and then.

Your thoughts flit back and forth between God and the many pressing duties which await you. Your prayer hour becomes really the most restless hour of the day. Your mind is literally torn to shreds. Joy, peace and rest are as far from you as the east is from the west. And the longer you prolong the session, the more you feel that you are neglecting your work. To put it plainly, you feel as though the time you are spending on your knees is just that much time wasted. Then you stop praying. The enemy has won a very neat victory!

Here is where we are face to face with enemies who are vastly superior to us. And they will defeat us every time, without any doubt whatsoever, if we do not learn the true secret of prayer: to open our hearts to Jesus and give Him access to our needs.

He has power also over my restless thoughts. He can rebuke the storm in my soul and still its raging waters.

There is a profound and beautiful passage bearing on this in Philippians 4:7, "And the peace of God, which passeth all understanding, shall guard your hearts and your thoughts in Christ Jesus." The only way in which we can gather and keep collected our distracted minds and our roaming thoughts is to center them about Jesus Christ. By that I mean that we should let Christ lay hold of, attract, captivate and gather about Himself all our interests.

OLE HALLESBY, IN *PRAYER*

PRAYER AND HOLINESS

As he who called you is holy, you also be holy in all your conduct, since it is written, "You shall be holy, for I am holy."

(1 PETER 1:15-16)

As holiness of heart and of life is thoroughly impregnated with prayer, so consecration and prayer are closely allied in personal religion. It takes prayer to bring one into such a consecrated life of holiness to the Lord, and it takes prayer to maintain such a life. Without much prayer, such a life of holiness will break down. Holy people are praying people. Holiness of heart and life puts people to praying. Consecration puts people to praying in earnest.

Prayerless people are strangers to anything like holiness of heart and cleanness of heart. Those who are unfamiliar with the closet are not at all interested in consecration and holiness. Holiness thrives in the place of secret prayer. The environments of the closet of prayer are favourable to its being and its culture. In the closet holiness is found. Consecration brings one into holiness of heart, and prayer stands hard by when it is done.

The spirit of consecration is the spirit of prayer. The law of consecration is the law of prayer. Both laws work in perfect harmony without the slightest jar or discord. Consecration is the practical expression of true prayer. People who are consecrated are known by their praying habits. Consecration thus expresses itself in prayer. He who is not interested in prayer has no interest in consecration. Prayer creates an interest in consecration, then prayer brings one into a state of heart where consecration is a subject of delight, bringing joy of heart, satisfaction of soul, contentment of spirit. The consecrated soul is the happiest soul. There is no friction whatever between him who is fully given over to God and God's will. There is perfect harmony between the will of such a man and God, and His will. And the two wills being in perfect accord, this brings rest of soul, absence of friction, and the presence of perfect peace.

E. M. BOUNDS, IN *THE ESSENTIALS OF PRAYER*

ENCOURAGEMENT FROM THE WORD

Faith comes from hearing, and hearing through the word of Christ.

(Romans 10:17)

Through reading of the word of God, and especially through meditation on the word of God, the believer becomes more and more acquainted with the nature and character of God, and thus sees more and more, besides his holiness and justice, what a kind, loving, gracious, merciful, mighty, wise, and faithful being he is, and, therefore, in poverty, affliction of body, bereavement in his family, difficulty in his service, want of a situation or employment, he will repose upon the ability of God to help him, because he has not only learned from his word that he is of almighty power and infinite wisdom, but he has also seen instance upon instance in the Holy Scriptures in which his almighty power and infinite wisdom have been actually exercised in helping and delivering his people; and he will repose upon the willingness of God to help him, because he has not only learned from the Scriptures what a kind, good, merciful, gracious, and faithful being God is, but because he has also seen in the word of God, how in a great variety of instances he has proved himself to be so. And the consideration of this, if God has become known to us through prayer and meditation on his own word, will lead us, in general at least, with a measure of confidence to rely upon him: and thus the reading of the word of God, together with meditation on it, will be one especial means to strengthen our faith.

GEORGE MÜLLER, IN *ANSWERS TO PRAYER*

God in All the Business of Life

Whether you eat or drink, or whatever you do, do all to the glory of God.

(1 Corinthians 10:31)

Brother Lawrence told me that the foundation of the spiritual life in him had been a high notion and esteem of God in faith; which when he had once well conceived, he had no other care at first, but faithfully to reject every other thought, that he might perform all his actions for the love of God. That when sometimes he had not thought of God for a good while, he did not disquiet himself for it; but after having acknowledged his wretchedness to God, he returned to Him with so much the greater trust in Him, by how much he found himself more wretched to have forgot Him.

That the trust we put in God honors Him much, and draws down great graces.

That it was impossible, not only that God should deceive, but also that He should long let a soul suffer which is perfectly resigned to Him, and resolved to endure everything for His sake.

That he had so often experienced the ready succors of Divine Grace upon all occasions, that from the same experience, when he had business to do, he did not think of it beforehand; but when it was time to do it, he found in God, as in a clear mirror, all that was fit for him to do. That of late he had acted thus, without anticipating care; but before the experience above mentioned, he had used it in his affairs.

When outward business diverted him a little from the thought of God, a fresh remembrance coming from God invested his soul, and so inflamed and transported him that it was difficult for him to contain himself.

That he was more united to God in his outward employments, than when he left them for devotion in retirement.

Brother Lawrence, in *The Practice of the Presence of God*

STRIVING IN PRAYER

You, beloved, building yourselves up in your most holy faith and
praying in the Holy Spirit, keep yourselves in the love of God.
(JUDE 20-21)

Instinctive as is our dependence upon God, no duty is more earnestly impressed upon us in Scripture than the duty of continual communion with Him. The main reason for this unceasing insistence is *the arduousness of prayer*. In its nature it is a laborious undertaking, and in our endeavor to maintain the spirit of prayer we are called to wrestle against principalities and powers of darkness. The arduousness of prayer lies in the fact that we are spiritually hindered: there is "the noise of archers in the places of drawing water." St. Paul assures us that we shall have to maintain our prayer energy "against the rulers of the darkness of this world, against spiritual wickedness in high places." Dr. Andrew Bonar used to say that, as the King of Syria commanded his captains to fight neither with small nor great, but only with the King of Israel, so the prince of the power of the air seems to bend all the force of his attack against the spirit of prayer. If he should prove victorious there, he has won the day.

Sometimes we are conscious of a satanic impulse directed immediately against the life of prayer in our souls. Sometimes we are led into "dry" and wilderness-experiences, and the face of God grows dark above us. Sometimes, when we strive most earnestly to bring every thought and imagination under obedience to Christ, we seem to be given over to disorder and unrest. Sometimes the inbred slothfulness of our nature lends itself to the evil one as an instrument by which he may turn our minds back from the exercise of prayer. Because of all these things, therefore, we must be diligent and resolved, watching as a sentry who remembers that the lives of men are lying at the hazard of his wakefulness, resourcefulness, and courage. "And what I say unto you," said the Lord to His disciples, "I say unto all, Watch!"

DAVID MCINTYRE, IN *THE HIDDEN LIFE OF PRAYER*

HIS UNCHANGING LOVE

In this the love of God was made manifest among us, that God sent
his only Son into the world, so that we might live through him.

(1 JOHN 4:9)

The love of God in itself is the eternal purpose and act of his will. This is no more changeable than God himself: if it were, no flesh could be saved; but it changeth not, and we are not consumed. What then? Loves he his people in their sinning? Yes; his people, not their sinning. Alters he not his love towards them? Not the *purpose* of his will, but the *dispensations* of his grace. He *rebukes* them, he *chastens* them, he *hides* his face from them, he *smites* them, he *fills* them with a sense of his indignation; but woe, woe would it be to us, should he change in his love, or take away his kindness from us! Those very things which seem to be demonstrations of the change of his affections towards his, do as clearly proceed from love as those which seem to be the most genuine issues thereof. "But will not this encourage to sin?" He never tasted of the love of God that can seriously make this objection. The *doctrine* of grace may be turned into wantonness; the *principle* cannot. I shall not wrong the saints by giving another answer to this objection: Detestation of sin in any may well consist with the acceptation of their persons, and their designation to life eternal.

But now our love to God is ebbing and flowing, waning and increasing. We lose our first love, and we grow again in love; scarce a day at a stand. What poor creatures are we! How unlike the Lord and his love! When ever was the time, where ever was the place, that our love was one day equal towards God?

JOHN OWEN, IN *OF COMMUNION WITH GOD THE FATHER, SON AND HOLY GHOST*

STUDY TO PRAY

Keep back your servant also from presumptuous sins; let them not have dominion over me! Then I shall be blameless, and innocent of great transgression. Let the words of my mouth and the meditation of my heart be acceptable in your sight, O LORD, my rock and my redeemer.

(PSALM 19:13-14)

David was so troubled sometimes that he could not speak: "I remembered you, O God, and I groaned; I mused, and my spirit grew faint. You kept my eyes from closing; I was too troubled to speak" (Psalm 77:3-4, NIV). But this might comfort all sorrowful hearts, that though you cannot through the anguish of your spirit speak much, yet the Holy Spirit stirs up in your heart groans and sights so much more effectively. When your mouth is hindered, yet your spirit is not hindered. Moses made heaven ring with his prayers in his deepest agony of heart, yet not one word came from his mouth.

If you would more fully express yourself before the Lord, study; first, study your sinful condition; second, study God's promises; and third, study the loving heart of Christ. You may discern the heart of Christ by pondering his condescension and shed blood. You may think of the mercy he has shown to sinners in former times. Then in your prayer plead your own sinfulness and unworthiness, bemoan your condition before God, plead Christ's shed blood, plead for the mercy that he extended to other sinners, plead with his many rich promises of grace, and let these things be upon your heart in your meditations.

Yet, let me counsel you. Take heed that you do not content yourself with mere words. Take heed lest you think that God looks only upon your words. Whether your words be few or many, let your heart and soul go with them to God. You shall seek and find him when you seek him with your whole heart and being: "For I know the plans I have for you," declares the Lord, "plans to prosper you and not to harm you, plans to give you hope and future. Then you will call upon me and come and pray to me, and I will listen to you. You will seek me and find me when you seek me with all your heart" (Jeremiah 29:11-13, NIV).

JOHN BUNYAN, IN *PILGRIM'S PRAYER BOOK*

Citizens of the Kingdom

> *Let us be grateful for receiving a kingdom that cannot be*
> *shaken, and thus let us offer to God acceptable worship,*
> *with reverence and awe, for our God is a consuming fire.*
> (Hebrews 12:28-29)

When Jesus told His followers to pray, "Your kingdom come," He was making them participants in His own mission to spread the reign of God on this planet so that it might reflect the way God's reign is established in heaven to this day. When He came, Jesus inaugurated God's kingdom. He didn't consummate it, but He started it. And when He ascended into heaven, He went there for His coronation, for His investiture as the King of kings and Lord of lords.

So Jesus' kingship is not something that remains in the future. Christ is King right this minute. He is in the seat of the highest cosmic authority. All authority in heaven and on earth has been given to God's anointed Son (Matthew 28:18). Unless and until the name of God is regarded as holy, His kingdom will not and cannot come to this world. But we who do regard His name as holy then have the responsibility to make the kingdom of God manifest.

John Calvin said it is the task of the church to make the invisible kingdom visible. We do that by living in such a way that we bear witness to the reality of the kingship of Christ in our jobs, our families, our schools, and even our checkbooks, because God in Christ is King over every one of these spheres of life. The only way the kingdom of God is going to be manifest in this world before Christ comes is if we manifest it by the way we live as citizens of heaven and subjects of the King.

R. C. Sproul, in *The Prayer of the Lord*

JUST ASK!

Whatever you ask in prayer, you will receive, if you have faith.
(MATTHEW 21:22)

How often we go to prayer meetings without really asking for anything! Our prayers go all round the world, without anything definite being asked for. We do not expect anything. Many people would be greatly surprised if God did answer their prayers. I remember hearing of a very eloquent man who was leading a meeting in prayer. There was not a single definite petition in the whole. A poor, earnest woman shouted out: "Ask Him somethin', man." How often you hear what is called prayer without any asking! "Ask, and ye shall receive."

I believe if we put all the stumbling blocks out of the way, God will answer our petitions. If we put away sin and come into His presence with pure hands, as He has commanded us to come, our prayers will have power with Him. In Luke's Gospel we have as a grand supplement to the Disciples' Prayer, "Ask and it shall be given you; seek, and ye shall find; knock, and it shall be opened unto you." Some people think God does not like to be troubled with our constant coming and asking. The only way to trouble God is not to come at all. He encourages us to come to Him repeatedly, and press our claims.

Our Lord teaches us here that we are not only to ask, but we are to wait for the answer; if it does not come, we must seek to find out the reason. I believe that we get a good many blessings just by asking; others we do not get, because there may be something in our life that needs to be brought to light.

D. L. MOODY, IN *PREVAILING PRAYER*

A Test for Faith

I will meditate on your precepts and fix my eyes on your ways.

(Psalm 119:15)

My fellow classmates had been preparing for this exam for months. As it is a comprehensive exam covering everything we studied for four years it was quite challenging. As I prayed about the situation, the Lord brought Isaiah 43:2 to my attention, "When you pass through the waters, I will be with you; and when you pass through the rivers, they will not sweep over you. When you walk through the fire, you will not be burned; the flames will not set you ablaze." As I studied this passage and meditated on it, the Lord spoke to me from it, encouraging me that He would carry me through the exam. It was because of His leading that we were staying in West Lafayette and by His grace, the job was already provided. Now what was needed was a license, and He would provide that as well. In prayer, I asked the Lord to help me "pass through" the exam, to bring to my mind what I had previously studied, and to help me testify to His goodness in the midst of it.

On the day of the exam, everyone was very tense. The written exam, though long, was finished with time to spare. But now came ten stations where we were to be questioned by examiners or asked to perform some skill. Each time as I waited in line to be examined, I would silently review Isaiah 43:2, reminding the Lord of His promise to be with me and to help me pass through these troubled "waters" and "flames" of testing. I watched as my classmates exited the exam rooms with pale faces, and some in tears. My anxiety level was rising with each moment. But to my great delight, my examiners were very friendly and the questions they asked were things that I knew. Several were believers and asked me questions about the ministry that I had started in the veterinary school for students and the faculty. I passed the exam and went home rejoicing once again that the Lord had proved Himself faithful.

Thomas R. Yeakley, in *Praying Over God's Promises*

Praying Is Service

What thanksgiving can we return to God for you, for all the
joy that we feel for your sake before our God, as we pray
most earnestly night and day that we may see you face to face
and supply what is lacking in your faith? Now may our God
and Father himself, and our Lord Jesus, direct our way to you.

(1 Thessalonians 3:9-11)

Paul does not simply pray that the faith of the Thessalonians might be strengthened, leaving the means unstated; rather, he prays that he himself might do it. He is like Isaiah after his vision of the Almighty: "Here am I. Send me!" (Isaiah 6:8, NIV).

For Paul, prayer is not a substitute for Christian service; it is part of it. And apparently he cannot long pray for believers without longing to serve them himself. This was true even with respect to believers Paul had not yet met but for whom he nevertheless prayed (Romans 1:11).

This mindset ought to be in all of us. Relatively few of us are called to cross-cultural ministry; few of us will be able to minister personally to all the believers for whom we ought to be praying. But the mindset of service should belong to all of us, especially when we pray. Certainly all of us can be doing something. As we pray for believers we know, we may be able to write an encouraging letter, befriend a teenager who is beginning to go adrift, take a fatherless child fishing, start an inductive Bible study for young Christians in the subdivision, quietly administer a humble word of admonition to someone who is doing damage with unguarded speech, send some free books to a pastor in the so-called Third World. These things ought not to be done without prayer; conversely, praying with Paul will impel us to do some of these things, and more. Both in our praying and in our immediate, personal service, we will strive to make up what is lacking in someone's faith.

D. A. Carson, in *A Call to Spiritual Reformation*

BEWARE OF FAINTNESS

> *Moses' hands grew weary, so they took a stone and put it under him, and he sat on it, while Aaron and Hur held up his hands, one on one side, and the other on the other side. So his hands were steady until the going down of the sun.*
>
> (EXODUS 17:12)

So mighty was the prayer of Moses, that all depended upon it. The petitions of Moses discomfited the enemy more than the fighting of Joshua. Yet both were needed. So, in the soul's conflict, force and fervour, decision and devotion, valour and vehemence, must join their forces, and all will be well. You must wrestle with your sin, but the major part of the wrestling must be done alone in private with God. Prayer, like Moses', holds up the token of the covenant before the Lord. The rod was the emblem of God's working with Moses, the symbol of God's government in Israel. Learn, O pleading saint, to hold up the promise and the oath of God before him. The Lord cannot deny his own declarations. Hold up the rod of promise, and have what you will.

Moses grew weary, and then his friends assisted him. When at any time your prayer flags, let faith support one hand, and let holy hope uplift the other, and prayer seating itself upon the stone of Israel, the rock of our salvation, will persevere and prevail. Beware of faintness in devotion; if Moses felt it, who can escape? It is far easier to fight with sin in public, than to pray against it in private. It is remarked that Joshua never grew weary in the fighting, but Moses did grow weary in the praying; the more spiritual an exercise, the more difficult it is for flesh and blood to maintain it. Let us cry, then, for special strength, and may the Spirit of God, who helpeth our infirmities, as he allowed help to Moses, enable us like him to continue with our hands steady "until the going down of the sun;" till the evening of life is over; till we shall come to the rising of a better sun in the land where prayer is swallowed up in praise.

CHARLES SPURGEON, IN *MORNING BY MORNING*

Time to Pray

I wait for your salvation, O Lord.

(Genesis 49:18)

There are few instant answers in matters of spiritual importance. God has performed miracles in response to urgent, on-the-spot pleas, of course, but many spiritual battles take much time. You cannot earn God's blessing by virtue of the amount of time you pray. Yet no one ever became mighty in prayer without spending much time praying.

Listen to Isaiah's testimony: "For Zion's sake I will not keep silent, for Jerusalem's sake I will not remain quiet, till her righteousness shines out like the dawn, her salvation like a blazing torch. . . . I have posted watchmen on your walls, O Jerusalem; they will never be silent day or night. You who call on the Lord, give yourselves no rest, and give him no rest till he establishes Jerusalem and makes her the praise of the earth" (Isaiah 62:1, 6-7, NIV).

Nehemiah prevailed day and night in prayer: "Let your ear be attentive and your eyes open to hear the prayer your servant is praying before you day and night for your servants, the people of Israel" (Nehemiah 1:6, NIV).

Daniel prayed regularly at stated times, but spent as much as three weeks in prevailing at a time of special need (Daniel 10:2). Paul prayed night and day, prevailing for his converts and his new churches (1 Thessalonians 3:10). We will do no less when we learn how to prevail.

Jesus often prayed all night. "One of those days Jesus went out to a mountainside to pray, and spent the night praying to God" (Luke 6:12, NIV). "Will not God bring about justice for his chosen ones, who cry out to him day and night? Will he keep putting them off? I tell you, he will see that they get justice, and quickly. However, when the Son of Man comes, will he find faith on the earth?" (18:7-8, NIV).

Wesley Duewel, in *Touch the World Through Prayer*

Your Circumstances in the Hand of God

The LORD is in his holy temple; the LORD's throne is in heaven;
his eyes see, his eyelids test the children of man.

(Psalm 11:4)

The circumstances of a saint's life are ordained by God, and not by happy-go-lucky chance. There is no such thing as chance in the life of a saint, and we shall find that God by His providence brings our bodies into circumstances that we cannot understand a bit, but the Spirit of God understands; He is bringing us into places and among people and under conditions in order that the intercession of the Holy Spirit in us may take a particular line. Do not, therefore, suddenly put your hand in front of the circumstances and say, "No, I am going to be my own amateur providence, I am going to watch this and guard that." "Trust in the Lord with all thine heart; and lean not unto thine own understanding." The point to remember is that all our circumstances are in the hand of God. The Spirit imparts a solemnity to our circumstances and makes us understand something of the travail of Jesus Christ. It is not that we enter into the agony of intercession, it is that we utilize the common-sense circumstances into which God has put us, and the common-sense people He has put us among by His providence, to present their cases before Him and give the Holy Spirit a chance to intercede for them. We bring the particular people and circumstances before God's throne, and the Holy Spirit in us has a chance to intercede for them. That is how God is going to sweep the whole world by His saints. Are we making the Holy Spirit's work difficult by being indefinite, or by trying to do His work for Him? We must do the human side of the intercession, and the human side is the circumstances we are in, the people we are in contact with. We have to use our common sense in keeping our conscious life and our circumstances as a shrine of the Holy Ghost, and as we bring the different ones before God, the Holy Spirit presents them before the Throne all the time.

Oswald Chambers, in *If You Will Ask*

GOD LOVES A MAN AFLAME

Zeal for your house has consumed me.
(PSALM 69:9)

It is not every kind of praying that works wonders. It takes a man of prayer to pray as Elijah and George Müller prayed. It is the energized prayer of the righteous man that is of great force. The widow knew that Elijah was a man of God when he prayed her boy back to life (1 Kings 17:24). It is always the crowning proof and the ultimate test. Nothing would turn the nation back to God so surely and so quickly as a church that prayed and prevailed. The world will never believe in a religion in which there is no supernatural power. A rationalized faith, a socialized church, and a moralized gospel may gain applause, but they awaken no conviction and win no converts.

There is passion in the praying that prevails. Elijah was a man of passions all compact. There was passion in all he did. All there was of him went into everything he did. God loves a man aflame. The lukewarm he cannot abide. He never keeps hot hearts waiting. "When ye shall search for me with all your heart . . . I will be found of you" (Jeremiah 29:13-14, KJV). When he prayed, he prayed in his prayer. Is there not much praying in which there is no prayer? The praying man was in his petition. Listen to his praying in the death chamber. Watch him on Carmel. Hear him plead the honor of God and cry unto the Lord for the affliction of the people. It is always the same: Abraham pleading for Sodom, Jacob wrestling in the stillness of the night, Moses standing in the breach, Hannah intoxicated with sorrow, David heartbroken with remorse and grief—Jesus in a sweat of blood. Add to the list from the records of the church, personal observation and experience, and always there is the cost of passion unto blood. It prevails. It turns ordinary mortals into men of power. It brings power. It brings fire. It brings rain. It brings life. It brings God. There is no power like that of prevailing prayer.

SAMUEL CHADWICK, IN *THE PATH OF PRAYER*

SURRENDERED TO GOD AT THE SEA

The earth shall be full of the knowledge of
the LORD as the waters cover the sea.

(ISAIAH 11:9)

So Hudson Taylor was alone on the sands of Brighton beach that Sunday morning when he met the crisis of his life. He had gone to church with others, but the sight of multitudes rejoicing in the blessings of salvation was more than he could bear. "I have other sheep that are not of this sheep pen" — the lost and perishing in China, for whose souls no man cared — "I must bring them also" (John 10:16). The tones of the master's voice and the love in the master's face pleaded silently. Taylor knew that God was speaking. He knew that if he yielded to his will and prayed under his guidance, God would give evangelists for inland China. He had no anxiety about their support. He who called and sent them would not fail to give them daily bread. But what if they should fail? Hudson Taylor was not facing an unknown situation. He was familiar with conditions in China, the real temptations they would meet, and the real enemy entrenched on his own ground. What if the fellow workers could not manage under the weight and they laid the blame on him? "It was just a bringing in of self through unbelief; the devil getting one to feel," he recalled, "that while prayer and faith would bring one into the fix, one would have to get out of it as best one might. And I did not see that the power that would give the men and the means would be sufficient to keep them also, even in the far interior of China." Meanwhile, a million a month were dying in that great, waiting land — dying without God. This burned into Taylor's soul. He had to make a decision and he knew it, because he could no longer endure the conflict. It was comparatively easy to pray for workers, but would he, could he, accept the burden of leadership? "In great spiritual agony, I wandered out on the sands alone. And there the Lord conquered my unbelief, and I surrendered myself to God for this service."

DR. AND MRS. HOWARD TAYLOR, IN *HUDSON TAYLOR'S SPIRITUAL SECRET*

TEACH ME TO PRAY

> *Jesus was praying in a certain place, and when he finished,*
> *one of his disciples said to him, "Lord, teach us to pray."*
> (LUKE 11:1)

Blessed Lord! You live eternally to pray, and can teach me, too, to live eternally to pray. You want me to share Your glory in heaven by sharing this unceasing prayer with You, standing as a priest in the presence of my God.

Lord Jesus! Enroll my name among those who confess that they don't know how to pray as they should, and who especially ask you for a course of teaching in prayer. Lord! Teach me to be patient in Your school, so that You will have time to train me. I am ignorant of the wonderful privilege and power of prayer, of the need for the Holy Spirit to be the spirit of prayer. Lead me to forget my thoughts of what I think I know, and make me kneel before You in true teachableness and poverty of spirit.

Fill me, Lord, with the confidence that with You for my Teacher, I will learn to pray. Then I will not be afraid, because my Teacher prays continuously to the Father, and by His prayer rules the destinies of His Church and the world. Unfold for me everything I need to know about the mysteries of the prayer-world. When there is something I may not know, teach me to be strong in faith, giving glory to God.

Blessed Lord! I know that You won't put that student to shame who trusts You. And, with Your grace, that student won't shame You, either. Amen.

ANDREW MURRAY, IN *WITH CHRIST IN THE SCHOOL OF PRAYER*

THE JOINT WORK

Faith is the assurance of things hoped for, the conviction of things not seen.
(HEBREWS 11:1)

We must not encourage in ourselves or others any tendency to work up a subjective state which, if we succeeded, we should describe as "faith," with the idea that this will somehow insure the granting of our prayer. We have probably all done this as children. But the state of mind which desperate desire working on a strong imagination can manufacture is not faith in the Christian sense. It is a feat of psychological gymnastics.

It seems to me we must conclude that such promises about prayer with faith refer to a degree or kind of faith which most believers never experience. A far inferior degree is, I hope, acceptable to God. Even the kind that says "Help thou my unbelief" may make way for a miracle. Again, the absence of such faith as insures the granting of the prayer is not even necessarily a sin; for Our Lord had no such assurance when He prayed in Gethsemane.

How or why does such faith occur sometimes, but not always? We, or I, can only guess. My own idea is that it occurs only when the one who prays does so as God's fellow-worker, demanding what is needed for the joint work.

It would be idle presumption for us who are habitually suitors and do not often rise to the level of servants, to imagine that we shall have any assurance which is not an illusion — or correct only by accident — about the event of our prayers. Our struggle is — isn't it? — to achieve and retain faith on a lower level. To believe that, whether He can grant them or not, God will listen to our prayers, will take them into account. Even to go on believing that there is a Listener at all. For as the situation grows more desperate, the grisly fears intrude. Are we only talking to ourselves in an empty universe? The silence is so emphatic. And we have prayed so much already.

C. S. LEWIS, IN *LETTERS TO MALCOLM*

WITH CHRIST

The life I now live in the flesh I live by faith in the
Son of God, who loved me and gave himself for me.
(GALATIANS 2:20)

The heaven of the child of God, the man whose soul is born from above, the man whose heart is instructed with divine truth, is described in one sentence: "To be with Christ, and to behold his glory." The great Apostle of the Gentiles was caught up to the third heaven, and saw what he could not describe; but you will observe that ever after his thought of heaven was this — *to be with Christ*: "I have a desire to depart, and to be with Christ, which is far better" (Philippians 1:23, KJV). Our blessed Lord Jesus Himself seems to have had no more perfect way of expressing what heaven was than, "where I am." When He would cheer the forgiven, and dying thief, and awaken the note of triumph in his heart, the promise was, "Today shalt thou be *with me* in paradise" (Luke 23:43, KJV).

If this is the heaven we anticipate, what is our meetness for it? Would we be happy there? It is a very solemn question, and one we ought in all sincerity to ask ourselves. Suppose the God of all grace were this moment to introduce us to where Christ is, that we might be with Christ, beholding His glory, would serving Him be our happiness? Would the employments of heaven suit our taste? Alas, the employments which most suit the tastes of many have no place there; where Jesus is all in all. Do we care for His society here? The long days of eternity in heaven are spent in praise, ascribing "Blessing and honour . . . and power . . . to him that sitteth upon the throne" (Revelation 5:13, KJV), magnifying His holy name, and with unspeakable adoration worshiping Him that "made us kings and priests to God and to his Father" (Revelation 1:6, KJV).

Do we enjoy this sort of thing now? If not, what reason have we for supposing we would enjoy it there? "Ye must be born again" (John 3:3, KJV) if the heaven Jesus speaks of — as being with Him, and beholding His glory — is to be our consummated happiness.

MARCUS RAINSFORD, IN *OUR LORD PRAYS FOR HIS OWN*

What We Really Need

*I have learned in whatever situation I am to be content. I know how to be
brought low, and I know how to abound. In any and every circumstance, I
have learned the secret of facing plenty and hunger, abundance and need.*

(Philippians 4:11-12)

Can the guidance of God actually take a person into a wilderness? It took
Israel into one. It took them to Marah, where the water was too bitter to
drink. It took Jesus into forty days and nights of harrowing temptation by
his archenemy.

How such leading could possibly be the will of God for anyone, even
for Jesus, would be a total mystery if we were to try to understand the case
in isolation from others. But it was, according to Jesus' own words later,
"for their sakes" that he sanctified himself.

We are not Jesus. We are not even a part of that huge mob of Israelites
that moved through the deserts toward the promised land. But what we
learn from them is meant for us, because we are going in the same direction—Home. I have found it true that obedience may lead me not to the
fulfillment of my own ideals of spirituality but to very unexpected situations, very "unspiritual" situations, in my view, that are meant to teach me
to be meek and lowly in heart. If I want to learn of him, this is what I am
going to have to learn. And there, to my surprise, I find rest. I find the
chance to recall once more (how many, many times I have to review my
lessons) that if I am serious about my primary aim, I may be led elsewhere
than my lesser aims would take me, for I do not know what I really need.
God sees the "one thing needful," and he alone knows the path that will
take me there.

Elisabeth Elliot, in *God's Guidance*

GOD'S GREAT DESIRE

As one trespass led to condemnation for all men, so one act
of righteousness leads to justification and life for all men.
(ROMANS 5:18)

God's heart is set on the salvation of all men. This concerns God. He has declared this in the death of His Son by an unspeakable voice, and every movement on earth for this end pleases God. And so He declares that our prayers for the salvation of all men are well pleasing in His sight. The sublime and holy inspiration of pleasing God should ever move us to prayer for all men. God eyes the closet, and nothing we can do pleases Him better than our large-hearted, ardent praying for all men. It is the embodiment and test of our devotion to God's will and of our sympathetic loyalty to God.

In 1 Timothy 2:13 the apostle Paul does not descend to a low plane, but presses the necessity of prayer by the most forceful facts. Jesus Christ, a man, the God-man, the highest illustration of manhood, is the Mediator between God and man. Jesus Christ, this Divine man, died for all men. His life is but an intercession for all men. His death is but a prayer for all men. On earth, Jesus Christ knew no higher law, no holier business, no diviner life, than to plead for men. In Heaven He knows no more royal estate, no higher theme, than to intercede for men. On earth He lived and prayed and died for men. His life, His death and His exaltation in Heaven all plead for men.

Is there any work, higher work for the disciple to do than His Lord did? Is there any loftier employment, more honourable, more divine, than to pray for men? To take their woes, their sins, and their perils before God; to be one with Christ? To break the thrall which binds them, the hell which holds them and lift them to immortality and eternal life?

E. M. BOUNDS, IN *THE REALITY OF PRAYER*

FOR CHRIST'S SAKE

It was to show his righteousness at the present time, so that he might be just and the justifier of the one who has faith in Jesus.
(ROMANS 3:26)

There is a sense in which some things are done only "for Christ's sake" — because of His atoning death. Those who do not believe in the atoning death of Christ cannot pray "in His name." They may use the words, but without effect. For we are "justified by His blood" (Romans 5:9), and "we have redemption through His blood, even the forgiveness of sins" (Ephesians 1:7; Colossians 1:14). Let us illustrate this point by an experience which happened quite early in Mr. Moody's ministry. The wife of an infidel judge — a man of great intellectual gifts — begged Mr. Moody to speak to her husband. Moody, however, hesitated at arguing with such a man, and told him so quite frankly. "But," he added, "if ever you are converted will you promise to let me know?" The judge laughed cynically, and replied, "Oh, yes, I'll let you know quick enough if I am ever converted!" Moody went his way, relying upon prayer. That judge was converted, and within a year. He kept his promise and told Moody just how it came about. "I began to grow very uneasy and miserable one night when my wife was at a prayer meeting. I went to bed before she came home. I could not sleep all that night. Getting up early the next morning, I told my wife I should not need any breakfast, and went off to my office. Telling the clerks they could take a holiday, I shut myself up in my private room. But I became more and more wretched. Finally, I fell on my knees and asked God to forgive me my sins, but I would not say 'for Jesus' sake,' for I was Unitarian, and I did not believe in the atonement. In an agony of mind I kept praying, 'O God, forgive me my sins,' but no answer came. At last, in desperation, I cried, 'O God, for Christ's sake forgive my sins.' Then I found peace at once."

AN UNKNOWN CHRISTIAN, IN *THE KNEELING CHRISTIAN*

The Age of Complexity

Know that the LORD, he is God! It is he who made us,
and we are his; we are his people, and the sheep of his pasture.
(PSALM 100:3)

Every age has its own characteristics. Right now we are in an age of religious complexity. The simplicity which is in Christ is rarely found among us. In its stead are programs, methods, organizations and a world of nervous activities which occupy time and attention but can never satisfy the longing of the heart. The shallowness of our inner experience, the hollowness of our worship, and the servile imitation of the world which marks our promotional methods all testify that we, in this day, know God only imperfectly, and the peace of God scarcely at all.

If we would find God amid all the religious externals we must first determine to find Him, and then proceed in the way of simplicity. Now as always God discovers Himself to "babes" and hides Himself in thick darkness from the wise and the prudent. We must simplify our approach to Him. We must strip down to essentials (and they will be found to be blessedly few). We must put away all effort to impress, and come with the guileless candor of childhood. If we do this, without doubt God will quickly respond.

When religion has said its last word, there is little that we need other than God Himself. The evil habit of seeking God-and effectively prevents us from finding God in full revelation. In the "and" lies our great woe. If we omit the "and," we shall soon find God, and in Him we shall find that for which we have all our lives been secretly longing.

We need not fear that in seeking God only we may narrow our lives or restrict the motions of our expanding hearts. The opposite is true. We can well afford to make God our All, to concentrate, to sacrifice the many for the One.

A. W. TOZER, IN *THE PURSUIT OF GOD*

Deliver Us from Idols

> *Put to death therefore what is earthly in you: sexual immorality,*
> *impurity, passion, evil desire, and covetousness, which is*
> *idolatry. On account of these the wrath of God is coming.*
>
> (Colossians 3:5-6)

The elders of Israel had come to Ezekiel to pray for them; it was seemingly a day of great triumph for Ezekiel. For a long time, for days and months, perhaps for years, Ezekiel had been longing for the time when the elders of Israel would come to their senses and come to him and ask him to pray for them, and the time seemed to have come. With a glad heart Ezekiel was about to go to God in prayer for them, and for the people. But God suddenly stops him, He says, "Ezekiel, do not pray for these men, *they have set up their idols in their heart,* and put the stumbling-block of their iniquity before their face: *should I be inquired of at all by them?*" Here we are clearly told that *idols in the heart make it impossible for God to attend to our prayers.*

In Japan, China, and India and other non-Christian lands they set up their idols in their temples and in their homes, but the Jews, and we Christians also today, set up our idols in our hearts. There are no hideous images on our mantels or in other places in our homes, but there are idols in the hearts of many of us which make it just as impossible for God to answer our prayers as if we had the most hideous images in our homes or in our churches.

What is an idol? An idol is anything that a man puts before God. Oh, if you covet power in prayer, go alone with God and let Him search you; ask Him to show you if there is any idol in your heart, and when He shows it to you do away with it today.

> The dearest idol I have known,
> Whate'er that idol be,
> Help me to tear it from its throne
> And worship only Thee.

R. A. Torrey, in *The Power of Prayer*

A Holy Watchfulness

*Understand this, that in the last days there will come
times of difficulty. For people will be lovers of self.*
(2 Timothy 3:1-2)

The real hindrance to intercessory prayer is, of course, the fact that we live and move in such a narrow circle about ourselves and those nearest us that the Spirit of prayer cannot create in our hearts true zeal for others. The result is that our labors in intercessory prayer often become very circumscribed, and in many cases utterly impossible.

However, the Spirit can convict us also of this sin. And as soon as I acknowledge my selfish indifference, He will save me from it. The Spirit of prayer will then fill my empty heart with holy zeal and remind me of one thing after another for which I should make my poor and humble intercessions!

But if we wish to preserve this Spirit, we must be willing to struggle.

Jesus said, "Watch and pray, that ye enter not into temptation: the spirit is indeed willing, but the flesh is weak." Without holy watchfulness we will soon lose our zeal for others. All watchful intercessors know themselves and therefore keep close to Him who daily fills their hearts with loving zeal for others. It was love of ease which overcame the apostles that night. And it is love of ease which overcomes us. We begin by praying for something for ourselves or for others, and all goes well until our love of ease begins to make itself felt.

Then we get tired of praying, and little by little our praying ceases. How many such humiliating experiences can we not all look back upon!

That is why Jesus admonishes us to watch and pray.

OLE HALLESBY, IN *PRAYER*

PRAYING SCRIPTURE

I keep your precepts and testimonies, for all my ways are before you.

(PSALM 119:168)

Throughout the book of Nehemiah he prays eleven times. He never mentions the wall in his prayers. Nehemiah's main concern is not a wall around Jerusalem but that the people will be brought back together. That is why he reminds God of what He said to Moses. Was Nehemiah's prayer answered?

Yes, a large number of Israelites came back and were united in Jerusalem. The fulfillment started with a man bringing God's Word in prayer to God.

Daniel's great prayer of intercession is quoted in Daniel 9. Why did he pray as he did? Daniel tells us why in verse 2: "In the first year of his reign, I, Daniel, understood from the Scriptures, according to the word of the Lord given to Jeremiah the prophet, that the desolation of Jerusalem would last seventy years." Daniel knew his prayer would have to be answered because he was responding to the very words of God. His prayer was one of great humility. We do not threaten God with His Word, but we humbly ask Him to carry out that which He Himself has spoken.

Allow God to initiate the conversation. The most straightforward way to do this is to have a Bible-reading program where each day you ask God to speak to you through His Word. As you are prayerfully reading, mark those things that stand out to you. Then go back and talk to God about those thoughts He has spoken. In such a conversation with God, you might ask Him questions, or make statements of agreement with Him. In this process, you may be led to confess something for you or someone else. Or, you may be led to offer praise to God from your heart of thanksgiving. The better you know the Scriptures, the deeper the conversation will go.

LEE BRASE, IN *PRAYING FROM GOD'S HEART*

Pray with Emotion

You shall love the Lord your God with all your heart
and with all your soul and with all your might.
(Deuteronomy 6:5)

O, the heat, strength, life, vigor, and affection that are in right prayer! "As the deer pants for streams of water, so my soul pants for you, O God" (Psalm 42:1, niv). "How I long for your precepts! Renew my life in your righteousness" (119:40, niv). "I long for your salvation, O Lord, and your law is my delight" (verse 174, niv). "My soul yearns, even faints for the courts of the Lord; my heart and my flesh cry out for the living God" (84:2, niv). Oh, what affection — passion, emotion — there must be in prayer! It is similar with Daniel: "O Lord, listen! O Lord, forgive! O Lord, hear and act! For your sake, O my God, do not delay, because your city and your people bear your Name" (Daniel 9:19, niv). Every syllable carries a mighty intensity and urgency in it. This is called the fervent, or the working prayer, by the Apostle James. And so again it is reported of Jesus, "And being in anguish, he prayed more earnestly, and his sweat was like drops of blood falling to the ground" (Luke 22:44, niv). Jesus had his emotions more and more drawn out after God's helping hand.

But far away from the Bible's example are most people when they pray! Prayer with earnestness and urgency is genuine *prayer* in God's account. Alas, the greatest number of people are not conscious at all of the duty of prayer. And as for those who are, it is to be feared that many of them are very great strangers to sincere, sensible, and affectionate — emotional — pouring out of their hearts or souls to God. Too many content themselves with a little lip-service and bodily exercise, mumbling over a few imaginary prayers. When the emotions are involved in such urgency that the soul will waste itself rather than go without the good desired, there is communion and solace with Christ. And hence it is that the saints have spent their strength, and lost their lives, rather than go without the blessings God intended for them.

John Bunyan, in *Pilgrim's Prayer Book*

Talking with God Too

He is actually not far from each one of us,
for "In him we live and move and have our being."
(Acts 17:27-28)

One never-to-be-forgotten afternoon, we knelt in my little Chinese apartment to pray for several of these students by name, and for the class that evening.

As I remember, Mildred was praying for Ming-lee in a situation that concerned her sister-in-law. Now I'd forgotten to tell Mildred that Ming-lee had sent a little note to me that morning, and that the situation for which Mildred was praying had already been cleared up. Her prayer was already answered and she didn't know it!

Without thinking, I interrupted her prayer, and continued it as mine, "We thank Thee, Lord, that Thou hast already answered that prayer. Ming-lee has already been able to forgive her sister-in-law."

I stopped, startled by my own audacity at interrupting Mildred's prayer. There was a moment of silence, and then with great relief both of us sat back and laughed.

"Why, isn't that something!" said Mildred, meaning both the early answer to her prayer, *and* the natural, spontaneous way in which the news about Ming-lee had popped out.

We settled down to pray again, but with a sense of joy, of lightness, of the Lord's presence very near.

I prayed, "Lord, art Thou trying to teach us something through this incident? Should we give Thee more opportunity while we are praying to get Thy ideas through to us? Would that give the Holy Spirit more opportunity to guide us as we pray?"

Then with the freedom which comes with a new discovery, I stopped praying and spoke to Mildred.

"Do you know what? I believe the Lord taught us something just now! Instead of each of us making a prayer-speech to Him, let's talk things over with Him, back and forth, including Him in it, as we do when we have a conversation."

Rosalind Rinker, in *Prayer: Conversing with God*

PROMISES, FAITH, PATIENCE

> *To those who by patience in well-doing seek for glory*
> *and honor and immortality, he will give eternal life.*
> (ROMANS 2:7)

One of our family traditions for Thanksgiving is the making of fresh butter. We purchase the cream and place it in a jar with a tight lid and then begin to shake it vigorously. The shaking usually wears out several people as it seems that the cream will never turn to butter. And then suddenly, in the instant of one shake, what was cream is now a lump of delicious butter in the jar. Boy, does it taste good!

In Hebrews 6:12, the author writes, "We do not want you to become lazy, but to imitate those who through faith and patience inherit what has been promised." In this verse, we find the three elements necessary to seeing God answer our prayers as we pray over the promises in His Word. Walking by faith is like our making butter; it takes three elements: promises (cream), faith (jar), and patience (vigorous shaking over time). Though it seems to take forever, the end result is worth the effort!

All three elements are necessary for a balanced, dynamic walk with God. Promises and faith, without patience, will lead to compromise and our attempt to answer our own prayers. Promises and patience without faith will result in walking by sight, trusting in what is seen, and there will be lack of the dynamic in our lives. Faith and patience without the promises of God is presumption and can lead to great hardship and error. We must have all three: promises, faith, and patience, if we are to realize the blessings of God.

THOMAS R. YEAKLEY, IN *PRAYING OVER GOD'S PROMISES*

ACCEPTING HIS PERFECT WILL

> *Our great God and Savior Jesus Christ, who gave himself for us to*
> *redeem us from all lawlessness and to purify for himself a people*
> *for his own possession who are zealous for good works.*
> (TITUS 2:13-14)

There have been times, no doubt, in the life of each one of us, when the Spirit of God granted us enlargement of affection and desire. Our prayers soared through heavenly distances, and were about to fold their wings before the throne. When, suddenly, there was brought to our remembrance some duty unfulfilled, some harmful indulgence tolerated, some sin unrepented of. It was in order that we might forsake that which is evil, and follow that which is good, that the Holy Spirit granted us so abundantly His assistance in prayer. He designed that, in that good hour of His visitation, we should be enabled to purify ourselves from every stain, that henceforth we might live as His "purchased possession." And, perhaps, in such a case, we shunned the light, and turned back from the solicitation of God. Then darkness fell upon our face; the Divine Comforter, "who helpeth our infirmities," being grieved, withdrew. And to that hour, it may be, we can trace our present feebleness in the holy exercise of prayer. "If I regard iniquity in my heart, the Lord will not hear me" (Psalm 66:18, KJV). "He that turneth away his ear from hearing the law, even his prayer shall be abomination" (Proverbs 28:9, KJV). "Your iniquities have separated between you and your God, and your sins have hid His face from you, that He will not hear" (Isaiah 59:2, KJV). "And when ye spread forth your hands, I will hide Mine eyes from you; yea, when ye make many prayers, I will not hear" (Isaiah 1:15, KJV).

In wireless telegraphy if the receiver is not attuned to the transmitter, communication is impossible. In true prayer God and the suppliant must be "of one accord." Now, what God requires of those who seek His face is "a right intention" — a deliberate, a resigned, a joyful acceptance of His good and perfect will. All true prayer must fall back upon the great atonement, in which the Man of Sorrows translated into "active passion" the supplication of His agony, "O My Father, if it be possible, let this cup pass from Me; nevertheless, not as I will, but as Thou wilt" (Matthew 26:39, KJV). He has transmitted to us His own prayer: we offer it in the power of His sacrifice.

DAVID MCINTYRE, IN *THE HIDDEN LIFE OF PRAYER*

Too Dry to Pray

*Lift your drooping hands and strengthen your weak knees,
and make straight paths for your feet, so that what is
lame may not be put out of joint but rather be healed.*

(Hebrews 12:12-13)

Some of us may set aside a time to pray, only to find that when the time comes we feel too discouraged, or too unbelieving, or too empty — in short, too dry — to pray. We may then be tempted to put off praying until we feel like it a little more.

Whether or not we have given in to our feelings, all of us have sometimes felt that way. What triggers our discouragement or spiritual dryness may be one of a hundred things. . . .

Hidden behind this excuse are two presuppositions that are really quite monstrous. The first is that the acceptability of my approach to God in prayer ought to be tied to how I feel. But is God especially impressed with us when we feel joyful or carefree or well rested or pious? Is not the basis of any Christian's approach to the heavenly Father the sufficiency of Christ's mediating work on our behalf? Is not this a part of what we mean when we pray in "Jesus' name"? Are we not casting a terrible slur on the cross when we act as if the usefulness or acceptability of our prayers turns on whether we feel full or dry? True, when we feel empty and dispirited we may have to remind ourselves a little more forcefully that the sole reason why God accepts us is the grace that he has bestowed upon us in the person and work of his Son. But that is surely better than giving the impression that we are somehow more fit to pray when we feel good.

The second unacceptable presupposition behind this attitude is that my obligation to pray is somehow diminished when I do not feel like praying. This is to assign to my mood or my feelings the right to determine what I ought to do. And that, of course, is unbearably self-centered. It means that I, and I alone, determine what is my duty, my obligation. In short, it means that I am my own god. It is to act as if the Bible never says, "Be joyful in hope, patient in affliction, *faithful in prayer*" (Romans 12:12, NIV, emphasis added).

D. A. Carson, in *A Call to Spiritual Reformation*

WHAT GOD EXPECTS

God's kindness is meant to lead you to repentance.

(ROMANS 2:4)

Spend the remainder of your life only in worshipping God. He requires no great matters of us: a little remembrance of Him from time to time; a little adoration; sometimes to pray for His grace, sometimes to offer Him your sufferings, and sometimes to return Him thanks for the favors He has given you, and still gives you, in the midst of your troubles, and to console yourself with Him the oftenest you can. Lift up your heart to Him, sometimes even at your meals, and when you are in company; the least little remembrance will always be acceptable to Him. You need not cry very loud; He is nearer to us than we are aware of.

It is not necessary for being with God to be always at church. We may make an oratory of our heart wherein to retire from time to time to converse with Him in meekness, humility, and love. Everyone is capable of such familiar conversation with God, some more, some less: He knows what we can do. Let us begin then; perhaps He expects but one generous resolution on our part. Have courage. We have but little time to live; you are near sixty-four, and I am almost eighty. Let us live and die with God: sufferings will be sweet and pleasant to us, while we are with Him; and the greatest pleasures will be, without Him, a cruel punishment to us. Use yourself then by degrees thus to worship Him, to beg His grace, to offer Him your heart from time to time, in the midst of your business, even every moment if you can. Do not always scrupulously confine yourself to certain rules, or particular forms of devotion; but act with a general confidence in God, with love and humility.

BROTHER LAWRENCE, IN *THE PRACTICE OF THE PRESENCE OF GOD*

Faith, Grace, and Prayer

Let him ask in faith, with no doubting, for the one who doubts is like a wave of the sea that is driven and tossed by the wind.

(James 1:6)

Saint Paul expounds the law of faith in relation to grace, and Saint James expounds the same law in the realm of prayer. There is no controversy between them. Faith to both is more than an intellectual conviction, however sincere. It is a moral and spiritual attitude that commits the whole being to accepted and assured truth. Faith is more than belief. The devils believe and tremble, but they do not trust. Faith is trust. It is not an opinion, not a fiction, not a supposition. It is a faculty of vision, a process of verification, an assurance of knowledge, a logic of life. It demands an honest and impartial mind, a pure and disinterested motive, a loyal and steadfast obedience. This is the faith that works by law to the justification of the ungodly, to the sanctification of the unholy, and to the mighty power that prevails in prayer.

The teaching of James consists chiefly of amplifications and applications of our Lord's teaching in the Sermon on the Mount. He begins where our Lord began on the subject of prayer with the simple command to ask. "If any man lack, let him ask of God." The reach of the privilege of asking covers the whole man's need as well as his lack of wisdom. God gives to all that ask, liberally and without upbraiding, therefore "ask, and ye shall receive." There is no limit to the range of prayer. "Whatsoever" is promised to "whosoever," and the largest liberty is given to those who pray. "In nothing be anxious; but in everything by prayer and supplication with thanksgiving let your requests be made known unto God" (Philippians 4:6, KJV). "Ask, and ye shall receive" (John 16:24, KJV). Prayer is asking. "Your Father knoweth what things ye have need of, before ye ask him. After this manner therefore pray ye" (Matthew 6:8-9, KJV). Why pray if He knows? Because asking is something different from giving information. God waits to be asked, before He gives the gifts that supply man's deepest needs.

Samuel Chadwick, in *The Path of Prayer*

"PRAY FOR ME"

> *For the sake of Christ, then, I am content with weaknesses,*
> *insults, hardships, persecutions, and calamities.*
> *For when I am weak, then I am strong.*
>
> (2 CORINTHIANS 12:10)

At one of our missions in England the audience was extremely small, results seemed impossible, but I received a letter from a missionary that an American missionary, known as Praying Hyde, would be in the place to pray God's blessing down upon our work. Almost instantly the tide changed — the Hall was packed and my first invitation meant fifty for Jesus Christ. As we were leaving I said, "Mr. Hyde I want you to pray for me." He came to my room, turned the key in the door, dropped on his knees, waited five minutes without a single syllable coming from his lips. I could hear my own heart thumping and his beating. I felt the hot tears running down my face. I knew I was with God. Then with upturned face, down which tears streamed he said, "Oh! God!" Then for five minutes at least he was still again, and then when he knew that he was talking to God, his arm went round my shoulder, and then came up from the depth of his heart such petitions for men as I have never heard before, and I rose from my knees to know what *real* prayer was. We have gone round the world and back again, believing that prayer is mighty, and we believe it as never before.

Mr. Hyde remained in the place for a whole week and then crawled back to us. I saw at once that he had been wrestling with the Lord and had gained the victory, but it had almost been too much for his physical strength. The following day he could scarcely speak, he was so weak! But he smiled and whispered to me as I bent over him, "The burden was very heavy, but my dear Savior's burden for me took Him down to the grave."

CAPTAIN E. G. CARRÉ, IN *A PRESENT-DAY CHALLENGE TO PRAYER*

GOD'S WORKING THROUGH PRAYER

May the God of peace who brought again from the dead our Lord Jesus,
the great shepherd of the sheep, by the blood of the eternal covenant,
equip you with everything good that you may do his will.

(HEBREWS 13:20-21)

The rulers of the Church which the Scriptures reveal have had preeminence in prayer because God was with and in what they did, for prayer always carries us back to God. It recognizes God and brings God into the world to work and save and bless. The most efficient agents in disseminating the knowledge of God, in prosecuting His work upon the earth, and in standing as breakwater against the billows of evil, have been praying Church leaders. God depends upon them, employs them and blesses them.

Prayer cannot be retired as a secondary force in this world. To do so is to retire God from the movement. It is to make God secondary. The prayer ministry is an all-engaging force. It must be so, to be a force at all. Prayer is the sense of God's need and the call for God's help to supply that need. The estimate and place of prayer is the estimate and place of God. To give prayer the secondary place is to make God secondary in life's affairs. To substitute other forces for prayer, retires God and materializes the whole movement.

Prayer is an absolute necessity to the proper carrying on of God's work. God has made it so. This must have been the principal reason why in the early Church, when the complaint that the widows of certain believers had been neglected in the daily administration of the Church's benefactions, that the twelve called the disciples together, and told them to look out for seven men, "full of the Holy Ghost, and wisdom," who they would appoint over that benevolent work, adding this important statement, "But we will give ourselves continually to prayer and to the ministry of the Word." They surely realized that the success of the Word and the progress of the Church were dependent in a preeminent sense upon their "giving themselves to prayer." God could effectively work through them in proportion as they gave themselves fully to prayer.

E. M. BOUNDS, IN *PURPOSE IN PRAYER*

SAMUEL RUTHERFORD'S TRIALS

Count it all joy, my brothers, when you meet trials of various kinds,
for you know that the testing of your faith produces steadfastness.

(JAMES 1:2-3)

Rutherford beautifully writes, in reference to the value of sanctified trial, and the wisdom of submitting in it to God's will:

"Oh, what owe I to the file, to the hammer, to the furnace of my Lord Jesus, who hath now let me see how good the wheat of Christ is that goeth through His mill and His oven, to be made bread for His own table! Grace tried is better than grace; and it is more than grace; it is glory in its infancy. I now see that Godliness is more than the outside, and this world's passments and their bushings. Who knoweth the truth of grace without a trial? Oh, how little getteth Christ of us, but that which He winneth to speak so with much toil and pains! And how soon would faith freeze without a cross! How many dumb crosses have been laid upon my back, that had never a tongue to speak the sweetness of Christ, as this hath! When Christ blesseth His own crosses with a tongue, they breathe out Christ's love, wisdom, kindness, and care for us. Why should I start at the plough of my Lord, that maketh deep furrows on my soul? I know that He is no idle husbandman; He purposeth a crop. Oh that this white withered lea-ground were made fertile to bear a crop for Him, by whom it is so painfully drest, and that this fallow ground were broken up! Why was I (a fool!) grieved that He put His garland and His rose upon my head — the glory and honor of His faithful witnesses? I desire now to make no more pleas with Christ. Verily He hath not put me to a loss by what I suffer; He oweth me nothing; for in my bonds how sweet and comfortable have the thoughts of Him been to me, wherein I find a sufficient recompense of reward! How blind are my adversaries who sent me to a banqueting house, to a house of wine, to the lovely feasts of my lovely Lord Jesus, and not to a prison, or place of exile!"

D. L. MOODY, IN *PREVAILING PRAYER*

Prayer for Humility

This is the one to whom I will look: he who is humble
and contrite in spirit and trembles at my word.

(Isaiah 66:2)

Whole sections of our Protestantism have lost the virtue of humility or the understanding of it. It means for them no more than modesty or diffidence. It is the humility of weakness, not of power. To many useful, and even strong, people no experience seems to bring this subtle, spiritual intelligence, this finer discipline of the moral man. No rebukes, no rebuffs, no humiliations, no sorrows, seem to bring it to them.

We are not humble in God's sight, partly because in our prayer there is a point at which we cease to pray, where we do not turn everything out into God's light. It is because there is a chamber or two in our souls where we do not enter in and take God with us. We hurry Him by the door as we take Him along the corridors of our life to see our tidy places or our public rooms. We ask from our prayers too exclusively comfort, strength, enjoyment, or tenderness and graciousness, and not often enough humiliation and its fine strength. We want beautiful prayers, touching prayers, simple prayers, thoughtful prayers; prayers with a quaver or a tear in them, or prayers with delicacy and dignity in them. But searching prayer, humbling prayer, which is the prayer of the conscience, and not merely of the heart or taste; prayer which is bent on reality, and to win the new joy goes through new misery if need be — are such prayers as welcome and common as they should be? Too much of our prayer is apt to leave us with the self-complacency of the sympathetically incorrigible, of the benevolent and irremediable, of the breezy octogenarian, all of whose yesterdays look backward with a cheery and exasperating smile.

P. T. Forsyth, in *The Soul of Prayer*

To Value Christ

Come to him, a living stone rejected by men
but in the sight of God chosen and precious.
(1 Peter 2:4)

Christ and a dungeon, Christ and a cross, is infinitely sweeter than a crown, a sceptre without him, to their souls. So was it with Moses, Hebrews 11:26, "He esteemed the reproach of Christ greater riches than the treasures in Egypt." The reproach of Christ is the worst consequent that the wickedness of the world or the malice of Satan can bring upon the followers of him. The treasures of Egypt were in those days the greatest in the world; Moses despised the very best of the world, for the worst of the cross of Christ. Indeed, himself hath told believers, that if they love any thing better than him, father or mother, they are not worthy of him. A despising of all things for Christ is the very first lesson of the gospel. "Give away all, take up the cross and follow me," was the way whereby he tried his disciples of old; and if there be not the same mind and heart in us, we are none of his.

"My life is not dear, that I may perfect my course with joy, and the ministry I have received of the Lord Jesus;" (Acts 20:24) — "Let life and all go, so that I may serve him; and, when all is done, enjoy him, and be made like to him." It is known what is reported of Ignatius when he was led to martyrdom: "Let what will," said he, "come upon me, only so I may obtain Jesus Christ." Hence they of old rejoiced when whipped, scourged, put to shame, for his sake, Acts 5:41; Hebrews 11. All is welcome that comes from him, or for him. The lives they have to live, the death they have to die, is little, is light, upon the thoughts of him who is the stay of their lives and the end of their death. Were it not for the refreshment which daily they receive by thoughts of him, they could not live.

John Owen, in *Of Communion with God the Father, Son and Holy Ghost*

PRIESTS IN HIS PRESENCE

Let us draw near with a true heart in full assurance of faith,
with our hearts sprinkled clean from an evil conscience
and our bodies washed with pure water.

(HEBREWS 10:22)

When the believer, who had been content to think chiefly of the blood sprinkled on the mercy-seat as what he needs for pardon, is led to seek full priestly access to God, he feels the need of a fuller and more abiding experience of the power of the blood, as really sprinkling and cleansing the heart from an evil conscience, so that he has "no more conscience of sin" (Hebrews 10:2) as cleansing from all sin. And it is as he gets to enjoy this, that the consciousness is awakened of his wonderful right of most intimate access to God, and of the full assurance that his intercessions are acceptable.

And as the blood gives the right, the Spirit gives the power, and fits for believing intercession. He breathes into us the priestly spirit — burning love for God's honour and the saving of souls. He makes us so one with Jesus that prayer in His Name is a reality. He strengthens us to believing, importunate prayer. The more the Christian is truly filled with the Spirit of Christ, the more spontaneous will be his giving himself up to the life of priestly intercession. Beloved fellow-Christians! God needs, greatly needs, priests who can draw near to Him, who live in His presence, and by their intercession draw down the blessings of His grace on others. And the world needs, greatly needs, priests who will bear the burden of the perishing ones, and intercede on their behalf.

Are you willing to offer yourself for this holy work? You know the surrender it demands — nothing less than the Christ-like giving up of all, that the saving purposes of God's love may be accomplished among men. Oh, be no longer of those who are content if they have salvation, and just do work enough to keep themselves warm and lively. O let nothing keep you back from giving yourselves to be wholly and only priests — nothing else, nothing less than the priests of the Most High God.

ANDREW MURRAY, IN *WITH CHRIST IN THE SCHOOL OF PRAYER*

Resolved to Pray

May the Lord give you increase, you and your children!
May you be blessed by the Lord, who made heaven and earth!
(Psalm 115:14-15)

I had daily prayed for the needed helpers and assistants for the various departments. Before a stone was laid, I began to pray for this; and, as the building progressed, I continued day by day to bring this matter before God, feeling assured, that, as in everything else, so in this particular also, He would graciously be pleased to appear on our behalf and help us, as the whole work is intended for His honour and glory. At last the time was near when the house could be opened, and the time therefore near when the applications, which had been made in writing during more than two years previously, should be considered, for the filling up of the various posts. It now, however, was found that, whilst there had been about 50 applications made for the various situations, some places could not be filled up, because either the individuals who had applied for them were married, or were, on examination, found unsuitable. This was no small trial of faith; for day by day, for years, had I asked God to help me in this particular.

What was now to be done, dear Reader? Would it have been right to charge God with unfaithfulness? Would it have been right to distrust Him? Would it have been right to say, it is useless to pray? By no means. This, on the contrary, I did; I thanked God for all the help, He had given me in connection with the whole of the enlargement; I thanked Him for enabling me to overcome so many and such great difficulties and instead of distrusting God, I looked upon this delay of the full answer to prayer, only as a trial of faith, and therefore resolved, that, instead of praying once a day with my dear wife about this matter, as we had been doing day by day for years, we should now meet daily three times, to bring this before God. I also brought the matter before the whole staff of my helpers in the work requesting their prayers. Thus I have now continued for about four months longer in prayer, day by day calling upon God three times on account of this need, and the result has been, that one helper after the other has been given, without the help coming too late, or the work getting into confusion; or the reception of the children being hindered; and I am fully assured, that the few who are yet needed will also be found, when they are really required.

George Müller, in *Answers to Prayer*

The Act of Faith

*Whoever humbles himself like this child is
the greatest in the kingdom of heaven.*
(Matthew 18:4)

Before a man begins building he must make sure of the foundation. Hearing and doing the Word — this is the bedrock of faith. Jesus made this simple enough for children to understand in his story of the two men who built houses, one on rock, one on sand. We all know what happened in the storm. The stability of one house is the picture of the man who hears the Word of God and does it. For me, it is wonderfully reassuring to know that this does not mean knowing all the Word, being perfectly obedient to all the Word, at one time. Hearing one thing, doing that one thing, is what is required. This puts me in touch with God, which is precisely what we mean when we speak of an "act of faith." "It is only when we obey God's laws that we can be quite sure that we really know him," John wrote.

When a child begins to walk, his first step is reason enough, in his parents' eyes, for enthusiastic praise. The step is not a very successful one. It is wobbly and may take the child where he didn't mean to go faster than he wanted. But it contains the elements of walking — putting one foot in front of the other. Doing this over and over will eventually get the child somewhere.

To believe one thing — this one promise that God will guide us, for example — is a baby step. It is a beginning of a walk with God. The steps that follow will be like the first one in that they contain the element of faith. If God means it this time, he means it the next time. I take him at his word now, and I will hear another word tomorrow.

Elisabeth Elliot, in *God's Guidance*

COOPERATE WITH GOD

He made from one man every nation of mankind to live on all the face of the earth, having determined allotted periods and the boundaries of their dwelling place, that they should seek God, and perhaps feel their way toward him and find him.

(ACTS 17:26-27)

God has left man many things to do for himself. He promises seedtime and harvest. Yet man must prepare the soil, sow, and till, and reap in order to allow God to do His share. God provides us with food and drink. But He leaves us to take, and eat, and drink. There are some things God cannot, or at least will not, do without our help. God cannot do some things unless we think. He never emblazons His truth upon the sky. The laws of science have always been there. But we must think, and experiment, and think again if we would use those laws for our own good and God's glory.

God cannot do some things unless we work. He stores the hills with marble, but He has never built a cathedral. He fills the mountains with iron ore, but He never makes a needle or a locomotive. He leaves that to us. We must work.

If, then, God has left many things dependent upon man's thinking and working, why should He not leave some things dependent upon man's praying? He has done so. "Ask and ye shall receive." And there are some things God will not give us unless we ask. Prayer is one of the three ways in which man can cooperate with God; and the greatest of these is prayer.

Men of power are without exception men of prayer. God bestows His Holy Spirit in His fullness only on men of prayer. And it is through the operation of the Spirit that answers to prayer come. Every believer has the Spirit of Christ dwelling in him. For "if any have not the Spirit of Christ, he is none of his." But a man of prevailing prayer must be filled with the Spirit of God.

AN UNKNOWN CHRISTIAN, IN *THE KNEELING CHRISTIAN*

DRAWING STRENGTH FROM THE SCRIPTURES

If you faint in the day of adversity, your strength is small.
(PROVERBS 24:10)

We do well to wait upon the Lord's mercy. After all, the Lord has waited a lot longer upon us than we have waited upon him! "I waited patiently for the Lord," David said, "he turned to me and heard my cry" (Psalm 40:1, NIV). And the best help in patient waiting is an understanding well-informed and enlightened.

Alas! How many poor souls are there in the world, who, because they are not well-informed in their understanding, are often ready to give up all for lost because of the tricks and temptations of Satan! The Lord pity them! The Lord help them to pray with the spirit and with the understanding also. This is true to much of my own experiences. When I have been in my fits of agony of spirit, I have often been strongly persuaded to quit and to ask the Lord no longer to answer my request. But then I remember and understand what great sinners the Lord has had mercy upon, and how large his promises are still to sinners. And I remember that it was not the whole and healthy, but the sick; not the righteous, but the sinners; not the full, but the empty that he intended to give his grace and mercy. When I remember these things my patience is renewed and I persevere in prayer until I receive the blessing. Remembering and understanding the teachings of the Scriptures has made me, through the assistance of the Holy Spirit, to cleave to him, hang upon him, and continue to cry, though for the present he made no answer — and he has helped me! May the Lord help all of his poor, tempted, and afflicted people to do the same and to continue, though it be long, according to the saying of the prophet: "For the revelation awaits an appointed time; it speaks of the end and will not prove false. Though it linger, wait for it; it will certainly come and not delay" (Habakkuk 2:3, NIV). May the Lord help those who pray to that end, not by the inventions of men and their rituals, but with the spirit and the understanding also.

JOHN BUNYAN, IN *PILGRIM'S PRAYER BOOK*

At Peace Before Him

The Lord make his face to shine upon you and be gracious to you;
the Lord lift up his countenance upon you and give you peace.
(Numbers 6:25-26)

The infant hanging at the mother's breast is a lively illustration of our subject: it begins to draw the milk by moving its little lips; but when the milk flows abundantly, it is content to swallow, and suspends its suction: by doing otherwise it would only hurt itself, spill the milk, and be obliged to quit the breast.

We must act in like manner in the beginning of Prayer, by exerting the lips of the affections; but as soon as the milk of Divine Grace flows freely, we have nothing to do but, in repose and stillness, sweetly to imbibe it; and when it ceases to flow, we must again stir up the affections as the infant moves its lips. Whoever acts otherwise cannot turn this grace to advantage, which is bestowed to allure and draw the soul into the repose of Love, and not into the multiplicity of Self.

But what becometh of this child, who gently and without motion drinketh in the milk? Who would believe that it can thus receive nourishment? Yet the more peacefully it feeds, the better it thrives. What, I say, becomes of this infant? It drops gently asleep on its mother's bosom. So the soul that is tranquil and peaceful in prayer, sinketh frequently into a mystic slumber, wherein all its powers are at rest; till at length it is wholly fitted for that state, of which it enjoys these transient anticipations. In this process the soul is led naturally, without effort, art, or study.

If any will thus pursue the little path I have pointed out, it will lead them to intuitive prayer. God demands nothing extraordinary nor difficult; on the contrary, He is best pleased by a simple and child-like conduct. Would you go to God, follow this sweet and simple path, and you will arrive at the desired object, with an ease and expedition that will amaze you.

Jeanne Guyon, in *A Short and Easy Method of Prayer*

DRAWN DEEP INTO PRAYER

I cry out to God Most High, to God who fulfills his purpose for me.
(PSALM 57:2)

We may perfect the structure and efficiency of our organizations. We may increase the number of people involved in our evangelistic efforts. We may increase our use of literature, radio, or other media. We may advertise widely — all without spiritual results. We may use all the right words, the right Scriptures, the right methods, and even the right people. But unless God gives His anointing, empowering, and help, our results will be only human results. Spiritually we will remain barren.

When God desires to do a mighty work of salvation and spiritual harvest, He calls His people to their knees. The Holy Spirit places a deep hunger in the heart of those of God's children who are close enough to Him to hear His voice. As their hearts cry out to Him, He leads them to spend more and more time in prayer. He leads them to join with others who share a similar prayer burden. God may lead them to add fasting to their prayer burden because their heart's desire is so intense that they want to take this extra, more costly step in seeking God's supernatural visitation.

Many times God uses pastors or other Christian leaders to issue calls for special prayer or to set aside days for prayer and fasting. More often God leads people, one by one, to take steps to deepen their own personal prayer life. Many a local revival visitation by the Holy Spirit was assisted by the prayer preparation of two or three people in one or more places, praying individually or together for months or even years. As they have humbled themselves before God, asking for God's mercy, claiming God's promises, they have been used by the Spirit to prepare for a mighty work of God. This is the role for which God needs you and your prayer.

WESLEY DUEWEL, IN *TOUCH THE WORLD THROUGH PRAYER*

Weeping for the People

> *Be wretched and mourn and weep. Let your laughter be turned to mourning and your joy to gloom. Humble yourselves before the Lord, and he will exalt you.*
>
> (James 4:9-10)

It was while Nehemiah was in Babylon, in the king's palace, that one day his brethren came from Jerusalem, and very naturally Nehemiah desired news from the people there and information concerning the city itself. The distressing information was given him that the walls were broken down, the gates were burned with fire, and the remnant who were left there at the beginning of the captivity were in great affliction and reproach.

Just one verse gives the effect of this sad news upon this man of God:

"And it came to pass when I heard these words, that I sat down and wept, and mourned certain days and fasted, and prayed before the God of heaven."

Here was a man whose heart was in his own native land far away from where he now lived. He loved Israel, was concerned for the welfare of Zion, and was true to God. Deeply distressed by the information concerning his brethren at Jerusalem, he mourned and wept. How few the strong men in these days who can weep at the evils and abominations of the times! How rare those who, seeing the desolations of Zion, are sufficiently interested and concerned for the welfare of the Church to mourn! Mourning and weeping over the decay of religion, the decline of revival power, and the fearful inroads of worldliness in the Church are almost an unknown quantity. There is so much of so-called optimism that leaders have no eyes to see the breaking down of the walls of Zion and the low spiritual state of the Christians of the present day, and have less heart to mourn and cry about it. Nehemiah was a mourner in Zion. And possessing this state of heart, distressed beyond measure, he does that which other praying saints had done — he goes to God and makes it a subject of prayer.

E. M. Bounds, in *Prayer and Praying Men*

The Law of Prayer

If my people who are called by my name humble themselves, and pray
and seek my face and turn from their wicked ways, then I will hear
from heaven and will forgive their sin and heal their land.

(2 Chronicles 7:14)

Prayer life has its own laws, as all the rest of life has. The fundamental law in prayer is this: Prayer is given and ordained for the purpose of glorifying God. Prayer is the appointed way of giving Jesus an opportunity to exercise His supernatural powers of salvation. And in so doing He desires to make use of us.

We should through prayer give Jesus the opportunity of gaining access to our souls, our bodies, our homes, our neighborhoods, our countries, to the whole world, to the fellowship of believers and to the unsaved.

If we will make use of prayer, not to wrest from God advantages for ourselves or our dear ones, or to escape from tribulations and difficulties, but to call down upon ourselves and others those things which will glorify the name of God, then we shall see the strongest and boldest promises of the Bible about prayer fulfilled also in our weak, little prayer life. Then we shall see such answers to prayer as we had never thought were possible.

It is written, "And this is the boldness which we have toward him, that, if we ask anything according to his will, he heareth us: and if we know that he heareth us whatsoever we ask, we know that we have the petitions which we ask of him" (1 John 5:14-15, KJV).

The apostle establishes the fact from his own prayer-experience as well as that of his readers, that if we pray for anything according to the will of God, we already have what we pray for the moment we ask it. It is immediately sent from heaven on its way to us. We do not know exactly when it will arrive while we are asking for it; but he who has learned to know God through the Spirit of God, has learned to leave this in His hands, and to live just as happily whether the answer arrives immediately or later.

Ole Hallesby, in *Prayer*

GOD'S POINT OF VIEW

All mine are yours, and yours are mine, and I am glorified in them.
(JOHN 17:10)

Some people pray and long and yearn for the experience of sanctification, but never get anywhere near it; others enter in with a sudden marvelous realization. Sanctification is an instantaneous, continuous work of grace; how long the approach to it takes depends upon ourselves, and that leads some to say sanctification is not instantaneous. The reason why some do not enter in is because they have never allowed their minds to realize what sanctification means.

When we pray to be caught up into God's purpose behind this intercession of the Apostle Paul, we must see that we are willing to face the standard of these verses. Are we prepared for what sanctification will cost? It will cost an intense narrowing of all our interests on earth, and an immense broadening of our interest in God. In other words, sanctification means an intense concentration on God's point of view—every power of spirit, soul and body chained and kept for God's purpose only. Sanctification means being made one with God, even as the Lord Jesus Christ was one—"that they may be one, even as We are one." That is much more than union, it is one in identity; the same disposition that ruled in Jesus rules in me.

Am I prepared for what that will cost? It will cost everything that is not God in me. Am I prepared for God to separate me for His work in me, as He separated Jesus, and after His work is done, am I prepared to separate myself to God even as Jesus did? It is this settling down into God's truth that is needed.

The type of sanctified life is the Lord Jesus Christ, and the characteristic of His life was subordination to His Father. The only way to get right with God is to soak in the atmosphere of the life of the Lord Jesus.

OSWALD CHAMBERS, IN *IF YOU WILL ASK*

Prayer, Not Independence

Clothe yourselves, all of you, with humility toward one another,
for "God opposes the proud but gives grace to the humble."
(1 Peter 5:5)

Few of us are so crass that we self-consciously reason, "I am too important to pray. I am too self-confident to pray. I am too independent to pray." Instead, what happens is this: Although abstractly I may affirm the importance of prayer, in reality I may treat prayer as important only in the lives of other people, especially those whom I judge to be weaker in character, more needy, less competent, less productive. Thus, while affirming the importance of prayer, I may not feel deep need for prayer in my own life. I may be getting along so well without much praying that my self-confidence is constantly being reinforced. That breeds yet another round of prayerlessness.

What is God's response? If Christians who shelter beneath such self-assurance do not learn better ways by listening to the Scriptures, God may address them in the terrible language of tragedy. We serve a God who delights to disclose himself to the contrite, to the lowly of heart, to the meek. When God finds us so puffed up that we do not feel our need for him, it is an act of kindness on his part to take us down a peg or two; it would be an act of judgment to leave us in our vaulting self-esteem.

This lesson is taught in countless passages of Scripture. It is painfully easy for us to come to all kinds of critical points in ministry, service, family development, changes in vocation, and precisely because we have enjoyed spiritual victories in the past, approach these matters with sophisticated criteria but without prayer. We love our independence. As a result we may repeatedly stumble and fall, because although we have exercised all our intellectual ingenuity we have not sought God's face, we have not begged him for wisdom.

D. A. Carson, in *A Call to Spiritual Reformation*

An Opportunity to Trust

Though he slay me, I will hope in him; yet I will argue my ways to his face.
(Job 13:15)

Many times, God seems to be slow in answering our prayers. We have the promises, we pray over the promises by faith, and seek to meet any conditions stated. Yet, God still does not answer. Why is He so slow? Is it that He is hard of hearing or asleep when we pray? Definitely not! Is it that we must convince God of our sincerity by praying for a long time? God sees our hearts and knows the end from the beginning, thus He knows our motives. Then why? It is because when God allows a delay, we are given more opportunities to trust, to walk by faith; we have more time to exercise our muscle of faith. For once the answer comes, the opportunity to grow in faith is past. God is more interested in the process than the result.

We need to learn to enjoy the times of waiting for the answer, knowing that God is using this to build our confidence and belief in Him and His promises. Our natural desire is to run from the pressure and avoid the testing of our faith. It is painful under the pressure of trials, but this will bring beneficial results. Do not always complain when God seems slow to answer. It has been said, "The mark of maturity is being able to enjoy the trip, even when you are on a detour." "But he knows the way that I take; when he has tested me, I will come forth as gold" (Job 23:10, NASB).

We must also recognize that our enemy, the devil, is actively opposing us in our walk by faith. He is seeking to sow seeds of unbelief in the promises of God and to get us to doubt His reliability (Daniel 10:1-14). We too are often not aware of the cosmic forces that are in combat as we pray. Trust that the Lord will answer in His perfect time; He has not forgotten!

Thomas R. Yeakley, in *Praying Over God's Promises*

NO ACCUSATION CAN STAND

If anyone does sin, we have an advocate with
the Father, Jesus Christ the righteous.
(1 JOHN 2:1)

We're familiar with the role of Satan as the tempter, and that's certainly his stock-in-trade. But if anything is his trademark in terms of the work he does in the life of the Christian, it's not so much the work of temptation as the work of accusation. Satan seeks to do everything he can to paralyze believers with unresolved guilt. In that sense, he's standing in direct opposition to the truth of God, which, of course, has been his role from the beginning. Ever since Eden, Satan has been about contradicting what God says.

God makes a simple but profound promise to Christians: "If we confess our sins, He is faithful and just to forgive us our sins and to cleanse us from all unrighteousness" (1 John 1:9, NKJV). When a child of God confesses his sin, God forgives it — it's as simple as that. But as soon as God says that believer is forgiven, Satan shows up and says: "Oh, no, you're not. You are still guilty." When a Christian listens to him, he becomes burdened and weighed down with a paralyzing load of guilt. That guilt, in turn, robs the believer of his assurance of salvation.

Paul addresses this problem when he writes, almost triumphantly: "Who shall bring a charge against God's elect? It is God who justifies. Who is he who condemns?" (Romans 8:33-34, NKJV). God has justified us on the basis of the righteousness of Christ. Thus, when Satan brings his accusations against us, we should respond: "Yes, Satan, I sinned, but now my guilt is covered and my sin is washed away. Be gone!"

Peter referred to Satan as the believer's "adversary" (1 Peter 5:8). But we are assured that if we "resist the devil . . . he will flee" (James 4:7, NKJV), and prayer is a key weapon in our resistance.

R. C. SPROUL, IN *THE PRAYER OF THE LORD*

Revival in the Home

> *Whatever prayer, whatever plea is made by any man or by all your*
> *people Israel, each knowing the affliction of his own heart and*
> *stretching out his hands toward this house, then hear in heaven*
> *your dwelling place and forgive and act and render to each whose*
> *heart you know, according to all his ways (for you, you only, know*
> *the hearts of all the children of mankind), that they may fear you*
> *all the days that they live in the land that you gave to our fathers.*
>
> (1 Kings 8:38-40)

The nation [of Israel] fortunately had a man who could pray, who knew the place and the worth of prayer, and a leader who had the ear of God and who could influence God. But Samuel's praying did not stop there. He judged Israel all the days of his life, and had occasion from year to year to go in circuit to Bethel, Gilgal and Mizpeh. Then he returned home to Ramah, where he resided. "And there he built an altar unto the Lord." Here was an altar of sacrifice but as well was it an altar of prayer. And while it may have been for the benefit of the community where he lived, after the fashion of a town church, yet it must not be overlooked that it must have been a family altar, a place where the sacrifice for sin was offered but at the same time where his household gathered for worship, praise and prayer. Here Almighty God was acknowledged in the home, here was the advertisement of a religious home, and here father and mother called upon the name of the Lord, differentiating this home from all the worldly and idolatrous homes about them.

Here is an example of a religious home, the kind so greatly needed in this irreligious, godless age. Blessed is that home which has in it an altar of sacrifice and of prayer, where daily thanksgivings ascend to heaven and where morning and night praying is done.

Samuel was not only a praying priest, a praying leader and a praying teacher and leader, but he was a praying father. And any one who knows the situation so far as family religion is concerned knows full well that the great demand of these modern times is religious homes and praying fathers and mothers. Here is where the breakdown in religion occurs, where the religious life of a community first begins to decay, and where we must go first to beget praying men and women in the Church of God. It is in the home that the revival must commence.

E. M. Bounds, in *Prayer and Praying Men*

One with Christ!

You have died, and your life is hidden with Christ in God.

(Colossians 3:3)

The highest blessing and source of blessing that even God Himself can bestow upon us is union with Himself; and this is more than *all grace* and *all glory*, because all grace in time and glory in eternity shall flow from this. We read in John 17:22 a passage which, I conceive, contains one of the deepest of the many deep sayings of Christ: "And the glory which thou gavest me I have given them; *that they may be one, even as we are one.*" Evidently, this union is more than the glory given, which is but a means to it. It is a divine reality; and by-and-by when it shall be fully manifested, Jesus shall "see of the travail of his soul, and shall be satisfied." Meantime, faith may take its highest range, hope may soar to its loftiest flight, and love embrace its fullest portion; yet nothing that faith can reach or hope or aspire to, nothing that love itself is able to comprehend, can possibly exceed what this union with God secures—"That they also may be one *in us*" forevermore. Wonderful! wonderful! the believer's union with God in Christ! It is the foundation gospel truth of revelation; and it is well adapted to fill our thoughts, hearts, hopes, and affections with Christ, by whom "God dwelleth in us and we in God," and who thus introduces it in His prayer that we, listening to Him by faith, may be lifted out of the things of time, and that our desires may soar away unto the things of eternity. Oh, how humbly ought we to walk with our God—how loosely to the things of earth! What manner of persons ought we to be, in all holy conversation and godliness! And if the Holy Ghost could say that "God will be sanctified in those who draw near to him," how much more in those who are not only "redeemed by the blood" of Jesus, not only made near to God, but are one with Him in God.

Marcus Rainsford, in *Our Lord Prays for His Own*

Into the Presence of God

Let us then with confidence draw near to the throne of grace,
that we may receive mercy and find grace to help in time of need.
(Hebrews 4:16)

Very much of so-called prayer, both public and private, is not unto God. In order that a prayer should be really unto God, there must be a definite and conscious approach to God when we pray; we must have a definite and vivid realization that God is bending over us and listening as we pray. In very much of our prayer there is really but little thought of God. Our mind is taken up with the thought of what we need, and is not occupied with the thought of the mighty and loving Father of whom we are seeking it. Oftentimes it is the case that we are occupied neither with the need nor with the One to whom we are praying, but our mind is wandering here and there throughout the world. There is no power in that sort of prayer. But when we really come into God's presence, really meet Him face to face in the place of prayer, really seek the things that we desire FROM HIM, then there is power.

If, then, we would pray aright, the first thing that we should do is to see to it that we really get an audience with God, that we really get into His very presence. Before a word of petition is offered, we should have the definite and vivid consciousness that we are talking to God, and should believe that He is listening to our petition and is going to grant the thing that we ask of Him. This is only possible by the Holy Spirit's power, so we should look to the Holy Spirit to really lead us into the presence of God, and should not be hasty in words until He has actually brought us there.

R. A. Torrey, in *How to Pray*

LIVING ABOVE THE WORLD

Do not love the world or the things in the world.
If anyone loves the world, the love of the Father is not in him.
(1 JOHN 2:15)

Professed Christians are bound to maintain a life consistent with their profession, they ought to deny worldly lusts; and not, by seeking to gratify them, give occasion to the world to scoff and say that Christians love the world as well as they do. If professors of religion are backslidden in heart, and entertain a longing for worldly sports and amusements, they are bound by every consideration of duty and decency to abstain from all outward manifestation of such inward lustings. Some have maintained that we should conform to the ways of the world somewhat — at least, enough to show that we can enjoy the world and religion too; and that we make religion appear repulsive to unconverted souls by turning our backs upon what they call their innocent amusements. But we should represent religion as it really is — as living above the world, as consisting in a heavenly mind, as that which affords an enjoyment so spiritual and heavenly as to render the low pursuits and joys of worldly men disagreeable and repulsive. It is a sad stumbling-block to the un-converted to see professed Christians seeking pleasure or happiness from this world. Such seeking is a misrepresentation of the religion of Jesus. It misleads, bewilders, and confounds the observing outsider. If he ever reads his Bible, he cannot but wonder that souls who are born of God and have communion with Him should have any relish for worldly ways and pleasures. The fact is that thoughtful unconverted men have little or no confidence in that class of professing Christians who seek enjoyment from this world. They may profess to have, and may loosely think of such as being liberal and good Christians. They may flatter them, and commend their religion as being the opposite of fanaticism and bigotry, and as being such a religion as they like to see; but there is no real sincerity in such professions on the part of the impenitent.

CHARLES FINNEY, IN *POWER FROM ON HIGH*

QUIT PRETENDING

*I am afraid that as the serpent deceived Eve by his cunning, your
thoughts will be led astray from a sincere and pure devotion to Christ.*

(2 CORINTHIANS 11:3)

Most people live in secret fear that some day they will be careless and by
chance an enemy or friend will be allowed to peep into their poor empty
souls. So they are never relaxed. Bright people are tense and alert in fear
that they may be trapped into saying something common or stupid.
Traveled people are afraid that they may meet some Marco Polo who is able
to describe some remote place where they have never been.

This unnatural condition is part of our sad heritage of sin, but in our
day it is aggravated by our whole way of life. Advertising is largely based
upon this habit of pretense. "Courses" are offered in this or that field of
human learning frankly appealing to the victim's desire to shine at a party.
Books are sold, clothes and cosmetics are peddled, by playing continually
upon this desire to appear what we are not. Artificiality is one curse that
will drop away the moment we kneel at Jesus' feet and surrender ourselves
to His meekness. Then we will not care what people think of us so long as
God is pleased. Then what we are will be everything; what we appear will
take its place far down the scale of interest for us. Apart from sin we have
nothing of which to be ashamed. Only an evil desire to shine makes us
want to appear other than we are.

The heart of the world is breaking under this load of pride and pretense.
There is no release from our burden apart from the meekness of Christ.
Good keen reasoning may help slightly, but so strong is this vice that if we
push it down one place it will come up somewhere else. To men and women
everywhere Jesus says, "Come unto me, and I will give you rest." The rest
He offers is the rest of meekness, the blessed relief which comes when we
accept ourselves for what we are and cease to pretend.

A. W. TOZER, IN *THE PURSUIT OF GOD*

All My Desire

> The woman, knowing what had happened to her, came in fear
> and trembling and fell down before him and told him the whole
> truth. And he said to her, "Daughter, your faith has made
> you well; go in peace, and be healed of your disease."

(Mark 5:33-34)

What are your deep personal needs? Have you prayed about them? Have you asked the Person who can take care of them, to do it? Have you had your prayers answered? Or do you just grumble, and rebel, and blame other people?

Ask, says Jesus, ask largely, that your joy may be full (John 16:24).

How shall you ask?

When we look at the sick woman in Mark 5 the answer to this question is simple, too. Ask in His presence. Get close to the Lord Jesus. Touch Him. He is the answer. He is my answer and He is your answer. He Himself is the answer.

"If you live in Me [abide vitally united to Me] and My words remain in you *and* continue to live in your hearts, ask whatever you will, and it shall be done for you" (John 15:7, AMP).

What does "if you live in Me" mean? It means that all my desire is centered in the Person of Jesus Christ, and apart from Him nothing permanently influences the real me.

How shall you ask?

In the dramatic account of her conversion story in *The Burden Is Light* Eugenia Price prayed only two words over and over from the depths of her heart and He heard. "Oh, God! Oh, God! Oh, God!" Her heart was so heavy there was nothing else she could do but call on His Name. It is not the actual words we pray, it is the condition of our hearts when we pray that brings the answer. In her case, as in all others, He Himself was the answer.

How great is your need?

How deep is your desire?

Will it bring you to His side? Will it carry you past all that keeps you from Him? Will you stop what you are doing now, and kneel at His feet, in His presence? He is there. Ask, seek, knock. There *is* Someone on the other side of the door, and He will open it and give you all that He is.

ROSALIND RINKER, IN *PRAYER: CONVERSING WITH GOD*

ASSISTED IN PRAYER

> *The Spirit helps us in our weakness. For we do not*
> *know what to pray for as we ought, but the Spirit himself*
> *intercedes for us with groanings too deep for words.*
>
> (Romans 8:26)

Tuesday, June 26. In the morning my desires seemed to rise, and ascend up freely to God. Was busy most of the day in translating prayers into the language of the Delaware Indians; met with great difficulty, by reason that my interpreter was altogether unacquainted with the business. But though I was much discouraged with the extreme difficulty of that work, yet God supported me; and especially in the evening gave me sweet refreshment. In prayer my soul was enlarged, and my faith drawn into sensible exercise; was enabled to cry to God for my poor Indians; and though the work of their conversion appeared impossible with man, yet with God I saw all things were possible. My faith was much strengthened, by observing the wonderful assistance God afforded his servants Nehemiah and Ezra, reforming his people, and reestabling his ancient church. I was much assisted in prayer for dear Christian friends, and for others that I apprehended to be Christless; but was more especially concerned for the poor heathen, and those of my own charge: was enabled to be instant in prayer for them; and hoped that God would bow the heavens and come down for their salvation. It seemed to me there could be no impediment sufficient to obstruct that glorious work, seeing the living God, as I strongly hoped, was engaged for it. I continued in a solemn frame, lifting up my heart to God for assistance and grace, that I might be more mortified to this present world, that my whole soul might be taken up continually in concern for the advancement of Christ's kingdom: longed that God would purge me more, that I might be as a chosen vessel to bear his name among the heathens. Continued in this frame till I dropped asleep.

Jonathan Edwards, in *The Life and Diary of David Brainerd*

A SACRED PARTNERSHIP

*I came from you; and they have believed
that you sent me. I am praying for them.*

(JOHN 17:8-9)

Prayer brings you into a sacred partnership with Jesus Christ, the enthroned Son of God. If God had not revealed this to you in His Word, it would have been blasphemous to suggest that you could share such partnership. "The Lord worked with them" is a succinct history of the early church (Mark 16:20). Further, Scripture calls all Christians "God's fellow workers" (1 Corinthians 3:9; 2 Corinthians 6:1).

There are many ways to "work" with God—through obedience, through service to others, and through sharing His love. But He wants to have even more intimate contact with you. He wants to bring you into His inner circle where you can hear His great heart beating for a lost world. He has created you with the ability to speak to Him and fellowship with Him. Above all else, as His "fellow worker," you were created to pray—as He prays.

We are told repeatedly in Scripture that Jesus prayed and that He continues to pray today. But why is prayer necessary for Jesus who spoke worlds into existence (John 1:3) and sustains all things (Hebrews 1:3)? Why must He pray? Why not merely command? No demon from hell or combination of demonic forces could stand against His powerful word. Why does Jesus not just rebuke them, stop them, or consume them by His word?

One day He will (2 Thessalonians 2:8). One day He will rule with an iron scepter (Revelation 12:5), and so will we (2:27). But today Christ has chosen to rule the world by prayer. This is the day of grace, not the day of His power and glory. Christ is already enthroned at the right hand of the Father. What is He doing? He is reigning. But how is He reigning? Not by His scepter, but by prayer! Even before His death and resurrection, when He forewarned Peter that Satan had asked permission to sift the disciples as wheat (Luke 22:31-32), Christ did not say, "I will stop Satan." Instead, He said, "I have prayed for you."

WESLEY DUEWEL, IN *TOUCH THE WORLD THROUGH PRAYER*

THE HARD, EASY COMMANDS

*Take my yoke upon you, and learn from me, for I am gentle
and lowly in heart, and you will find rest for your souls.*

(MATTHEW 11:29)

We can only achieve perfect liberty and enjoy fellowship with Jesus when
his command, his call to absolute discipleship, is appreciated in its entirety.
Only the man who follows the command of Jesus single-mindedly, and
unresistingly lets his yoke rest upon him, finds his burden easy, and under
its gentle pressure receives the power to persevere in the right way. The
command of Jesus is hard, unutterably hard, for those who try to resist it.
But for those who willingly submit, the yoke is easy, and the burden is light.
"His commandments are not grievous" (1 John 5:3, KJV). The commandment of Jesus is not a sort of spiritual shock treatment. Jesus asks nothing
of us without giving us the strength to perform it. His commandment
never seeks to destroy life, but to foster, strengthen and heal it.

But one question still troubles us. What can the call to discipleship
mean today for the worker, the business man, the squire and the soldier?
Does it not lead to an intolerable dichotomy between our lives as workers in
the world and our lives as Christians? If Christianity means following
Christ, is it not a religion for a small minority, a spiritual elite? Does it not
mean the repudiation of the great mass of society, and a hearty contempt
for the weak and the poor? Yet surely such an attitude is the exact opposite
of the gracious mercy of Jesus Christ, who came to the publicans and
sinners, the weak and the poor, the erring and the hopeless.

And if we answer the call to discipleship, where will it lead us? What
decisions and partings will it demand? To answer this question we shall
have to go to him, for only he knows the answer. Only Jesus Christ, who bid
us follow him, knows the journey's end. But we do know that it will be a
road of boundless mercy. Discipleship means joy.

DIETRICH BONHOEFFER, IN *THE COST OF DISCIPLESHIP*

THOUGHTS OF SIN AND GRACE

If many died through one man's trespass, much more
have the grace of God and the free gift by the grace
of that one man Jesus Christ abounded for many.

(ROMANS 5:15)

Above all, we dare not, in confessions which are addressed to a holy God, simulate an experience which we have never known. But let us, as far as God has revealed it to us, confess the deep sin of our nature. It has been said with much truth that the only sign of one's being in Christ which Satan cannot counterfeit is the grief and sorrow which true believers undergo when God discloses to them the sinfulness of inbred sin.

But, on the other hand, the love of Christ at times so fills the heart that, though the remembrance of sin continues, the sense of sin is lost — swallowed up in a measureless ocean of peace and grace. Such high moments of visitation from the living God are surely a prelude to the joy of heaven. For the song of the redeemed in glory is unlike the praises of earth in this, that while it also celebrates the death of the Lamb of God there is in it no mention of sin. All the poisonous fruits of our iniquity have been killed; all the bitter consequences of our evil deeds have been blotted out. And the only relics of sin which are found in heaven are the scarred feet and hands and side of the Redeemer. So, when the saved from earth recall their former transgressions, they look to Christ; and the remembrance of sin dies in the love of Him who wore the thorny-crown, and endured the cross.

The fouler was the error, the sadder was the fall,
The ampler are the praises of Him who pardoned all.

DAVID MCINTYRE, IN *THE HIDDEN LIFE OF PRAYER*

GIVING THANKS TO GOD

Let the peace of Christ rule in your hearts, to which
indeed you were called in one body. And be thankful.

(COLOSSIANS 3:15)

What do we thank God for? Paul tells us to set our hearts on things above (Colossians 3:1). If what we highly cherish belongs to the realm of heaven, our hearts and minds will incline to heaven and all its values; but if what we highly cherish belongs to the realm of earth and the merely transitory, our hearts and minds will incline to the merely transitory. After all, the Master himself taught us that our hearts will run to where our treasure lies (Matthew 6:19-21).

So what does this have to do with our praying?

If in our prayers we are to develop a mental framework analogous to Paul's, we must look for signs of grace in the lives of Christians, and give God thanks for them. It is not simply that Paul gives thanks for whatever measure of maturity some group of Christians has achieved, before he goes on to ask for yet more maturity (though in part that is what he is doing). Rather, the specific elements in his thanksgiving show the framework of values he brings to his intercession — and we urgently need to develop the same framework.

For what have we thanked God recently? Have we gone over a list of members at our local church, say, or over a list of Christian workers, and quietly thanked God for signs of grace in their lives? Do we make it a matter of praise to God when we observe evidence in one another of growing conformity to Christ, exemplified in trust, reliability, love, and genuine spiritual stamina?

D. A. CARSON, IN *A CALL TO SPIRITUAL REFORMATION*

USING GOD'S PROMISES

I entreat your favor with all my heart;
be gracious to me according to your promise.
(PSALM 119:58)

The trustworthy character of God stands behind His promises. He is holy and true. He cannot lie or go back on His promises. He is faithful and will continue to be faithful and worthy of our trust. Therefore, "since we have these promises, dear friends, let us purify ourselves from everything that contaminates body and spirit, perfecting holiness out of reverence for God" (2 Corinthians 7:1, NIV). As a response to His wonderful promises, we should pursue personal purity with all our hearts. We live to honor Him because He has done so much for us. A God-honoring life flows from a grateful heart.

Chief Crowfoot was a Canadian Blackfoot Indian chief who lived in Alberta. In 1885, there was a large Indian uprising, the Saskatchewan Rebellion, but Chief Crowfoot led his people in a path of peace; they did not join the rebellion. As a token of the Canadian government's appreciation for his help and service, Chief Crowfoot was given a lifetime free pass to ride on the Trans-Canadian Railroad. Crowfoot acknowledged the receipt of the free pass by putting it in a leather pouch, which he hung around his neck. He died with the pouch around his neck, never having ridden on the railroad once!

The promises of God are like that lifetime railroad pass. They are given to be used, not stored for future reference. They are given to be believed, trusted, tried and proved. Let us launch out into the adventure of claiming the promises of God in prayer so that we see Him glorify Himself as He does "immeasurably more than all we ask or imagine, according to His power that is at work within us." (Ephesians 3:20, NIV).

THOMAS R. YEAKLEY, IN *PRAYING OVER GOD'S PROMISES*

Alone with Him

Let us know; let us press on to know the LORD;
his going out is sure as the dawn; he will come to us
as the showers, as the spring rains that water the earth.

(HOSEA 6:3)

"If you were shipwrecked on a desert island, whom would you like to be your companion?" is a tired old question. For most of us, the idea of prolonged isolation with anybody we didn't like is a thing to be avoided at all cost. With someone we love it may look like heaven. With anyone else it looks like hell. We don't care to be "taken aside" or given any "quiet talks," to be subjected to any situation that will lead to heart-to-heart conversation, especially if the person holds any kind of power over us. We'd rather stick with the crowd. The presence of other people is a protection. Issues can more easily be avoided.

I have sometimes been afraid to be alone with God. This fear, John tells us, would be "cast out" if I loved God perfectly, but of course I don't. Issues I have been successfully avoiding might come up if I were to get alone with him. I know quite well that something awkward may arise between us that I would just as soon not deal with. But what if the kind Shepherd takes me aside somewhere because he has something special for me, something he did not want to bring out until he got me alone?

When Jesus was in the region called the Decapolis, a deaf and dumb man was brought to him for healing. Quite a crowd had collected to see the fun, but what Jesus planned to do he wanted to do in private. What if the man had said "Oh, no, you don't get me off by myself!" But the deaf-mute was willing to take the risk. What he had heard of Jesus gave him hope; he took him at his word and got healed. We ought to be willing to allow God to do "special" things for us if he wants to and to accept them quietly, confident that whatever he does fits into the working out of his purposes for us all.

ELISABETH ELLIOT, IN *GOD'S GUIDANCE*

HIS INFINITE FATHERLINESS

> *Jesus answered her, "If you knew the gift of God, and who
> it is that is saying to you, 'Give me a drink,' you would have
> asked him, and he would have given you living water." The woman
> said to him, "Sir, you have nothing to draw water with, and
> the well is deep. Where do you get that living water?"*
>
> (JOHN 4:10-11)

Jesus is full of grace and truth; the Holy Spirit is the Spirit of truth; through Him the grace that is in Jesus is ours in deed and truth, a positive communication out of the Divine life. And so worship in spirit is worship in truth; actual living fellowship with God, a real correspondence and harmony between the Father, who is a Spirit, and the child praying in the spirit.

What Jesus said to the woman of Samaria, she could not at once understand. Pentecost was needed to reveal its full meaning. We are hardly prepared at our first entrance into the school of prayer to grasp such teaching. We shall understand it better later on. Let us only begin and take the lesson as He gives it. We are carnal and cannot bring God the worship He seeks. But Jesus came to give the Spirit: He has given Him to us. Let the disposition in which we set ourselves to pray be what Christ's words have taught us. Let there be the deep confession of our inability to bring God the worship that is pleasing to Him; the childlike teachableness that waits on Him to instruct us; the simple faith that yields itself to the breathing of the Spirit. Above all, let us hold fast the blessed truth — we shall find that the Lord has more to say to us about it — that the knowledge of the Fatherhood of God, the revelation of His infinite Fatherliness in our hearts, the faith in the infinite love that gives us His Son and His Spirit to make us children, is indeed the secret of prayer in spirit and truth. This is the new and living way Christ opened up for us. To have Christ the Son, and the Spirit of the Son, dwelling within us, and revealing the Father, this makes us true, spiritual worshippers.

ANDREW MURRAY, IN *WITH CHRIST IN THE SCHOOL OF PRAYER*

KEEP YOUR MIND IN HIS PRESENCE

Let the words of my mouth and the meditation of my heart
be acceptable in your sight, O LORD, my rock and my redeemer.

(PSALM 19:14)

Our mind roves; but as the will is mistress of all our faculties, she must recall them, and carry them to God, as their last end. When the mind, for want of being sufficiently reduced by recollection, at our first engaging in devotion, has contracted certain bad habits of wandering and dissipation, they are difficult to overcome, and commonly draw us, even against our wills, to the things of the earth.

I believe one remedy for this is, to confess our faults, and to humble ourselves before God. I do not advise you to use multiplicity of words in prayer; many words and long discourses being often the occasions of wandering: hold yourself in prayer before God, like a dumb or paralytic beggar at a rich man's gate: let it be your business to keep your mind in the presence of the Lord. If it sometimes wander, and withdraw itself from Him, do not much disquiet yourself for that; trouble and disquiet serve rather to distract the mind, than to re-collect it; the will must bring it back in tranquility; if you persevere in this manner, God will have pity on you.

One way to recollect the mind easily in the time of prayer, and preserve it more in tranquility, is not to let it wander too far at other times: you should keep it strictly in the presence of God; and being accustomed to think of Him often, you will find it easy to keep your mind calm in the time of prayer, or at least to recall it from its wanderings.

BROTHER LAWRENCE, IN *THE PRACTICE OF THE PRESENCE OF GOD*

PASSION FOR GOD

Do not be slothful in zeal, be fervent in spirit, serve the Lord.
(ROMANS 12:11)

The ardour of devotion is in prayer. In Revelation 4:8, we read: "And they rest not day nor night, saying, Holy, Holy, Holy, Lord God Almighty, which was, and is, and is to come." The inspiration and centre of their rapturous devotion is the holiness of God. That holiness of God claims their attention, inflames their devotion. There is nothing cold, nothing dull, nothing wearisome about them or their heavenly worship. "They rest not day nor night."

What zeal! What unfainting ardour and ceaseless rapture! The ministry of prayer, if it be anything worthy of the name, is a ministry of ardour, a ministry of unwearied and intense longing after God and after His holiness.

The spirit of devotion pervades the saints in heaven and characterizes the worship of heaven's angelic intelligences. No devotionless creatures are in that heavenly world. God is there, and His very presence begets the spirit of reverence, of awe, and of filial fear. If we would be partakers with them after death, we must first learn the spirit of devotion on earth before we get there.

These living creatures in their restless, tireless, attitude after God, and their rapt devotion to His holiness, are the perfect symbols and illustrations of true prayer and its ardour.

Prayer must be aflame. Its ardour must consume. Prayer without fervour is as a sun without light or heat, or as a flower without beauty or fragrance. A soul devoted to God is a fervent soul, and prayer is the creature of that flame. He only can truly pray who is all aglow for holiness, for God, and for heaven.

Activity is not strength. Work is not zeal. Moving about is not devotion. Activity often is the unrecognised symptom of spiritual weakness. It may be hurtful to piety when made the substitute for real devotion in worship. Enthusiasm is more active than faith, though it cannot remove mountains nor call into action any of the omnipotent forces which faith can command.

E. M. BOUNDS, IN *THE ESSENTIALS OF PRAYER*

WANT OF THE SPIRIT

Be filled with the Spirit, addressing one another in psalms
and hymns and spiritual songs, singing and making melody
to the Lord with your heart, giving thanks always and for
everything to God the Father in the name of our Lord Jesus Christ.

(EPHESIANS 5:18-20)

Have you ever noticed the "wondering-ness" (if I may coin a word) of the people who go on with God? They never seem to be over-anxious or over-concerned, and they always seem to be getting younger. What is the characteristic of the people of this world who have not got the child-heart? They are always sighing; they have mental and spiritual rheumatism and neuralgia, moral twists and perversities, and nothing can rouse them. Why? They want the child-spirit, the Spirit that was given to the disciples after the Resurrection, and in its fullness at Pentecost, then nothing will turn them aside. After Pentecost there was the sword and great persecution, and they were all scattered abroad, but nothing could stop them preaching the word. There was a hilarious shout all through these men's lives because of the mighty baptism of the Holy Ghost and fire. There was running then! No power on earth or heaven above or hell beneath could stop the tremendous strength of the child-life of the Holy Ghost in them. Have you got the wonder in your heart tonight, my brother, or are you sighing, "Thank God I have managed to squeeze enough grace out of God to last through this day"? Blessed be the Name of God, all the unsearchable riches of Christ are at your disposal!

Thank God for every life that is running in the strength of the tremendous vision. Keep your eyes on your file Leader, Jesus only, Jesus ever, "and make straight paths for your feet." Watch for His goings. When He stands and hides Himself in a cloud — stand, watch and wait. When the meaning is clear, then you will run. A vision puts enthusiasm into you, a thrilling understanding of God's Word and you soar above in a tremendous ecstasy; then you come down and run without being weary, and then you come to the grandest days and walk without fainting.

OSWALD CHAMBERS, IN *IF YOU WILL ASK*

GOD'S GIFTS OF LOVE

Love bears all things, believes all things,
hopes all things, endures all things.

(1 CORINTHIANS 13:7)

The essence of love is to give: give all it has to give, give all it can give without bringing harm to the loved one, give all it can persuade the loved one to accept.

That God gives some gifts to men without their prayer and other gifts only to those who pray, can be accounted for by the simple fact that there is a wide difference in kind between these gifts. All people accept some of God's gifts; this is true, for instance, of temporal gifts. They are given without our prayer.

But men close their hearts to some of God's other gifts; this is true of all the gifts which pertain to our salvation. These gifts God cannot bestow upon us before He can persuade us to open our hearts and receive them voluntarily. And, as we have seen above, prayer is the organ whereby we open our hearts to God and let Him enter in.

Here we see why prayer is essential.

It is not for the purpose of making God good or generous. He is that from all eternity. Nor is it for the purpose of informing God concerning our needs. He knows what they are better than we do. Nor is it for the purpose of bringing God's gifts down from heaven to us. It is He who bestows the gifts, and by knocking at the door of our hearts, He reminds us that He desires to impart them to us.

No, prayer has one function, and that is to answer "Yes," when He knocks, to open the soul and give Him the opportunity to bring us the answer.

This throws light on the struggles and strivings, the work and the fasting connected with prayer. All these things have but one purpose: to induce us to open our hearts and to receive all that Jesus is willing to give, to put away all those things which would distract us and prevent us from hearing Jesus knock, that is, from hearing the Spirit of prayer when He tries to tell us what God is waiting to give us if we will only ask for it.

OLE HALLESBY, IN *PRAYER*

Our Sufficient God

How then will they call on him in whom they have not believed?
And how are they to believe in him of whom they have never
heard? And how are they to hear without someone preaching?

(Romans 10:14)

Taylor was a man burdened with a God-given message, and he moved from place to place, awakening other hearts to the same God-consciousness.

It was a new thing, in those days, to talk about faith as a sufficient financial basis for missionary work at the other end of the world. "Faith missions" were unheard of, as the only organizations that existed were the regular denominational boards. But Hudson Taylor, even though he was young, had learned to know God and his faithfulness in a very real way. He had seen him calm storms, stop the actions of would-be murderers and pacify enraged men in answer to prayer. He had seen God heal sickness and revive the dying when all hope of recovery seemed gone. For more than eight years God had proved his faithfulness in supplying the needs of his family and work in answer to prayer, unforeseen as many of those needs had been.

Hudson Taylor was eager to call others to trust God and his unfailing faithfulness. "We have to do with one," he reminded his hearers, "who is Lord of all power and might, whose arm is not shortened that it cannot save, nor his ear heavy that it cannot hear; with one whose unchanging word directs us to ask and receive that our joy may be full, to open our mouths wide, that he may fill them. And we do well to remember that this gracious God, who has condescended to place his almighty power at the command of believing prayer looks not lightly on the blood-guiltiness of those who neglect to avail themselves of it for the benefit of the perishing. To those who have never been called to prove the faithfulness of the covenant-keeping God . . . it might seem a hazardous experiment to send evangelists to a distant heathen land 'with only God to look to'; but in one whose privilege it has been, through many years, to put that God to the test — at home and abroad, by land and sea, in sickness and in health, in dangers, necessities, and at the gates of death — such apprehensions would be wholly inexcusable."

Dr. and Mrs. Howard Taylor, in *Hudson Taylor's Spiritual Secret*

PRAYER'S PLACE

Lift your drooping hands and strengthen your weak knees,
and make straight paths for your feet, so that what is lame
may not be put out of joint but rather be healed.

(HEBREWS 12:12-13)

God's great storehouse is full of blessings. Only prayer can unlock that storehouse. Prayer is the key, and faith both turns the key and opens the door, and claims the blessing. Blessed are the pure in heart, for they shall see God. And to see Him is to pray aright.

Listen! All our past failure, all our past inefficiency and insufficiency, all our past unfruitfulness in service, can be banished now, once and for all, if we will only give prayer its proper place. Do it today. Do not wait for a more convenient time.

Everything worth having depends upon the decision we make. Truly God is a wonderful God! And one of the most wonderful things about Him is that He puts His all at the disposal of the prayer of faith. Believing prayer from a wholly-cleansed heart never fails. God has given us His word for it. Yet vastly more wonderful is the amazing fact that Christian men and women should either not believe God's word, or should fail to put it to the test.

When Christ is "all in all" — when He is Savior and Lord and King of our whole being, then it is really He Who prays our prayers. We can then truthfully alter one word of a well-known verse and say that the Lord Jesus ever liveth to make intercession in us. Oh, that we might make the Lord Jesus "marvel" not at our unbelief but at our faith! When our Lord shall again "marvel," and say of us, "Verily . . . I have not found so great faith, no, not in Israel" (Matthew 8:10, KJV), then indeed shall "palsy" — paralysis — be transformed into power.

AN UNKNOWN CHRISTIAN, IN *THE KNEELING CHRISTIAN*

Pray with Earnestness

O Lord, God of my salvation; I cry out day and night before you.
(Psalm 88:1)

The prayer that prevails with God is the prayer into which we put our whole soul, stretching out toward God in intense and agonizing desire. Much of our modern prayer has no power in it because there is no heart in it. We rush into God's presence, run through a string of petitions, jump up and go out. If someone should ask us an hour afterward for what we prayed, oftentimes we could not tell. If we put so little heart into our prayers, we cannot expect God to put much heart into answering them. We hear much in our day of the rest of faith, but there is such a thing as the fight of faith in prayer as well as in effort. Those who would have us think that they have attained to some sublime height of faith and trust because they never know any agony of conflict or of prayer, have surely gotten beyond their Lord, and beyond the mightiest victors for God, both in effort and prayer, that the ages of Christian history have known. When we learn to come to God with an intensity of desire that wrings the soul, then shall we know a power in prayer that most of us do not know now.

But how shall we attain to this earnestness in prayer?

Not by trying to work ourselves up into it. The true method is explained in Romans 8:26, "And in like manner the Spirit also helpeth our infirmity: for we know not how to pray as we ought; but the Spirit Himself maketh intercession for us with groanings which cannot be uttered." The earnestness that we work up in the energy of the flesh is a repulsive thing. The earnestness wrought in us by the power of the Holy Spirit is pleasing to God.

Here again, if we would pray aright, we must look to the Spirit of God to teach us to pray.

R. A. Torrey, in *How to Pray*

Closer Than a Brother

I am with you always, to the end of the age.
(Matthew 28:20)

It is well there is One who is ever the same, and who is ever with us. It is well there is one stable rock amidst the billows of the sea of life. O my soul, set not thine affections upon rusting, moth-eaten, decaying treasures, but set thine heart upon him who abides forever faithful to thee. Build not thine house upon the moving quicksands of a deceitful world, but found thy hopes upon this rock, which, amid descending rain and roaring floods, shall stand immovably secure. My soul, I charge thee, lay up thy treasure in the only secure cabinet; store thy jewels where thou canst never lose them. Put thine all in Christ; set all thine affections on his person, all thy hope in his merit, all thy trust in his efficacious blood, all thy joy in his presence, and so thou mayest laugh at loss, and defy destruction. Remember that all the flowers in the world's garden fade by turns, and the day cometh when nothing will be left but the black, cold earth. Death's black extinguisher must soon put out thy candle. Oh! how sweet to have sunlight when the candle is gone! The dark flood must soon roll between thee and all thou hast; then wed thine heart to him who will never leave thee; trust thyself with him who will go with thee through the black and surging current of death's stream, and who will land thee safely on the celestial shore, and make thee sit with him in heavenly places forever. Go, sorrowing son of affliction, tell thy secrets to the Friend who sticketh closer than a brother. Trust all thy concerns with him who never can be taken from thee, who will never leave thee, and who will never let thee leave him, even "Jesus Christ, the same yesterday, and today, and forever." "Lo, I am with you alway," is enough for my soul to live upon, let who will forsake me.

Charles Spurgeon, in *Morning by Morning*

Selling Out to God

I delight to do your will, O my God; your law is within my heart.

(Psalm 40:8)

"Be thou exalted" is the language of victorious spiritual experience. It is a little key to unlock the door to great treasures of grace. It is central in the life of God in the soul. Let the seeking man reach a place where life and lips join to say continually "Be thou exalted," and a thousand minor problems will be solved at once. His Christian life ceases to be the complicated thing it had been before and becomes the very essence of simplicity. By the exercise of his will he has set his course, and on that course he will stay as if guided by an automatic pilot. If blown off course for a moment by some adverse wind he will surely return again as by a secret bent of the soul. The hidden motions of the Spirit are working in his favor, and "the stars in their courses" fight for him. He has met his life problem at its center, and everything else must follow along. Let no one imagine that he will lose anything of human dignity by this voluntary sell-out of his all to his God. He does not by this degrade himself as a man; rather he finds his right place of high honor as one made in the image of his Creator. His deep disgrace lay in his moral derangement, his unnatural usurpation of the place of God. His honor will be proved by restoring again that stolen throne. In exalting God over all he finds his own highest honor upheld.

Anyone who might feel reluctant to surrender his will to the will of another should remember Jesus' words, "Whosoever committeth sin is the servant of sin." We must of necessity be servant to someone, either to God or to sin. The sinner prides himself on his independence, completely overlooking the fact that he is the weak slave of the sins that rule his members. The man who surrenders to Christ exchanges a cruel slave driver for a kind and gentle Master whose yoke is easy and whose burden is light.

A. W. Tozer, in *The Pursuit of God*

Bunyan's Dying Words on Prayer

Pray without ceasing.
(1 Thessalonians 5:17)

Before you enter into prayer, ask your soul these questions:

1. To what end, O my soul, am I retired into this place? Am I come to discourse with the Lord in prayer? Is he present, will he hear me? Is he merciful, will he help me? Is my business with him unimportant? Is it concerning the welfare of my soul? What words will I use to move him to compassion?

2. To make your preparation complete, consider that you are but dust and ashes, and he is the great God and Father of our Lord Jesus Christ. He clothes himself with light as with a garment, and you are but a sinner. He is a holy God, and you are but a sinful creature. He is the omnipotent Creator.

3. In all your prayers do not forget to thank God for all of his mercies.

4. When you pray, rather let your heart be without words than your words be without heart.

5. Prayer will make a man cease from sin or sin will entice a man to cease from prayer.

6. The spirit of prayer is more precious than treasures of gold and silver.

7. Pray often, for prayer is a shield to the soul, a sacrifice to God, and a scourge to Satan.

John Bunyan, in *Pilgrim's Prayer Book*

PRAYER AND POWER

Let everyone who is godly offer prayer to you at a time when you may
be found; surely in the rush of great waters, they shall not reach him.

(PSALM 32:6)

Imagine what it must have been like to have the privilege of following Jesus around day after day, listening to His teaching and watching Him perform His miracles. I can think of lots of things they could have asked Him to teach them. The disciples might have gone to Him and said, "Jesus, teach us how to turn water into wine." They might have asked, "Teach us how to walk on water." But the New Testament tells us of a different request that the disciples brought to Jesus. They came to Him on one occasion, as Luke records it for us in his Gospel, and said, "Lord, teach us to pray" (Luke 11:1, KJV). I find it fascinating that this was the burning question they brought to Jesus. They wanted to gain a special insight into prayer as a skill or an art.

Why did they ask Him this question? My guess is that they saw the link between Jesus' extraordinary prayer life and His power, His teaching, His character, His whole person. They must have noticed that after ministering to large crowds of people, Jesus often would withdraw by Himself. He must have felt drained from that ministry. During such times, Jesus would not simply withdraw for a half hour or so. Rather, He would go apart for long periods, and when He did so, He usually spent much of the time in intense seasons of prayer. We know of the intensity of His prayer in the Garden of Gethsemane, when He prayed with such stress and fervency that His sweat was like great drops of blood. We know that before He selected His disciples and called them to follow after Him, He spent the entire night alone in prayer. The disciples could not help but notice this commitment to prayer. They saw the intimacy Jesus had with the Father and made the connection between His prayer and His power.

R. C. SPROUL, IN *THE PRAYER OF THE LORD*

THE WORLD WAS MADE FOR PRAYER

We are his workmanship, created in Christ Jesus for good works,
which God prepared beforehand, that we should walk in them.

(EPHESIANS 2:10)

To think of our prayers as just "causes" would suggest that the whole importance of petitionary prayer lay in the achievement of the thing asked for. But really, for our spiritual life as a whole, the "being taken into account," or "considered," matters more than the being granted. Religious people don't talk about the "results" of prayer; they talk of its being "answered" or "heard." Someone said, "A suitor wants his suit to be heard as well as granted." In suits to God, if they are really religious acts at all and not merely attempts at magic, this is even more so. We can bear to be refused but not to be ignored. In other words, our faith can survive many refusals if they really are refusals and not mere disregards. The apparent stone will be bread to us if we believe that a Father's hand put it into ours, in mercy or in justice or even in rebuke. It is hard and bitter, yet it can be chewed and swallowed. But if, having prayed for our heart's desire and got it, we then became convinced that this was a mere accident—that providential designs which had only some quite different end just couldn't help throwing out this satisfaction for us as a by-product—then the apparent bread would become a stone. A pretty stone, perhaps, or even a precious stone. But not edible to the soul.

One of the purposes for which God instituted prayer may have been to bear witness that the course of events is not governed like a state but created like a work of art to which every being makes its contribution and (in prayer) a conscious contribution, and in which every being is both an end and a means. And since I have momentarily considered prayer itself as a means let me hasten to add that it is also an end. The world was made partly that there might be prayer; partly that our prayers might be answered.

C. S. LEWIS, IN *LETTERS TO MALCOLM*

THE LIVING LORD

You are my friends if you do what I command you.
(JOHN 15:14)

"Jesus Christ is not dead but alive and still speaking to us today through the testimony of scripture." Here he is, the same Christ whom the disciples encountered, the same Christ whole and entire. Yes, here he is already, the glorified, victorious and living Lord. Only Christ himself can call us to follow him. But discipleship never consists of this or that specific action: it is always a decision, either for or against Jesus Christ. Hence our situation is not a whit less clear than that of the disciple or the publican in the gospel. When Jesus called his first disciples, they obeyed and followed him because they recognized him as the Christ. But his Messiahship was as hidden to them as it is to us. By itself the call of Jesus could be taken in many different ways. How we take it depends on what we think of him, and he can be recognized only by faith. That was as true for the first disciples as it is to us. They saw the rabbi and the wonderworker, and believed on Christ. We hear the Word and believe on Christ.

But surely there is another way in which the disciples really had an advantage over us. When they had recognized the Christ, they were immediately given a simple and direct command from his very lips, telling them exactly what to do. But just at this crucial point of Christian obedience we are given no help whatever. Does not Christ speak to us differently now? If that were true, we should certainly be in a hopeless predicament. But it is far from true. Christ speaks to us exactly as he spoke to them. If Christ is the living Lord of my life, my encounter with him discloses his word for me, and indeed I have no other means of knowing him, but through his plain word and command.

DIETRICH BONHOEFFER, IN *THE COST OF DISCIPLESHIP*

The Great Physician

*Jesus answered them, "Those who are well have
no need of a physician, but those who are sick."*
(Luke 5:31)

I do not pray that you may be delivered from your pains; but I pray God earnestly that He would give you strength and patience to bear them as long as He pleases. Comfort yourself with Him who holds you fastened to the cross: He will loose you when He thinks fit. Happy those who suffer with Him: accustom yourself to suffer in that manner, and seek from Him the strength to endure as much, and as long, as He shall judge to be necessary for you. The men of the world do not comprehend these truths, nor is it to be wondered at, since they suffer like what they are, and not like Christians: they consider sickness as a pain to nature, and not as a favor from God; and seeing it only in that light, they find nothing in it but grief and distress. But those who consider sickness as coming from the hand of God, as the effects of His mercy, and the means which He employs for their salvation, commonly find in it great sweetness and sensible consolation. I wish you could convince yourself that God is often (in some sense) nearer to us and more effectually present with us, in sickness than in health. Rely upon no other Physician, for, according to my apprehension, He reserves your cure to Himself. Put then all your trust in Him, and you will soon find the effects of it in your recovery, which we often retard, by putting greater confidence in physic than in God.

Whatever remedies you make use of, they will succeed only so far as He permits. When pains come from God, He only can cure them. He often sends diseases of the body, to cure those of the soul. Comfort yourself with the sovereign Physician both of soul and body.

For the Glory of God

*By this my Father is glorified, that you bear
much fruit and so prove to be my disciples.*

(John 15:8)

The end of the dispensation of grace being to glorify the whole Trinity, the order fixed on and appointed wherein this is to be done, is, by *ascending to the Father's love through the work of the Spirit and blood of the Son*. The emanation of divine love to us begins with the Father, is carried on by the Son, and then communicated by the Spirit; the Father designing, the Son purchasing, the Spirit effectually working: which is their order. Our participation is first by the work of the Spirit, to an actual interest in the blood of the Son; whence we have acceptation with the Father.

This, then, is the order whereby we are brought to acceptation with the Father, for the glory of God through Christ:

1st. That the *Spirit may be glorified*, he is given unto us, to quicken us, convert us, work faith in us, Romans 8:11; Ephesians 1:19-20; according to all the promises of the covenant, Isaiah 4:4-5; Ezekiel 36:26.

2dly. This being wrought in us, *for the glory of the Son*, we are actually interested, according to the tenor of the covenant, at the same instant of time, in the *blood of Christ*, as to the benefits which he hath procured for us thereby; yea, this very work of the Spirit itself is a fruit and part of the purchase of Christ. But we speak of our sense of this thing, whereunto the communication of the Spirit is antecedent.

3dly. To the *glory of the Father*, we are accepted with him, justified, freed from guilt, pardoned, and have "peace with God," Romans 5:1. Thus, "through Christ we have access by one Spirit unto the Father," Ephesians 2:17. And thus are both Father and Son and the Holy Spirit glorified in our justification and acceptation with God; the Father in his free love, the Son in his full purchase, and the Holy Spirit in his effectual working.

John Owen, in *Of Communion with God the Father, Son and Holy Ghost*

PRAISE FIRST

You shall fear the LORD your God. You shall serve him and
hold fast to him, and by his name you shall swear. He is your
praise. He is your God, who has done for you these great
and terrifying things that your eyes have seen.

(DEUTERONOMY 10:20-21)

There is an aspect of praise that many of us have missed, a truth about praise that the saints of old understood. If we grasp this truth, it will greatly enhance the effectiveness of our prayers. That truth is that *praise opens the door for God's rule.*

The King of Kings is "enthroned on the praises" of His people (Psalm 22:3, NIV). When we offer praise, we open the door for God to rule. This is precisely what happened at the birth of Jesus. All that praise brought the throne of God, or the rule of God, to bear on all that surrounded our Lord's birth.

Not only was Jesus birthed amid praise, so was the church. From the ascension of Christ until Pentecost, the apostles "stayed continually at the temple, praising God" (Luke 24:53, NIV). According to Acts 13:1-3, the work of missions was also birthed "while they were worshipping the Lord and fasting."

The enemy cannot reign where God is enthroned. There can only be one ruler. Praise proclaims God's rule and displaces Satan's.

A clear example of praise opening the door for God's rule happened in Judah while Jehoshaphat was king. Three armies surrounded Judah. Jehoshaphat proclaimed a fast and a prayer meeting. After prayer, God's people were assured of victory. Then we are told, "Jehoshaphat appointed men to sing to the Lord and to praise him for the splendor of his holiness as they went out ahead of the army" (2 Chronicles 20:21, NIV). The very next verse says, "As they began to sing praise, the Lord set ambushes against" the enemy.

LEE BRASE, IN *PRAYING FROM GOD'S HEART*

PRAYER FOR EVERY MINUTE DETAIL

If you then, who are evil, know how to give good gifts
to your children, how much more will the heavenly
Father give the Holy Spirit to those who ask him!
(LUKE 11:13)

The Lord has been pleased to crown the prayers of his servant respecting the establishment of an Orphan House in this city. The subject of my prayer was, that he would graciously provide a house, either as a loan or as a gift, or that some one might be led to pay the rent for one; further, that he would give me one thousand pounds for the object, and likewise suitable individuals to take care of the children. A day or two after, I was led to ask, in addition to the above, that he would put it into the hearts of his people to send me articles of furniture, and some clothes for the children. In answer to these petitions, many articles of furniture, clothing, and food were sent, a conditional offer of a house, as a gift, was made, individuals proposed themselves to take care of the children, and various sums of money were given. It may be well to state that the above results have followed in answer to prayer, without any one having been asked by me for one single thing; from which I have refrained that I might see the hand of God so much the more clearly.

So far as I remember, I brought even the most minute circumstances concerning the Orphan House before the Lord in my petitions, being conscious of my own weakness and ignorance. There was, however, one point I never had prayed about, namely, that the Lord would send children; for I naturally took it for granted that there would be plenty of applications. The appointed time came, and not even one application was made. This circumstance now led me to lie low before my God in prayer, and to examine my heart once more as to all the motives concerning it; and being able, as formerly, to say, that I should rejoice in God being glorified in this matter, though it were by bringing the whole to nothing. I could then ask him heartily to send applications. The very next day the first application was made, and within a short time forty-three applied.

GEORGE MÜLLER, IN *THE AUTOBIOGRAPHY OF GEORGE MÜLLER*

Led by the Spirit

He makes me lie down in green pastures. He leads me beside still waters.
(Psalm 23:2)

Some persons, when they hear of the prayer of silence, falsely imagine, that the soul remains stupid, dead, and inactive. But, unquestionably, it acteth therein, more nobly and more extensively than it had ever done before; for God Himself is the mover, and the soul now acteth by the agency of His Spirit.

When Saint Paul speaks of our being led by the Spirit of God, it is not meant that we should cease from action; but that we should act through the internal agency of His Grace. This is finely represented by the Prophet Ezekiel's vision of the "wheels, which had a Living Spirit; and whithersoever the Spirit was to go, they went; they ascended, and descended, as they were moved; for the Spirit of Life was in them, and they returned not when they went" (Ezekiel 1:20-21). Thus the soul should be equally subservient to the will of that Vivifying Spirit wherewith it is informed, and scrupulously faithful to follow only as that moves. These motions now never tend to return, in reflection on the creatures or itself; but go forward, in an incessant approach towards the chief end.

This action of the soul is attended with the utmost tranquility. When it acts of itself, the act is forced and constrained; and, therefore, it can the more easily perceive and distinguish it: but when it acteth under the influence of the Spirit of Grace, its action is so free, so easy, and so natural, that it almost seems as if it did not act at all: "He hath set me at large, he hath delivered me, because he delighted in me" (Psalm 18:19).

Jeanne Guyon, in *A Short and Easy Method of Prayer*

WHEN JESUS ENTERS

God is faithful, by whom you were called into
the fellowship of his Son, Jesus Christ our Lord.

(1 CORINTHIANS 1:9)

He says, "If any man open the door, I will come in to him."

Notice carefully every word here. It is not our prayer which draws Jesus into our hearts. Nor is it our prayer which moves Jesus to come in to us. All He needs is access. He enters in of His own accord, because He desires to come in. And He enters in wherever He is not denied admittance.

As air enters in quietly when we breathe, and does its normal work in our lungs, so Jesus enters quietly into our hearts and does His blessed work there. He calls it to "sup with us." In Biblical language the common meal is symbolical of intimate and joyous fellowship. This affords a new glimpse into the nature of prayer, showing us that God has designed prayer as a means of intimate and joyous fellowship between God and man.

Notice how graciously prayer has been designed. To pray is nothing more involved than to let Jesus into our needs. To pray is to give Jesus permission to employ His powers in the alleviation of our distress. To pray is to let Jesus glorify His name in the midst of our needs.

The results of prayer are, therefore, not dependent upon the powers of the one who prays. His intense will, his fervent emotions, or his clear comprehension of what he is praying for are not the reasons why his prayers will be heard and answered. Nay, God be praised, the results of prayer are not dependent upon these things!

To pray is nothing more involved than to open the door, giving Jesus access to our needs and permitting Him to exercise His own power in dealing with them.

He who gave us the privilege of prayer knows us very well. He knows our frame; He remembers that we are dust. That is why He designed prayer in such a way that the most impotent can make use of it. For to pray is to open the door unto Jesus. And that requires no strength. It is only a question of our wills. Will we give Jesus access to our needs?

OLE HALLESBY, IN *PRAYER*

I Have Sinned

If we confess our sins, he is faithful and just to forgive
us our sins and to cleanse us from all unrighteousness.

(1 John 1:9)

Confession of sin is the first act of an awakened sinner, the first mark of a gracious spirit. When God desires an habitation in which to dwell, He prepares "a broken and a contrite heart." The altar of reconciliation stands at the entrance of the New Testament temple; from the altar the worshipper passes on, by way of the laver, to the appointed place of meeting: the blood-stained mercy-seat.

But we speak now rather of the confession of sin which is due by those who are justified, having found acceptance in Christ Jesus. Though they are children, they are sinners still. And if they walk in the light, they are conscious — as in their unregenerate state they never were — of the baseness of their guilt, the hatefulness of their iniquity. For now they bring their transgressions and apostasies into the light of God's countenance, and holding them up before Him, cry, "Against Thee, Thee only, have I sinned, and done this evil in Thy sight: that Thou mightest be justified when Thou speakest, and be clear when Thou judgest" (Psalm 51:4, KJV). So confession of sin should *be explicit.* The ritual law in Israel which provided for the transference of sin on the Day of Atonement presupposed definiteness of confession: "Aaron shall lay both his hands upon the head of the live goat, and confess over him *all* the iniquities of the children of Israel, and *all* their transgressions in all their sins" (Leviticus 16:21, KJV). In private sacrifices, also, while the hands of the offerer (1:4) were laid on the victim, the following prayer was recited: "I entreat, O Jehovah: I have sinned, I have done perversely, I have rebelled" then the special sin, or sins, were named, and the worshipper continued, "but I return in penitence: let this be for my atonement." A wise old writer says, "A child of God will confess sin in particular; an unsound Christian will confess sin by wholesale; he will acknowledge he is a sinner in general; whereas David doth, as it were, point with his finger to the sore: 'I have done *this* evil' (Psalm 51:4); he doth not say, 'I have done evil,' but '*this* evil.' He points to his blood-guiltiness."

David McIntyre, in *The Hidden Life of Prayer*

PRAY IN HIM, LIKE HIM

By this we know that we abide in him and he in us,
because he has given us of his Spirit.
(1 JOHN 4:13)

Blessed Lord! In lowly adoration I again bow before You. All of Your work of redemption has now passed into prayer. You are completely occupied with praying, to maintain and dispense what You purchased with Your blood. You live to pray. And because we abide in You, we have direct access to the Father. Our lives can be lives of unceasing prayer, and the answer to our prayer is certain.

Blessed Lord! You have invited Your people to be Your fellow-workers in a life of prayer. You have united Yourself with Your people. As Your Body, they share the ministry of intercession with You. Only through this ministry can the world be filled with the fruit of Your redemption and the glory of the Father. With more liberty than ever I come to You, my Lord, and plead with You to teach me to pray. Your life is prayer; Your life is mine. Lord! Teach me to pray in You and like You.

And, O my Lord! Let me know, just as You promised Your disciples, that You are in the Father, I am in You, and You are in me. Let the uniting power of the Holy Spirit make my whole life an abiding in You and in Your intercession. May my prayer be its echo, so that the Father hears me in You and You in me. Lord Jesus! In everything, let Your mind be in me! In everything, let my life be in You! In this way, I will be prepared to be the channel through which Your intercession pours its blessing on the world. Amen.

ANDREW MURRAY, IN *WITH CHRIST IN THE SCHOOL OF PRAYER*

COMPASSION AND PRAYER

Do not remember against us our former iniquities; let your compassion come speedily to meet us, for we are brought very low.

(PSALM 79:8)

Compassion is moved at the sight of sin, sorrow and suffering. It stands at the other extreme to indifference of spirit to the wants and woes of others, and is far removed from insensibility and hardness of heart, in the midst of want and trouble and wretchedness.

Compassion is silent but does not remain secluded. It goes out at the sight of trouble, sin and need. Compassion runs out in earnest prayer, first of all, for those for whom it feels, and has a sympathy for them. Prayer for others is born of a sympathetic heart. Prayer is natural and almost spontaneous when compassion is begotten in the heart. Prayer belongs to the compassionate man.

There is a certain compassion which belongs to the natural man, which expends its force in simple gifts to those in need, not to be despised. But spiritual compassion, the kind born in a renewed heart, which is Christly in its nature, is deeper, broader and more prayerlike.

Christly compassion always moves to prayer. This sort of compassion goes beyond the relief of mere bodily wants, and saying, "Be ye warmed — be ye clothed." It reaches deeper down and goes much farther.

Compassion is not blind. Rather we should say, that compassion is not born of blindness. He who has compassion of soul has eyes, first of all, to see the things which excite compassion. He who has no eyes to see the exceeding sinfulness of sin, the wants and woes of humanity, will never have compassion for humanity. It is written of our Lord that "when he saw the multitudes, he was moved with compassion on them." First, seeing the multitudes, with their hunger, their woes and their helpless condition, then compassion. Then prayer for the multitudes. Hard is he, and far from being Christlike, who sees the multitudes, and is unmoved at the sight of their sad state, their unhappiness and their peril. He has no heart of prayer for men.

E. M. BOUNDS, IN *THE ESSENTIALS OF PRAYER*

PRESENT THROUGH PRAYER

> *I am absent in body, yet I am with you in spirit, rejoicing to*
> *see your good order and the firmness of your faith in Christ.*
>
> (COLOSSIANS 2:5)

It is fully possible for any praying Christian to achieve such unity of love and holy desire through prolonged intercession that God will grant a special unity and identity of spirit and a reality of "prayer-presence."

For some twenty years whenever I returned home from college, missionary deputation, or on furloughs from India, it seemed every time we had family prayer my mother would begin to weep tears of longing love as she prayed for the mission fields, especially China and India. That was also the way she interceded for me, and I believe her praying spirit was often with me.

That was why God could call her to intercession at the exact hours when I was confronting danger during my service in India, even though she had no knowledge that I was in trouble. She was a real prayer warrior who spent several hours a day in true intercession and often experienced the prompting of the Holy Spirit. Through her prayer identity with me, she was reaching India for Christ!

Such faithfulness results in great opportunities for serving God. Through prayer you can enter halls of justice and place your affirming hand on the shoulder of the judge. Through prayer you can place your restraining hand on the arm of a criminal or terrorist anywhere in the world. Through prayer you place your guiding hand on the steering wheel of a car.

But you cannot breathe a half-minute prayer once a month for someone and do that. Your heart must be beating with the heart of Jesus as He intercedes. Your love must be flowing day after day with the love of the Holy Spirit. If you yearn deeply enough, if your prayer ministry is constant enough, if you are living in the Spirit and praying in the Spirit, you mediate God's blessing as truly as if you were there in body.

WESLEY DUEWEL, IN *TOUCH THE WORLD THROUGH PRAYER*

SOURCES

Bonhoeffer, Dietrich. *The Cost of Discipleship*. New York: Collier, 1963.

Bounds, E. M. *The Essentials of Prayer*. Public domain.

Bounds, E. M. *The Necessity of Prayer*. Public domain.

Bounds, E. M. *The Possibilities of Prayer*. Public domain.

Bounds, E. M. *Prayer and Praying Men*. Public domain.

Bounds, E. M. *Purpose in Prayer*. Public domain.

Bounds, E. M. *The Reality of Prayer*. Public domain.

Bounds, E. M. *The Weapon of Prayer*. Public domain.

Brase, Lee, with Henry Helsabek. *Praying from God's Heart*. Colorado Springs, CO: NavPress, 1993.

Bunyan, John. *Pilgrim's Prayer Book*. Edited by Louis Gifford Parkhurst Jr. Wheaton, IL: Tyndale, 1986.

Carré, Captain E. G. *A Present-Day Challenge to Prayer*. Public domain.

Carson, D. A. *A Call to Spiritual Reformation*. Grand Rapids, MI: Baker, 1992.

Chadwick, Samuel. *The Path of Prayer*. Fort Washington, PA: CLC Publications, 2000. Public domain.

Chambers, Oswald. *If You Will Ask*. Public domain.

Duewel, Wesley L. *Touch the World Through Prayer*. Grand Rapids, MI: Zondervan, 1986.

Edwards, Jonathan. *The Life and Diary of David Brainerd*. Public domain.

Elliot, Elisabeth. *God's Guidance*. Grand Rapids, MI: Revell, 1992.

Finney, Charles. *Power from on High*. Public domain.

Forsyth, P. T. *The Soul of Prayer*. Public domain.

Guyon, Jeanne. *A Short and Easy Method of Prayer*. Public domain.

Hallesby, Ole. *Prayer*. Minneapolis: Augsburg, 1959.

Brother Lawrence, *The Practice of the Presence of God*. Public domain.

Lewis, C. S. *Letters to Malcolm: Chiefly on Prayer*. San Diego: Harcourt, 1964.

McIntyre, David. *The Hidden Life of Prayer*. Public domain.

Moody, D. L. *Prevailing Prayer*. Public domain.

Müller, George. *Answers to Prayer*. Public domain.

Müller, George. *The Autobiography of George Müller*. Public domain.

Murray, Andrew. *With Christ in the School of Prayer*. Public domain.

Owen, John. *Of Communion with God the Father, Son and Holy Ghost*. Public domain.

Rainsford, Marcus. *Our Lord Prays for His Own*. Public domain.

Rinker, Rosalind. *Prayer: Conversing with God*. Public domain.

Sproul, R. C. *The Prayer of the Lord*. Lake Mary, FL: Reformation Trust, 2009.

Spurgeon, Charles. *Morning by Morning*. Public domain.

Taylor, Dr. Howard, and Mrs. Howard Taylor. *Hudson Taylor's Spiritual Secret*. Public domain.

Torrey, R. A. *How to Pray*. Public domain.

Torrey, R. A. *The Power of Prayer*. Public domain.

Tozer, A. W. *The Pursuit of God*. Public domain.

An Unknown Christian, *The Kneeling Christian*. Public domain.

Yeakley, Thomas R. *Praying Over God's Promises*. Colorado Springs, CO: NavPress, 2007.

ABOUT THE AUTHORS

DIETRICH BONHOEFFER was a German Lutheran pastor, theologian, and Nazi dissenter during World War II. His study of the Sermon on the Mount, *The Cost of Discipleship*, is one of the greatest testimonies to the power of Christian commitment in all of Christian literature. He was executed in the Flossenbürg concentration camp in 1945, just twenty-three days before the German surrender.

E. M. BOUNDS was a lawyer, an army chaplain during the Civil War, a Methodist pastor, and the author of nine books dedicated to the subject of prayer. He died in 1913 at the age of seventy-eight.

LEE BRASE is the director of The Navigators' International Prayer Ministry, in which he concentrates on mentoring leaders in prayer. For many years, Lee's passion has been to help people make God the primary focus of their prayers. He and his wife, Marilyn, live in Beaverton, Oregon.

JOHN BUNYAN was a preacher, prolific author, and evangelist working during the English Civil War. Best known for his epic allegory *The Pilgrim's Progress*, Bunyan's legacy is that of a man who suffered greatly and learned to comfort himself through the promises of Scripture. Charles Spurgeon once said of him, "Prick him anywhere—his blood is Bibline, the very essence of the Bible flows from him."

CAPTAIN E. G. CARRÉ was the Commodore captain of the British India Steam Navigation Company during the early 1920s. An acquaintance of the Reverend J. N. Hyde (known as "Praying Hyde," whose ministry of prayer and preaching in India is compared to that of his English counterparts Andrew Murray, George Müller, and Charles Finney), Captain Carré served as the editor of the first compilation of Hyde's letters and the anecdotes of his closest friends regarding his powerful ministry.

D. A. CARSON is research professor of New Testament at Trinity Evangelical Divinity School in Deerfield, Illinois, and the author of more than fifty relevant but expositional books. He has served as a pastor and lectures around the world in church and academic venues.

Samuel Chadwick was born in northern England in 1860, the son of a cotton miller. Called to the ministry in early life, Chadwick began as a lay pastor of a small Methodist congregation in Lancashire at age twenty-one. Some years later, he had a powerful experience of personal revival, at which time he began to write and evangelize most effectively. He spent his later years training young men for the ministry at Cliff College in England.

Oswald Chambers was a divinely gifted teacher and author who traveled and taught widely during World War I. His wife, Biddie, transcribed all of his lessons and spent the thirty years following his death in 1917 compiling his works, most notably *My Utmost for His Highest*.

Wesley L. Duewel is the former president of One Mission Society International. He was a missionary to India for twenty-five years and is the author of many books, including *Ablaze for God*, *Mighty Prevailing Prayer*, and *Revival Fire*.

Jonathan Edwards was a pastor, theologian, author, college president, and missionary who played a key role at the outset of the First Great Awakening in America from 1733 to 1735. Preeminent among his many important books, *The Life of David Brainerd* has served to inspire missions work throughout the nineteenth century.

Elisabeth Elliot is a Christian author and speaker whose first husband was killed in 1956 as he led a pioneering missionary effort to a native tribe in Ecuador. After working as a missionary for many years herself, Elliot has traveled the world inspiring many young people to enter international missions, live lives centered on the principles of Scripture, and walk in sexual purity. She has written more than twenty books.

Charles Finney was one of America's most powerful evangelists who led revivals between 1827 and 1832. A Presbyterian minister who traveled throughout the eastern U.S., Finney is best known for his teachings on the Holy Spirit and for his pioneering views on social issues such as slavery.

P. T. Forsyth was a Scottish pastor, seminary professor and principal, and prolific author of books and theological pamphlets. His ministry is credited for steering many away from the theological liberalism of the late 1800s in England.

JEANNE GUYON was a French author and dedicated Christian worker. She was sickly from childhood and then was widowed at a young age. While studying in Geneva, she began to share her revolutionary ideas about the Christian life. Although she was arrested and imprisoned several times, she continued to speak and write until her death in 1718.

OLE HALLESBY was one of Norway's leading theologically conservative Christian teachers and devotional writers. An outspoken opponent of the Nazi occupation of Norway, he was arrested and detained at a concentration camp during World War II. He worked as a seminary professor in Oslo until his death in 1961.

BROTHER LAWRENCE, whose real name was Nicholas Herman, ministered among the Carmelite monks in Paris in the 1600s. Little more is known about his life or the circumstances under which *The Practice of the Presence of God* was transcribed and prepared for publication.

C. S. LEWIS was a much-celebrated Christian author, professor, and traveling lecturer throughout the 1940s and 1950s. His works, both fiction and nonfiction, remain among the best-selling Christian books to this day.

DAVID MCINTYRE was apprentice and successor to pastor Andrew A. Bonar of Finnieston Church in Scotland. In 1913, he was appointed principal of the Bible Training Institute in Glasgow, Scotland. Loved by his students, parishioners, and many loyal readers, he passed into glory in 1936.

D. L. MOODY was an American evangelist, pastor, and publisher who founded the famous Moody Bible Church in downtown Chicago.

GEORGE MÜLLER was an evangelist and orphanage director in Bristol, England. His legacy includes the care of 10,024 orphans in five homes. He never solicited anyone for aid, nor did he accumulate debt during the many years of operation. Müller sought provision only through his earnest prayers to God, and God was faithful.

ANDREW MURRAY was a pastor and Bible teacher in South Africa in the late nineteenth and early twentieth centuries. He wrote scores of devotional volumes; besides *Waiting On God* and *Working for God*, these included *Abide in Christ, Absolute Surrender, The Deeper Christian Life,* and *The Spirit-Filled Life.* He died in 1917.

JOHN OWEN was one of the great Puritan pastors and theologians who served during the controversial insurgency of Oliver Cromwell. He later was dean of Christ Church in the University of Oxford. After his conversion in 1642, Owen married Mary Rooke, who bore eleven children, all but one of which died in childbirth. His literary legacy is perhaps the greatest of all the Puritan pastors, leaving nearly a hundred books in print.

MARCUS RAINSFORD was an Irish pastor and theologian who preached in Dundalk, Ireland, before taking the pulpit at St. John's Church in Belgrave Square, London, in 1866. A close associate of D. L. Moody's, Rainsford had a tremendous heart for outreach as well as exposition.

ROSALIND RINKER was an author and evangelist who spent much of her life working in China for the Oriental Mission Society. *Prayer: Conversing with God* was her most popular book. Listed among the top fifty books that have shaped evangelicals, it introduced many thousands of Christians to another level of intimacy with God through prayer. She died in 2002.

R. C. SPROUL, theologian and pastor, is the founder and president of Ligonier Ministries. He has written expositional commentaries on John, Romans, and 1 and 2 Peter. Besides *Pleasing God*, his numerous books include *Knowing Scripture*, *The Holiness of God*, *Chosen by God*, and *What Is Reformed Theology?* He also served as general editor of the *Reformation Study Bible*.

CHARLES SPURGEON, known to many as the "Prince of Preachers," served as pastor of the historic Metropolitan Tabernacle in London for nearly forty years. Always embroiled in controversy, Spurgeon continued faithfully to preach through the Bible, write and publish many helpful books, train young men for leadership, and reach out to the poor until his death in 1892.

DR. AND MRS. HOWARD TAYLOR were the compilers of Hudson Taylor's devotional biography. Many years after Hudson's death in 1905, Geraldine and Howard Taylor wrote the book in hopes that many who "long for just the joy and power that Hudson Taylor found" in Christ would be inspired by his fruitful labors in the land of China.

R. A. TORREY was an American evangelist and Bible scholar who studied at Yale College and Seminary. In 1889, he assumed the role of superintendent at Moody Bible Institute in Chicago.

A. W. Tozer was a twentieth-century pastor, serving churches in the United States and Canada. Besides *The Pursuit of God*, his books include *The Divine Conquest* and *The Knowledge of the Holy*. He died in 1963.

Thomas R. Yeakley has been involved in coaching and developing leaders for more than thirty years with The Navigators. He and his wife, Dana, served as missionaries to Indonesia, and upon their return to the United States in 1994, they have been involved in college ministry.

INDEX TO SCRIPTURAL CITATIONS

Topical Index

necessity of asking for, 280, 320
receiving, 190, 203, 307
giving, 29, 307
by God, 97, 145
of one's life, 212
glorification of God, 75, 99, 123, 124
in all business of life, 242
by answering need, 219
by answering prayer, 99, 138, 301
as only object, 191, 213
as purpose of grace, 318
as purpose of prayer, 285
through thanksgiving, 222
zealousness for, 130
glory, 15, 24, 54, 129
glory of God, 71, 94, 131
reflecting, 79, 213
goal of prayer, 48, 71, 204
God, 23, 43. *See also* Holy Spirit; Jesus Christ
access to, 24, 26, 106, 318, 324
attraction of, 208
character of, 117, 241

as Creator, 33
eternal, 143
as Father, 24, 41, 303
goodness of, 23, 52, 92
as guide, 84, 144
hearing of prayer, 16, 25, 116, 154, 256
manifestation of, 81
as Master, 94, 109
nature of, 87, 109
omnipotence of, 199
omniscience of, 19, 112, 143
perfection of, 27, 52, 143, 223
as Person, 57, 74, 117
as physician, 317
prayer by, 51
presence of. *See* presence of God
reality of, 57
security in, 90
as sole concern, 18, 23
as source of all, 61
sufficiency of, 133, 308
three Persons of, 117
timelessness of, 29, 143
unchanging, 20, 24, 27, 33, 138, 143

view of prayer, 192
God's love, 24, 77, 90
contrition and, 17
knowledge of, 42
power of, 187
unchanging nature of, 117, 200, 244
good, 42, 53, 90, 140
as God's purpose, 96
rejection of, 161
Gordon, A. J., 121
Gospel, advancement by prayer, 145
grace, 15, 36, 100, 299
access to, 312
crisis of, 150
faith corresponding to, 31
gauge of, 192
for glorification of God, 318
pardoning, 196
prayer as means of access to, 189
praying for, 23, 52
recipients of, 281
signs of, 213
suffering and, 138
Graham, Billy, 13
gratitude, 59, 222. *See also* thanksgiving
grief, 46, 299
grievances, 217
guidance, 84, 94, 122, 144, 176
asking for, 216
during prayer, 266
guilt, 235, 289

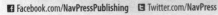

SUPPORT THE MINISTRY OF THE NAVIGATORS

The Navigators' calling is to advance the gospel of Jesus and His kingdom into the nations through spiritual generations of laborers living and discipling among the lost.

Navigators have invested their lives in people for more than 75 years, coming alongside them life on life to help them passionately know Christ and to make Him known.

The U.S. Navigators' ministry touches lives in varied settings, including college campuses, military bases, downtown offices, urban neighborhoods, prisons, and youth camps.

Dedicated to helping people navigate spiritually, The Navigators aims to make a permanent difference in the lives of people around the world. The Navigators helps its communities of friends to follow Christ passionately and equip them effectively to go out and do the same.

To learn more about donating to The Navigators' ministry, go to **www.navigators.org/us/support** or call toll-free at **1-866-568-7827**.

THE NAVIGATORS®